BUILDING LITERACY WITH
ENGLISH LANGUAGE LEARNERS

Also Available

Fluency Instruction, Second Edition:
Research-Based Best Practices
Edited by Timothy Rasinski,
Camille Blachowicz, and Kristin Lems

Building Literacy
with English
Language Learners

Insights from Linguistics

SECOND EDITION

Kristin Lems
Leah D. Miller
Tenena M. Soro

THE GUILFORD PRESS
New York   London

Copyright © 2017 Kristin Lems, Leah D. Miller, and Tenena M. Soro
Published by The Guilford Press
A Division of Guilford Publications, Inc.
370 Seventh Avenue, Suite 1200, New York, NY 10001
www.guilford.com

Printed in the United States of America

This book is printed on acid-free paper.

Last digit is print number: 9 8 7 6 5 4 3 2 1

Library of Congress Cataloging-in-Publication Data is available from the publisher.

ISBN 978-1-4625-3159-2 (paperback)
ISBN 978-1-4625-3160-8 (hardcover)

About the Authors

Kristin Lems, EdD, is Professor in the ESL/Bilingual Education Program at National Louis University, where she directed two 5-year grants from the U.S. Department of Education in ESL teacher education. A two-time Fulbright Scholar, Dr. Lems consults on literacy and ESL in area school districts and presents her research nationally. Her dissertation on adult ESL oral reading fluency was a finalist for Outstanding Dissertation of the Year from the International Literacy Association. She has coauthored or coedited several books, including *Fluency Instruction, Second Edition: Research-Based Best Practices*, which was a finalist for the Edward B. Fry Book Award of the Literacy Research Association.

Leah D. Miller, MA, was a full-time faculty member in the ESL/Bilingual Education Program at National Louis University before retiring in 2012. She taught linguistics, cross-cultural education, and reading courses at National Louis, and also taught composition at Northwestern University and linguistics at the University of Illinois at Chicago. She has presented on linguistics and ESL topics at state and national conferences, including TESOL and the American Educational Research Association.

Tenena M. Soro, PhD, teaches courses in linguistics, cross-cultural education, foundations, and reading in the ESL/Bilingual Education Program at National Louis University, where he received the Outstanding Adjunct Faculty Award. Dr. Soro has also taught courses in ethics and philosophy, linguistics, and social science at Columbia College, Northeastern Illinois University, and Northwestern University. He has presented on linguistics and ESL topics at state and national conferences.

Preface

Classroom teachers and educators who work with English language learners (ELLs) have come to recognize that effectively teaching ELLs is not "just good teaching" but a good deal more. Many teachers work in school districts whose language demographics have changed dramatically, and they want to learn about the first-language experiences of the children in their classes. Children enter school with many assets and abilities, and this fund of knowledge is coaxed, shaped, and developed over the course of their school experiences. Some of these resources are found within their first-language experiences. Other resources can be found in their cultural and community backgrounds and lived experiences. When ELLs enter the world of school, they are also joining the English-speaking community. Whether starting in the early grades or later on, English will become their primary means of instruction as they approach college and career readiness. Educators need to have deep disciplinary knowledge of linguistics as well as literacy in order to help ELLs hit the ground running in learning about many content areas.

The first edition of this book has allowed us to encourage thousands of educators, including preservice and inservice teachers, administrators, school staff, and colleagues at universities, to plunge into the field of linguistics to enrich our common understanding of languages and literacy. How are languages put together? What do they share in common? Which aspects of a child's first language can be easily applied to learning English as a new language, and which cannot? And how can we engage in best practices once we have a deeper understanding of language, literacy, and linguistics?

The literacy teaching profession has come a long way in the 7 years since the first edition of this book was published, in addressing the language-specific needs of different content disciplines, and we applaud that. We also applaud the heightened recognition of oracy, or oral language skills, as a precursor and "fellow traveler" as learners develop literacy—one of the biggest emphases of our first edition. In this new edition, we want to move the conversation forward in all of those key ideas around the basic concepts of linguistics, and a few new notions as well. What does it mean to say that we can now learn a new language with an app? How can ELLs develop their probabilistic reasoning to handle the proliferation of new English vocabulary that is being spawned by social media? And how can learners successfully navigate the many new literary genres, some of them still evolving, as both readers and writers?

Building Literacy with English Language Learners, Second Edition, addresses these areas of interest by increasing the knowledge base of educators involved with teaching ELLs.

Since the publication of the first edition, in 2010, we have learned a great deal from our students, and what we've learned has helped us refine our new edition. You will hear many new teacher voices, as well as some of our own new musings. Our book is intended for the following audiences: (1) instructional leaders in English as a second language (ESL) and bilingual education; (2) reading teachers and specialists who need to know more about the processes of developing reading in a new language; (3) current or future ESL teachers who need to develop expertise about literacy; and (4) general education teachers at all grade levels who need to know more about both ESL and reading in English for their ELL students. This book can be used in reading and language classes, ESL or applied linguistics classes, elementary or secondary language arts methods classes, and study groups for practicing teachers, coordinators, or principals.

We are proud to have been told by many students that our book is "challenging but very readable," and we hope to keep the same balance in the new edition.

Chapter 1 contains an overview of the second-language acquisition field, and it is somewhat vocabulary heavy because we want to establish a common set of understandings and terminology for our readers. Chapter 2 is devoted to the gnarly subject that is of great interest in school planning but is often oversimplified: What is the influence of a first language on learning a new language, especially in regard to reading? These two chapters also establish our conceptual framework for important issues that schools must address to ensure that they plan rigorous programs for their ELLs.

The seven chapters that follow address the specific components that must be built into a "syndrome of success" (see Chapter 1) in order for ELLs to enjoy and succeed in reading and writing in English:

- The critical development of oracy.
- Learning successful decoding of the English alphabet.
- Using morpheme study to increase vocabulary.
- Understanding word formation processes, cognates, and collocations in English.
- Developing reading fluency.
- Developing a set of flexible reading comprehension strategies.
- Learning to write in academic registers and using writing to learn.

Finally, there is a new concluding chapter that explores some of the implications of the digital revolution for the teaching and learning of languages and literacy.

At the beginning of each chapter, we include a list of new vocabulary introduced in the text. The meaning of each term can be found in the glossary at the end of the book. Within each chapter, we have interspersed teacher voices as well as our own. At the end of each chapter, a section titled "How Does This Look in the Classroom?" includes practical, fresh ideas about techniques, great and small, that can be used to put many of the ideas of the chapter into practice. Each chapter concludes with questions for further study, and the last question (or two) is a "Challenge Question" that might require more time and care to prepare. The challenge questions are especially designed for readers who have access to classrooms with ELLs. The questions can be used in a classroom for professional development or self-study.

This book may raise as many questions as it answers for you, and that's all right. Language is not an easily reducible subject—and why would we want it to be? However, we are confident that learning about the linguistic features of English will create many "aha moments" for you, and will provide both immediate and long-term benefits for your classroom teaching or instructional leadership. It is also likely to raise your curiosity about language in general. You will notice features about your own English language and literacy usage that you may never have thought about before! And in discussions with classmates, coworkers, and your students, you will find ways to incorporate your new understandings into your educational settings.

As authors, the more we learn about the subject of developing literacy in English as a new language, the more we enjoy the journey. Although we are glad to see the new edition of this book completed and ready to contribute to the education field, we are as motivated as ever and continue to be captivated by these compelling topics. If you had been a fly on the wall at any of our countless marathon sessions, you would have heard long, animated dialogues about details in the book that you might not notice—conversations that stimulated a lot of thought and helped us grow as educators and writers. We only wish we could have explored many of the topics and authors we introduce to you in much more detail, and we hope you will follow up on your own with whatever piques your interest. We wish you happy reading!

Acknowledgments

We'd like to thank the teachers and students who were kind enough to allow us to share their insights in this second edition: Sam Willingmyre, Rosario Gomez, Beatriz Lappay, Malitzina Salazar, Mary Helmstetter, Misty J. Richmond, Sylwia Bania, Thomas Bochnak, Clare Hourican, Kelly Miedwig, Patricia Grivas, Adriana Iuhas, Barb Prohaska, Joanne Lovaglia, Leah Cooper, Patricia Luna, Xiomara Guerrero, Katherine M. Lin, and Leticia Cortes.

Thanks also to the following colleagues and consultants: Xiaoning Chen, Jeanne Salis, Maria Marquez, Julia Takarada, Anthony Boen, and Neil Mercer.

We also thank the teachers, students, and scholars whose contributions to the first edition continue to illuminate the pages of this new edition. Your wisdom continues to light our way.

We greatly appreciate the fine team at The Guilford Press, who are a pleasure to work with. Special thanks to the always positive and insightful Craig Thomas, as well as to Katherine Sommer and Anna Nelson. Thanks also to the authors and artists whose materials we have included in the book.

Contents

Guide to Pronunciation
in This Book

We have chosen to avoid special symbols in favor of common, simplified forms that can be created on a standard keyboard, with the exception of the schwa sound, /ə/.

Consonants

Sound	as in
Voiced	
/b/	*bad*
/d/	*dog*
/g/	*go*
/j/	*job, fudge*
/l/	*lid*
/m/	*mad*
/n/	*not*
/r/	*red*
/v/	*van*
/w/	*win*
/z/	*zip*
/ng/	*sing*
/th/	*that*
/y/	*young*
/zh/	*measure*

Voiceless

/p/	*pin*
/t/	*tap*
/k/	*kid*
/f/	*fit*
/h/	*hat*
/s/	*sad*
/ch/	*chin*
/sh/	*shell*
/TH/	*think*

Vowels

Sound	as in	commonly called
Short vowels		
/ae/	*had*	short *a*
/e/	*bed*	short *e*
/i/	*bid*	short *i*
/a/	*father, hot*	short *o*
/oo/	*book*	alternate short *u*
/u/	*cut*	short *u*
/ə/	unstressed vowels (*across, zebra*)	schwa sound
Long vowels (all diphthongs in English)		
/ey/	*say*	long *a*
/iy/	*see, happy*	long *e*
/ay/	*I*	long *i*
/ow/	*go*	long *o*
/uw/	*you, food*	long *u*
/aw/	*saw, dog*	open *o*
Additional diphthongs		
/ou/	*house, crowd*	
/oy/	*toy*	
r-controlled vowels		
/ar/	*hard*	
/er/	*hurt*	
/ir/	*fear*	
/eyr/	*care*	
/ayr/	*fire*	
/owr/	*floor*	
/uwr/	*sure*	

CHAPTER ONE

Big Ideas and Research That Guide the Profession

New Vocabulary in This Chapter: *language-based theory of learning, grammar, phonology, morphology, syntax, semantics, orthography, linguistic capital, cultural capital, syndrome of success, language-specific, second-language acquisition (SLA), balanced literacy, communicative competence, input hypothesis, comprehensible input, motherese/caretaker speech, output hypothesis, comprehensible output, systemic functional linguistics (SFL), affect, affective filter, integrative motivation, instrumental motivation, assimilative motivation, intrinsic motivation, resilience, English as a foreign language (EFL), English as a second language (ESL), English language learners (ELLs), grammar translation approach, audiolingualism or audiolingual method (ALM), communicative approach, content-based instruction (CBI), content area, sheltered instruction, cognitive academic language learning approach (CALLA), specially designed academic instruction in English (SDAIE), sheltered instruction observation protocol (SIOP), socially constructed, zone of proximal development (ZPD), instructional conversation, dialect, deficit theory, realia*

Language is a fundamental part of how humans communicate with each other. It is no small thing! Through language, we "learn to mean" things (Halliday, 1993) and how to share those meanings with others. The story of how those meanings are created and shared is truly the story of the human family. Language is our distinctly human endowment.

I

Being able to share meanings with others in more than one language is an even more remarkable achievement. There is no doubt that biliteracy and bilingualism benefit both the individual and society. They create options for self-expression, open-mindedness, economic viability, and common problem solving across language groups. We unequivocally support bilingualism and biliteracy as core goals for an educated society.

That being said, however, we do not pretend that achieving this goal is easy, fast, or inexpensive! Many program models have been implemented in the United States and around the world to facilitate the development of biliteracy. Research about their effectiveness is beginning to be generalized, but there are still many unknowns. In this book, our specific goal is to help educators foster the growth of English academic proficiency by English language learners (ELLs) in the PreK–12 learning environment, regardless of the program model, or lack thereof, in which they find themselves.

Certain big ideas about learning, literacy, and second-language acquisition underlie and inform this book, so we will introduce them in this chapter in hopes that you will bear them in mind as you read the chapters that follow. In addition to these core linguistic and literacy concepts, we provide an overview of some of the research-based best practices for teaching English as a new language that emanate from the big ideas.

The Language-Based Theory of Learning

The *language-based theory of learning* (Halliday, 1993) is a good organizing principle for talking about second-language acquisition. Halliday, a renowned linguist, considered all learning as a linguistic process taking place in three interconnected areas: *learning language, learning through language,* and *learning about language.* Figure 1.1 shows these three areas of his language-based theory of learning.

Halliday (1993) explains his theory as follows:

> With this formulation I was trying to establish two unifying principles: that we should recognize not only a developmental continuity right through from birth to adult life, with language in home, neighborhood, primary school, secondary school, and place of work, but also a structural continuity running through all components and processes of learning. (p. 113)

Halliday recognized that language is more than a set of skills; it is also a tool for all other learning. Halliday's formulation nicely captures the concept of language both as a means to an end and an end in itself. It

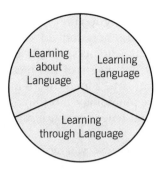

FIGURE 1.1. Three language functions of the language-based theory of learning (Halliday, 1993).

helps guide our thinking about how teaching English as a new language accounts for all of those functions. We can *learn language,* whether the first language or an additional language, in any setting, through social relationships, play, and performing many speech acts within a language community. However, we normally *learn about language* and *learn through language* in a more structured setting, such as school. Those of us who teach English as a new language need to be mindful of including activities in each of the three areas; conversely, learners will miss out on some areas of language competence if any one of these three aspects is overlooked over time.

Universals and Specifics of Language and Literacy

Language is a system that contains many small elements that can be combined in an infinite number of ways in order to make meanings. Human language has four universals: phonology, morphology, syntax, and semantics. These can be combined into the overall term *grammar.* Each language has its own grammar, and although some of the elements of one language can be found in other languages, the full inventory of characteristics is unique to that language.

The first universal is the inventory of sounds and sound combinations that belong to a language, the *phonology* of a language. It consists of the set of its sound patterns and the rules that govern how they can be combined. These patterns and rules give each language its distinct auditory identity. Another universal is that of units of meaning. *Morphology* can be defined as the units of meaning that make up the words of a language and the ways those units of meaning can be combined. A third universal is *syntax,* the set of rules governing the ways in which words can be ordered into phrases and sentences and, for some languages, the forms of the words within phrases or sentences. Finally, the *semantics* of a language is the fourth universal and consists of the meanings that emerge from the previous three elements: the sounds, word meanings, and word-order patterns. Even though the phonology, morphology, syntax, and semantics of every language differ, all languages have sounds, words, patterns, and meanings.

On the other hand, not every language has a writing system, or *orthography.* The first evidence of written records dates back only about 10,000 years; writing systems were invented, just as early civilizations invented the wheel, glass, and other cultural artifacts. Although orthographies take many forms, there is nothing inevitable about their invention. Orthography is a relatively recent development in human history.

The difference between the four inherent or universal aspects of language systems and writing systems is important because native speakers of a language naturally acquire the four universals, whereas literacy needs to be taught. Pinker (2007) says succinctly, "Language is an instinct, but reading is not" (p. 14). If reading and writing were universal and inevitable, all language groups would have a writing system, but we know that many societies, even some lasting several centuries, did not, and do not. The Mississippian peoples, living in the Cahokia region of Illinois around 1050 C.E., for example, created complex dwellings, a system of trade, games, many tools, and fine works of art, but never developed a writing system. Because reading and writing are not inevitable processes even in a first language, it stands to reason that considerable energy and effort are needed to learn to perform them in a new language.

Literacy: A Universal Human Right or a Privilege?

Reading and literacy empower both individuals and entire societies. Once literacy was an entitlement confined to elites, such as religious clergy and kings and ministers, but now there is an expectation that all societies should make literacy available to all their citizens. Literacy has come to be a measure of a society's worth. The right to universal literacy is not a new idea, but it is not a very old one, either, and it is not universally accepted even now. In fact, it is enshrined in the United Nations Educational, Scientific, and Cultural Organization's mission, as seen in the following statement.

> Literacy is a fundamental human right and the foundation for lifelong learning. It is fully essential to social and human development in its

ability to transform lives. For individuals, families, and societies alike, it is an instrument of empowerment to improve one's health, one's income, and one's relationship with the world. (*Literacy*, 2013, para 1)

Capital can be defined as a set of assets or resources available to people that gives them power or prestige in their society. Because we are social beings who use language for all manners of exchange, capital can be refined to include *linguistic capital,* the "amount of capital one can claim in the social world on the basis of one's linguistic ability and use" (Kanno & Kangas, 2014, p. 853). Literacy in a language enhances this linguistic capital; the skill of literacy can be considered a tool that confers great *cultural capital* upon its participants (Bourdieu, 1991). These grandiose claims are not overblown. Literacy greatly increases our ability to negotiate with others, through its ability to store, retrieve, analyze, and share information and ideas, and even to construct our identities.

The Interaction of Two Developing Systems

When ELLs strive to become literate in a new language, there are two large-scale, long-term developmental processes going on at the same time. One is the learning of the new language, and the other is the learning of literacy. The two processes develop, overlap, and interact in many complex ways over a period of years. Their successful dual achievement can be thought of almost as a kind of "syndrome." Normally, a syndrome is thought of as a group of factors that, taken together, characterize a disease or disorder. However, we'd like to flip that definition to describe a positive pattern. A positive syndrome, which we will call a *syndrome of success,* can be thought of as a synergy in which the presence of seemingly disconnected factors, working in combination, make success more likely. Because a syndrome of success for literacy in a new language includes complex factors, and there is a great deal of individual variation, researchers do not know all of the necessary ingredients or their proportions. However, we do know that a certain number of characteristics need to be "in the mix," and that some cannot be missing.

Let's look first at some key features of the syndrome of success in first-language literacy. This is not a short list! It includes listening comprehension, phonological and phonemic awareness, oral language production, the concept of word, sound–symbol matching (phonics), word recognition, the ability to construct meaning from print, fluent decoding, fluency, knowledge of morphology and syntax, vocabulary knowledge, knowledge of the function of punctuation, ability to spell, awareness of the diverse purposes of print, the ability to relate new information from prior experiences, writing for different purposes, and many other skills. The National Reading Panel (NRP) groups these features into five main categories: phonemic awareness, phonics, fluency, vocabulary, and comprehension. When the NRP findings were published in 2000, many called for the inclusion of writing as a core literacy skill as well.

Throughout this book, we use the term *L1* to represent the concepts "language one," "native language," "heritage language," or "first language," and the term *L2* to mean "second language," "new language," "subsequent language," or "additional language."

All of these same literacy features need to be developed in order to acquire literacy in a new language as well. Some aspects of these features can be learned once, in the first language, the L1, and positively applied to acquiring the same skill in a new language, the L2. Other features, however, require obtaining *language-specific* skills in the new language, that is, features that are unique to the structures of that particular language.

The skills needed may be acquired unconsciously in some cases, but in other cases must be consciously learned. Language-specific skills are not necessarily facilitated by knowing the same skill in the first language; they may sometimes even be hindered by it, depending on such factors as the structure of the two languages (Birch, 2015), the L1 and L2 proficiency levels of the learner, and the nature of the task.

Teachers of students who are becoming literate in a new language need to have special understandings and learn special strategies and skills that go above and beyond teaching literacy to native speakers. These special skills need to be part of an ESL teacher's toolkit. We have sketched some of them in Table 1.1.

English as a New Language:
Four Domains and the Fifth Domain

According to the language teaching field, four large domains are involved in learning a new language: listening, speaking, reading, and writing. These domains, stated in this order, also represent the common pattern of *second-language acquisition (SLA)*. Sometimes listening and reading are characterized as "receptive," and speaking and writing as "productive," but we caution against these labels because they fail to capture the active meaning making that takes place during both listening and reading. All instructional planning and assessment includes the four domains. In the same way, the three aspects of Halliday's language-based theory of learning need to be accounted for in any comprehensive literacy program.

Each one of the large domains has many skills nested within it. Furthermore, many language activities spill into more than one of the lan-

TABLE 1.1. ESL Teacher Toolkit

- Knowing the conventions of school and schooling
- Finding ways to work with families
- Honoring and including home languages
- Honoring and including home cultures
- Paying greater attention to students' oral language development
- Understanding L1 influence in phonology
- Structuring opportunities to practice speaking in many genres
- Understanding development of English decoding with knowledge of L1 decoding practices
- Helping students develop an extensive vocabulary
- Providing more scaffolding and greater practice time for writing
- Demonstrating explicit modeling, especially for writing
- Understanding L1 influence in spelling development
- Modeling and practicing appropriate and effective language in many different settings

guage domains—language is like that. There are times when one domain or skill should be the object of focus, and other times when the focus should be on constructing and communicating meaning through integrated activities that span the language domains. A sound instructional model can accommodate the development of both small skills that belong mainly to one domain, and large, integrated operations.

In a literacy curriculum, there are numerous small-skill areas across the four language domains, such as learning where to place a comma in a list or being able to anticipate the next word in a sentence. For example, native English speakers know that the word *of* belongs in the blank in the phrase "a box _____ crayons," or, at a more advanced level, that the word *nor* will come next when someone says, "Neither my family _____. . . . " (This is part of the pattern using *neither/ nor* that ELLs learn in advanced grammar classes.) However, the goal is ultimately to absorb each of these skills into the reading and writing process until they become automatic and unconscious. A pedagogical approach that favors mixing smaller skills within a framework of large meaning-based activities is usually called *balanced literacy*.

In addition to the domains mentioned here, a fifth domain, communicative competence, can be considered both a product of the other four and at the same time a contributor to their development (Hymes, 1981). *Communicative competence* is described as "the ability to know when, where, and how to use language in a variety of contexts or situations" (Rothenberg & Fisher, 2007, p. 38). Communicative competence is composed of many features. Linguists who developed the concept separate communicative competence into grammatical, sociolinguistic, discourse, and strategic competence (Canale, 1983), which, in turn, guide language users in making appropriate language choices for different social and academic functions. At the classroom level, this guidance fosters communicative competence.

People manifest communicative competence in many different ways, through word choices, syntax, vocal intonations, body language, and gestures. They can also demonstrate it through socially constructed rules that guide conversation and interaction in different social settings. We cannot take communicative competence for granted; it takes a long time to acquire, and its ingredients vary for differing purposes. Good L2 instruction infuses all the language domains with authentic activities that increase communicative competence in a natural, ongoing way. For example, when students learn the idiom "You're pulling my leg!," they need to learn not only its figurative meaning, but the kinds of settings in which it would be appropriate to say it.

Appendix 1.1 at the end of the chapter is a grid that can be used as a point of departure for thinking about ways to account for the five domains and the three functions of language learning in lesson planning. The chart can be used in the classroom and in curriculum planning as a kind of "quick check" of the domains and functions.

Language-Centered Factors Influencing SLA

What kinds of forces and factors contribute to creating proficiency in a new language? Research converges on several factors, which we briefly discuss here.

The Input Hypothesis and Comprehensible Input

Learners need sufficient exposure to a language, at a manageable level, to acquire it. Stephen Krashen (1985) grasped this concept in his revolutionary *input hypothesis,* which is one of the six hypotheses in his SLA theory. It states that people acquire a new language similarly to the way they acquire their native language, as long as they are exposed to enormous amounts of spoken language. He calls this language "input." Furthermore, the input needs not only to be very large; it must also be delivered at a level close to that at which learners can comprehend it. Krashen uses the term *comprehensible input* to describe language delivered to the learner at a level at which he or she can understand most of it.

We all deploy comprehensible input intuitively when we modify our speech for a specific listener. For example, we speak "baby talk" with an infant, using gestures and exaggerated intonation to get across our meanings (called *motherese* or *caretaker speech* by linguists). With careful planning, we can use our intuitive understanding of comprehensible input by modifying our language to assist limited English speakers. (If we are not mindful, it may sound like we're producing baby talk with learners who are not babies!) People may modify input for us when we travel to places where we don't know the language by adding gestures or throwing in a few shared words of English. Other ways people might make input comprehensible are by simplifying words, repeating words or phrases, speaking more slowly, speaking in a louder voice, breaking speech into smaller units, using exaggerated intonation or stress, or adding facial features or gestures. As learners gain proficiency, their level of comprehensible input becomes progressively more advanced as well. When learners are immersed in both oral and written language that is not too hard or overwhelming, they are able to internalize it.

Finally, the comprehensible input needs to be meaningful on some level. Look at this old joke:

PERSON A: What is the difference between ignorance and apathy?
PERSON B: I don't know and I don't care!

As is the case for these characters, people do not learn language for its own sake but to fulfill real purposes. If they don't know and they don't care, they won't learn! Even if it's comprehensible and there's enough of it, language acquisition requires some kind of authentic communicative purpose.

The input hypothesis and the concept of comprehensible input have been enormously influential in the ESL field. Both concepts have affected the development of all major ESL and bilingual programs and instructional materials.

The Output Hypothesis

For successful language learning, learners need opportunities not just to be exposed to spoken or written language, but also to interact with it. Swain's (2005) *output hypothesis* attempts to address this. Swain noticed that Canadian L1 English speakers in bilingual education programs, despite being immersed all day in French language content instruction over many years, did not speak and write French at the same level as their L1 French-speaking counterparts. The "input" was the same in quantity and quality; the missing piece was the "output." L1 English speakers were not being pushed to use French grammar accurately or meaningfully. This resulted in a lack of "urgency" to develop communicative competence.

Having lots of comprehensible input alone isn't enough to learn a new language, Swain reasoned; the learner needs abundant opportunities to create comprehensible output in situations that matter to the individual. *Comprehensible output* takes place through contact with a more competent other, such as a teacher or conversation partner, or in interactive situations such as collaborative dialogue (Swain, 2000, 2005, p. 478) or simple problem solving.

Comprehensible input helps explain the conditions for learning that are most likely to influence listening and reading, whereas comprehensible output helps explain the development of speaking and writing. Input and output are constantly interacting, however, and communicative competence is a constant overriding goal, no matter which processes are in play.

Systemic Functional Linguistics

One more influential approach is that of *systemic functional linguistics* (*SFL,* or "the functional approach"). This approach is an outgrowth of Halliday's language-based theory of learning and views language and linguistic content as two aspects of the same processes. These processes together form part of the sociocultural practices that occur within language communities. Functional linguists believe that "language users make choices based on their linguistic repertoires and these choices are related to the situations they participate in" (Achugar, Schleppegrell, & Oteiza, 2007, p. 12). When we look at language teaching as a way to help learners expand their linguistic repertoires in a variety of contexts, it creates a more holistic sense of the language user as a person who engages with many different communities for many different functions. For example, the language we use in the context of our immediate family is very different from the language we use in a job interview, or in a repair shop, or with a help desk over the phone. Becoming proficient in a range of functions within a new language greatly enlarges opportunities to interact with language communities.

Nonlinguistic Influences on SLA

Many nonlinguistic factors have been shown to influence success in learning a new language, and we have chosen to highlight three we consider to be very important.

The Affective Filter

Affect, or emotional state, is closely associated with language learning outcomes. The emotional aspects that influence language learning are referred to as the *affective filter* (Dulay & Burt, 1977), that is, the emotional response to the language learning situation. Krashen (1982) included this factor as one of the six hypotheses in his SLA theory. Stated briefly, many believe "the lower the level of anxiety, the better the language acquisition" (Krashen, 1987, p. 39). Learners' attitudes about their cultural or family background, the target language, the classroom climate, their feelings about their age or prior educational experiences, and many other factors influence the affective filter.

Motivation

The purposes that motivate a person to learn a new language are also at the forefront of language success, and can be grouped into four different categories: integrative motivation, instrumental motivation (Gardner & Lambert, 1972), assimilative motivation, and intrinsic motivation. *Integrative motivation* is the motivation a person feels when he or she wants to join a community. Voluntary immigrants have historically been those most interested in integrating into their new culture, and this attitude has an effect on the way they pursue language learning. *Instrumental motivation* occurs when a person needs to learn a language for a specific reason, such as communicating at school, at a job, or with a spouse. Students in foreign universities, people in international business, and those in English-dominant professions such as airplane pilots, international help desks, credit card IT desks, and air traffic controllers have instrumental motivation to learn English in the realms needed for their schooling or employment. When individuals wish to fully merge their identity with a target group (Richard-Amato, 2010), they are exhibiting *assimilative motivation*. Learners with assimilative motivation want to construct a new personal identify along with the new language. They are less likely to want to maintain their own heritage, language, and culture. This group of learners fits in more with the "melting pot" idea that everyone "melts" into a single national or language identity. Learners with integrative motivation, on the other hand, fit in more with the "salad bowl" concept: they prefer to mix in but retain their own identity, and not melt into the larger culture.

The fourth kind of motivation, which is less specific to language learning per se, is *intrinsic motivation*. People who have this kind of curiosity want to learn a new language or anything else for its own sake. Many of us who choose the language learning or language teaching profession have strong intrinsic motivation and find the study of languages captivating.

In addition, classroom motivational factors should never be discounted. The way teachers structure and present content has a measurable effect on the motivation level and the success of ELLs (Guilloteaux & Dornei, 2008).

Resilience

Resilience describes a person's ability to persevere to overcome possible obstacles. In research conducted about the differences between resilient and nonresilient students, resilient students were defined as high achievers who excelled on standardized tests and in daily schoolwork despite challenges, and nonresilient students were defined as low achievers who were not motivated and had poor attendance. Looking specifically at ELLs, Padrón, Waxman, Powers, and Brown (2002) found that resilient learners stayed on task more of the time in class, had higher satisfaction with their classes and a better self-image, got in trouble less, and had better relationships with their teachers. Significantly, resilient learners also used more metacognitive strategies while reading, and they did not consider reading to be their hardest subject. Resilient children were also found to speak more of their L1 with their parents and friends.

These findings suggest that reading proficiency and use of the L1 as a resource may be factors in building resilience and overall success for ELLs—or that resilience contributes to building them.

Padrón et al. (2002) suggest the following ways that teachers can build resilience in the classroom.

- Offering students opportunities to develop close relationships in the classroom.
- Increasing students' sense of mastery in their lives.
- Building social competencies in addition to academic skills.
- Reducing stress.
- Finding and generating school and community resources to serve the children's needs.

Language Teaching Approaches and Methods and the Role of Reading

Throughout history, there have been many approaches and methods to teaching new languages (we use the terms *approach* and *method* interchangeably in this section). We briefly highlight four important approaches used in a wide variety of ESL programs over the years, with particular reference to how they integrate the teaching of literacy in a new language: (1) grammar translation, (2) audiolingualism (Fries, 1945; Lado, 1977), (3) the communicative approach (Canale & Swain, 1980; Savignon, 1983), and (4) content-based instruction (CBI) (Brinton, Snow, & Wesche, 2003; Chamot & O'Malley, 1994; Peregoy & Boyle, 2005; Stoller & Grabe, 1997).

The language education field has an "alphabet soup" of constantly changing acronyms. When students learn English in a non-English-speaking country, it is called *English as a foreign language,* or *EFL.* Within an English-speaking country, learners of English are said to be studying *ESL,* or *English as a second language,* and the learners of English as a new language are commonly referred to as *English language learners (ELLs),* or often "ELs," shorthand for "English learners." These terms are widely used in the language teaching field. Some professional standards for teachers of ELLs, such as those in Illinois, for example, are called ENL ("English as a new language") standards. The terms L1 and L2, on the other hand, are used mainly in applied linguistics as a shorthand for the language being referred to at the moment.

The Grammar Translation Method

The grammar translation method, which has no instruction in listening or speaking, can be classified as "learning about language" in Halliday's language-based theory of learning. The focus of the grammar translation method is on reading and translating a text back and forth between the target language and one's first language. Once learners understand the specific grammar rules embedded in various reading passages, they begin reading and writing in the target language. Little or no attempt is made to build communicative competence. A grammar translation lesson usually consists of the teacher introducing a text in the new language and explaining the grammar rules that the text illustrates. Students often receive a list of vocabulary words and phrases to facilitate their reading. The *grammar translation approach* today is most widely used in language-learning methods designed for instrumental purposes. Its users include those training for the clergy or for advanced degrees in certain academic disciplines. Latin, Greek, Hebrew, and Sanskrit are often taught with this method. Grammar translation is also a component of language teaching in countries where there are not many native speakers of the target language, so that the book and its related exercises serve in many ways as the "teacher." Elements of grammar translation are even used for teaching very young children English as a foreign language.

Audiolingualism

Audiolingualism, or the *audiolingual method (ALM),* is a language-learning method in which listening and speaking in the target language takes precedence over reading and writing. This is reflected in its title—"audio" representing listening, and "lingual" representing speaking. It developed as a countermovement to the heavily text-centered nature of the grammar translation approach. The initial impetus for ALM in the United States was the need to develop fluent speakers of the world's languages for national defense purposes. A modified form of audiolingualism is still used in the United States to prepare people for the Peace Corps and for diplomatic and other international assignments. It is the method used by many independent language academies and in self-paced language-learning software programs.

An audiolingual lesson consists of students learning and repeating dialogues with the teacher and other students and practicing sentences based on the dialogues through oral drills. The dialogues used to be rehearsed in a language lab, but now a great deal of ALM study takes place through individualized programs using headphones. Students may memorize and perform a dialogue at the end of a unit. Rules are presented sequentially through the dialogues, and there is a strong emphasis on correction of errors, although they are not formally explained. Pronunciation gets a lot of attention in ALM. Reading is not a focus of audiolingualism and is not generally introduced until the third year of study. The audiolingual method, which focuses on imitating sentences, could be considered closest to the "learning language" concept in Halliday's theory, but ALM lacks the interactions found in a language community.

The Communicative Approach

The *communicative approach* changed the focus of ESL instruction by putting communicative competence at center stage. Canale and Swain (1980), Savignon (1983), and others recognized that the social functions of language and meaning making in language were too often missing from language teaching methods, particularly in ALM.

Brown (2001) describes the goals of communicative competence this way:

> Communicative goals are best achieved by giving due attention to language use and not just usage, to fluency and not just accuracy, to authentic language and contexts, and to students' eventual need to apply classroom learning to previously unrehearsed contexts. (p. 69)

The approach is learner centered and consistent with constructivist notions of education. Although reading and writing occur, they are seen as a means to greater communicative competence; academic language is not a focus. Students use authentic texts for speaking and reading activities from a wide variety of genres, such as menus, newspaper articles, or even medicine bottle labels. Grammar, when taught, is contextualized and is considered a means of enhancing communication. The communicative approach is widely used in EFL settings outside of English-speaking countries and with adult learners. Until the advent of content-based instruction, communicative language teaching was the most widely used approach in PreK–12 schools in the United States, and it is still widely practiced in the foreign-language classroom. The focus of the communicative approach, like the audiolingual approach, is also "learning language" from Halliday's theory, but the classrooms are consciously directed toward real-life or simulated social situations.

These three approaches, which started as methods for adult learners, have been successful in helping many people learn new languages. However, all of them presuppose a certain "grace period" before the language must be used for functional purposes, and these methods do not address the reality ELLs face in PreK–12 academic settings. Young people must learn English at the same time they are learning content matter through the medium of English in the areas of social studies, math, science, and language arts. In addition, students need to be able to use language to perform procedural tasks related to school, such as listening to directions and taking standardized tests.

Content-Based Instruction

Content-based instruction (*CBI*) (Chamot & O'Malley, 1994) addresses the pressing need of ELLs to perform at grade level on school curriculum while learning English. This paradigm shift is now the main instructional approach for teaching ELL students, whether the instruction takes place in a dual-language, bilingual, or ESL/EFL context. The central idea of CBI is to provide many avenues of support for teaching content and language. *Sheltered instruction,* which is a primary form that good content-based instruction takes, consists of building language proficiency and content knowledge by setting clearly defined language and content goals. This is done by means of an enriched curriculum, supplementary materials, flexible grouping options, authentic materials, technology enrichment, and classroom-based assessments.

For too long, it had been assumed that ELLs would naturally acquire the academic language that native speakers in schools are expected to possess, but all too often, this was not the case. Now, all teachers, whether they are ESL, bilingual, dual, or content teachers, are becoming knowledgeable about sheltering strategies and techniques. By the way, these same techniques also help in teaching native speakers of English! Good teachers need to shelter at every age and grade level in grade-appropriate ways.

The "language side" includes learning the forms of English (grammar), learning its functions, and becoming fluent in a wide range of spoken and written tasks. Learners need exposure to not only what is called basic "survival" English, social English, and academic English, but also to the language of general academic operations, such as the procedural language of school. Naturally, survival English and social English are part of the communicative approach, too, but CBI and sheltered instruction make content and language their explicit goals.

The "content side" includes learning the specific vocabulary of each unit of the curriculum in each of the *content areas* (for example, learning the names of laboratory equipment in science, such as "beaker" and "pipette,") as well as the content knowledge itself. The content vocabulary may be found not only in textbooks and lectures, but also in classroom interactions, such as a teacher modeling the thinking involved in solving a math problem, as well as in print and online materials such as video clips, WebQuests, and podcasts. The focus of the content-based approach is "learning through language" in Halliday's theory (see Figure 1.1). When using the content-based method, teachers must also include the other two aspects, learning language and learning about language, in order to provide language learners with a balanced approach.

In the past, teachers believed that introducing individual content words about a topic would address the language needs of learners, whether they were native speakers or ELLs. However, the missing ingredient for ELLs was accounting for the language activities that students required in order to perform the academic language tasks of the classroom. For example, third-grade ELLs learning about dinosaurs need two kinds of vocabulary. They need to learn the words to understand dinosaur species, their habitats, and the geological time periods in which dinosaurs lived. They also need academic language to process and demonstrate their understanding of the content, such as "Give reasons for and explain why the dinosaurs became extinct," or "Include supporting details about dinosaur habitats in the body of the report," or "Summarize what you have learned about brachiosaurus." These are complex academic operations and require explicit teaching and practice.

CBI can take place in a dual-language or bilingual setting in the student's native language or in a sheltered setting conducted in English. The content-based approach recognizes that the academic language demands to master content are just as important as the study of the content itself. In fact, learning these academic language strategies can transfer to the study of new content in different disciplines. For example, if a learner knows how to use a graphic organizer to represent the ways that modern birds possess the characteristics of theropod dinosaurs, that learner can also use the same kind of graphic organizer to list the ways that Charlotte the spider and Wilbur the pig show friendship, based on the classic text

Charlotte's Web (White, 1952). CBI is standards based, and the standards mirror the grade-level expectations for native English-speaking children in each subject area.

CBI-Based Instructional Models

Early sheltered approaches to teaching content to ELLs include the *cognitive academic language learning approach* (*CALLA*; Chamot & O'Malley, 1986) and *specially designed academic instruction in English* (*SDAIE*; California Department of Education, 1993). These approaches emphasize developing academic language and providing strategies students can use for independent learning. The best-known sheltered model, however, is the *sheltered instruction observation protocol* (*SIOP*; Echevarria, Vogt, & Short, 2000), which expands upon previous sheltered models with a full-scale design and eight major principles; its accompanying strategies aim to build students' language skills while learning grade-level content. This method, which involves intensive training, has been implemented in many school districts.

It's also important for CBI programs to provide adequate time for ELLs to engage in daily oral language activities that develop social skills and allow classroom friendships and a sense of community to unfold.

Many techniques and strategies accompany sheltered instructional designs and are summarized later in the chapter, in the section "Research into Effective Teaching Strategies for ELLs."

The Influence of Vygotsky's Theories on Second-Language Learning

Both Krashen's and Swain's hypotheses include the assumption that students' L2 proficiency increases when they engage in activities that will move them to understand or produce language at the next level. Therefore, they benefit from authentic opportunities to connect with a language user at a level just above their own current one. Their theories mesh nicely with those of Lev Vygotsky, a Russian psychologist whose works were largely unknown during his own lifetime but are becoming increasingly influential with language researchers, child psychologists, and educators.

Vygotsky's theories have contributed two important ideas to the field of L2 acquisition. One of these ideas is his characterization of learning as being *socially constructed*. Our social interactions and the language we use to perform them provide us with the mental tools that allow us to learn.

School settings are places where "socially organized events" are likely to occur, so they are important to our language growth, which is, in turn, the basis of our cognitive growth. This idea is applied through interactions that take place during schooling, family time, work, and play.

The other idea is Vygotsky's concept of the *zone of proximal development* (*ZPD*; Vygotsky, 1978), which he describes as "the discrepancy between a child's actual mental age and the level he reaches in solving problems with assistance" (Vygotsky, 1986, p. 187). Vygotsky described an effective learning setting as one in which the learner has multiple opportunities to grow within that zone. The teacher's role can be viewed as something like "collaborative coaching in the zone." Research on effective second-language instruction supports Vygotsky's idea that ELLs thrive when they engage in *instructional conversation* in the classroom (Tharp et al., 2003; Waxman & Téllez, 2002). Many educators have begun to embrace the powerful idea that a student can attain greater proficiency with assistance from a near peer or an "expert other" than with a teacher lecturing from the front of a classroom.

The concept of ZPD acknowledges the dynamic process of learning and also the importance of differentiating instruction among learners within a classroom. When we factor in the developmental continuum of human learning along with L2 acquisition, we should not be surprised at all the varieties of achievement that result! After all, no two people are alike, and no two language learners are ever at exactly the same stage.

> *The way I visualize learning a new language "in the zone" is by thinking of the formation of an island in the South Pacific. The island forms as more and more material is pushed up from below and becomes rich island soil. Following the metaphor, as we learn more language, more material is added to the rich soil, and that in turn increases the base. After a while, there is enough to stand on, and things begin to grow. In time, you might have enough space to live upon.*—KRISTIN

Deficit Theory

As we discuss best practices for building proficiency in English as a new language, we want to be sure to address the hidden assumptions that sometimes underlie the topic: the idea that English, or Standard English, is "better" than a student's home language or *dialect*. This assumption is an extension of the *deficit theory*, which has been identified and critiqued by many scholars with respect to the language use and academic success of learners from diverse backgrounds (e.g., Eller, 1989; Labov, 1972; Lakoff, 1973). Deficit theory is the idea that children enter school with "deficits," based on such factors as their family's interactional practices, their socioeconomic level, parent educational level, and/or home dialect. The role of the school is to correct these "deficits." Sociolinguists have demonstrated that family and community language use have strengths of their own and that educators need to become more aware of the language resources children already have in order to further develop them (Heath, 2012). Eller points out that it may be the nature of expected classroom exchanges, or teachers' own perceptions, that label children as linguistically deficient. She says, "Perhaps when classrooms become places where valid exchanges between teachers and learners can take place, we will stop labeling children 'verbally deficient' and begin to recognize their true competence as learners" (1989, p. 673).

Over time, the deficit model has been applied to children who speak a home language other than English. Instead of considering home languages as an asset or resource, home languages came to be seen as "problems" to be remediated. This view is reflected in the descriptors of linguistically and culturally diverse learners as "limited English proficient (LEP)," a term once used by the U.S. Department of Education.

Educators need to consider children's home languages and dialects as assets. Although this issue is powerfully addressed in discussions about the foundations of ESL and bilingual education (e.g., Baker, 1993, 2011; de Jong, 2011), we also feel it has important ramifications for literacy development.

Having covered the four major instructional models for learning English as a new language, we would be remiss not to mention the "non-method" of immersion. This "method," which consisted of immersing ELL children in an all-English classroom with no support or accommodations, was used for large numbers of new immigrants to the United States, especially when immigration was at its peak (around 1880–1920). However, the immersion method is still used today in many private and rural schools, and when a family declines existing support services for their child.

One of us had a language immersion experience:

I was first immersed into French at age 8 while living in my small town in Ivory Coast. There were over 100 kids in the classroom, and we were not allowed to use our mother tongues to communicate among ourselves. If you were caught speaking your language, you got punished and you had to wear the jaw of an animal hung around your neck, like a "scarlet letter," and everyone would make fun of you. On the first day of school, we went home for lunch at noon, and I told my parents I didn't want to go back because I was traumatized. My parents didn't want to hear it, so they whipped me and forcefully returned me to school. They told the teacher I didn't want to study. The teacher in turn gave me another whipping, and they all told me that my place was in school, and I must learn in French. That's one of the reasons I studied linguistics, so that my mother tongue could be taught too.—TENENA

Although it is true that immersion does work for some learners, especially very young children in a natural setting, as a method it has serious problems. First, one's first language is a resource that can inform and improve upon second-language study. Why not use it? "It's like asking a person to dance with one hand tied behind his or her back," said one of our students. Second, not allowing children to use their first language can have negative consequences for their identity and sense of well-being, as illustrated in Tenena's account. When children believe that the very words they say in their home environment are of lesser value than the language spoken in school, it creates a powerful negative subtext and can even make children think there is no place for them in school. Here is an example of the phenomenon from a second-grade bilingual Spanish teacher in a district that has bilingual education:

I work with a little girl who is completely ashamed of speaking Spanish. When I do Spanish interventions, she laughs and giggles. She purposely mispronounces words even if I know she knows the correct way. It saddens me to see that she is so ashamed to speak such a beautiful language.—LETICIA CORTES

Research into Effective Teaching Strategies for ELLs

In the past, research about best practices for teaching ELLs was spotty. Most of the research had been conducted on adults in academic settings, but far less was known about how children who speak a language other than English at home could achieve biliteracy and academic success. However, research about what teaching practices work best for ELLs has grown in recent years.

There are a number of metastudies (which look for trends and commonalities among individual research studies) that focus on ELLs (e.g., August & Shanahan, 2006; Gersten & Baker, 2000; Gersten et al., 2007; Téllez & Waxman, 2006; Tharp et al., 2003; Waxman & Téllez, 2002; Williams et al., 2007). From these studies, it is possible to extract a number of recurring characteristics that contribute to an ELL learner's "syndrome of success." Here is a brief description of some of the findings:

• *Collaborative learning communities.* ELLs thrive in cooperative learning and small-group settings because such settings lower the affective filter, give more opportunities to practice language, and provide motivation to use language for authentic communicative purposes.

• *Multiple representations of content.* ELLs benefit when they have several points of entry into content, including the use of visual images, audio files, videos, movies, and art forms such as music. If one method of presenting material doesn't make sense, another may.

• *Building on prior knowledge.* When learners activate their prior knowledge before engaging in reading, writing, or any kind of academic activity, it's easier for them to hook into many topic areas and respond positively. Students often have more extensive prior knowledge than teachers realize; it's just a matter of giving students opportunities for it to unfold.

• *Protracted instructional conversation.* Extended daily instructional conversation with both peers and with the teacher fosters ELL academic growth. In addition, the dialogue needs to be protracted. Téllez and Waxman (2006) found that "keeping the conversation going" (p. 261) as learners advance through school results in increased achievement among ELLs.

• *Culturally responsive instruction.* Like any students, ELLs need to see themselves and their home languages and cultures reflected in the curriculum. Although this is widely understood, many classrooms and schools have still not taken up the challenge to make available the many resources that respect and affirm ELL children's home languages and cultures.

• *Technology-enriched instruction.* Technology has opened vast new vistas for teaching ELLs. Programs, websites, and apps allow students to work at their own pace and on their own lessons, and allow differentiation in mixed-level or mixed-language classrooms.

• *Challenging curriculum.* When busily preparing lessons for ELLs at different English-proficiency levels, it's easy for teachers to become inadvertent "enablers." ELL students, like any students, can meet and exceed standards. Research indicates that all too often, ELL students are wrongly placed in special education or remedial level classes simply because they speak another language (Kanno & Kangas, 2014). Like all other students, ELL students will reflect a wide range of talents, abilities, and interests, and should be held to the highest standards. In fact, if anything, bilingualism and biliteracy can be considered a kind of "giftedness" because of the cognitive advantages that come from regularly using two languages (Dorner, Orellana, & Li-Grining, 2007).

- *Strong and explicit vocabulary development.* Vocabulary development in both oral and written forms is at the core of all academic learning for ELLs. Students need to learn the language of the content areas and to experience new words and concepts as they are modeled, heard, spoken, read, and written.

HOW DOES THIS LOOK IN THE CLASSROOM?

The first four items that follow serve as general reminders pertaining to the theories presented early in the chapter. The eight areas that follow them are brief classroom ideas that enhance the research-based best practices reviewed in the chapter. Future chapters include specific language and literacy activities.

Planning Work in the Five Domains

ELLs need daily experience using all five domains, both separately and in combination. Ask yourself, "Is each student in the class taking part in some listening, speaking, reading, writing, and communicative activity every day?"

Providing Comprehensible Input

The key word here is *comprehensible.* A person can have a TV with speakers of another language on all day and call it language "input," but that doesn't make it comprehensible! How can input be made comprehensible? Here are some of the ways: by breaking it up into smaller chunks, using visuals, providing repetition, simplifying language, adding captions, increasing expressive language, activating background knowledge, and checking comprehension regularly.

Pushing Output

Pushing output describes a classroom with less teacher talk and more pair work and small-group talk among students. Teachers can make sure desks and chairs are in pods rather than rows, experiment with flexible grouping so that learners will have many opportunities to interact, create cross-grade visits and collaborative projects, invite guests into the classroom, and encourage student artistic projects.

Lowering the Affective Filter

There are many ways to create a learning environment that is at once comforting, nurturing, and challenging. One teacher reports, "The atmosphere in my high school ESL class improved a lot when I dropped the closed-book tests and quizzes." In the area of assessments, we can give students choices about ways of responding, allow sufficient wait time for students to formulate answers, allow native language use, and provide opportunities for students to present in small groups instead of presenting to the entire class. Laughter, games, songs, skits, and brain teasers are the ticket! Culturally aware celebrations and parties also help to build community and contribute to an ambience that encourages resilience. Invite families and caregivers to be part of the classroom community.

• *Collaborative learning communities.* Students can design projects together through project-based learning, literature circles, group science experiments, performances, interviews, debates, and more. In classes of mixed ELLs and native speakers, structure activities carefully so that the ELL students have a specific role that they can competently perform—this may be better decided by the teacher than the students in some cases. As an example, young children can draw the progress as they watch ants build a home in a classroom ant farm installation over a period of several weeks, and discuss their drawings with others.

• *Multiple representations of content.* Audio and video sources can easily be brought in. *Realia,* or real-life material artifacts, can supplement any lesson. Ask students what they can bring in from home to illustrate a lesson. Realia might include bringing in a pair of knitting needles on the day you read a picture book featuring knitting, comics from the Sunday paper, or labels on clothing to collectively decode washing instructions. Formative assessment can ask for labeling, drawing, and filling in graphic organizers, and students can create their own visual products, including collages, photo essays, or posters.

• *Building on prior knowledge.* Coaxing out prior knowledge before beginning a new unit or book is part of any good lesson. However, don't forget that prior knowledge also means reviewing the previous day's lesson or the lesson from the previous week! The recycling helps embed the new language and concepts into the child's memory.

• *Protracted instructional conversation.* Waiting longer for responses and waiting after the second conversational exchange makes a big difference in both the quantity and quality of student work (Rowe, 1986). Instructional conversation can include reading and writing topics and also common classroom topics, such as planning activities for the day, setting up and maintaining a recycling program, discussing the physical setup of the classroom, or thinking through how to save or store student work. Don't do this for students—do it with them!

• *Culturally responsive instruction.* Inviting families and cultural representatives into the classroom as resources helps set a welcoming tone. Artifacts from other countries and cultures give children a chance to look at and touch creations from around the world, and encourages them to try to recreate similar items in art class. Having a good, attractive classroom library of multicultural and multilingual children's books deepens the level of commitment.

• *Technology-enriched instruction.* Digital technology has made colorful and engaging resources available at little cost. One good example is the catalogue of easy books from *www.raz-kids.com*, which are downloadable on a regular classroom printer. The short books can be read alone, in pairs, or chorally, and children can color and otherwise personalize their own copies of the books. Google images can pull up images of almost anything found in books, making it easier for students to visualize them. Learning to code is also "language learning" and can be done as a project. More technology ideas can be found in Chapter 10 and throughout the book.

• *Challenging curriculum.* Plan outside the box! Sometimes we may be so focused on "meeting or exceeding" standards that we overlook the talents and capabilities all around us. While students are still improving their English, you can set up projects that require a lot of thinking and problem solving, and you may be surprised. Making a simple movie together, creating a mural, building a toothpick fortress, creating a service project, or cowriting an alphabet book to go home to families are but a few of the ways you can encourage students to aspire to their creative potential. Instead of dwelling on the language that is still in development, it's great to look at the cognitive skills that already exist.

• *Strong and explicit vocabulary development.* There are many ways to "turbocharge" vocabulary learning. Chapter 8 of this book has many ideas. Children have the capability to learn thousands of words and phrases, so you can be "word-conscious" in your teaching setting, providing simple explanations of words and many repetitions of new words in different contexts. Students can practice new words in oral and written form, and they can illustrate them, too. Bilingual students can learn new meanings of words they know in L1 or in L2 and double the possibilities! Create a vocabulary learning system in the classroom, so it's systematic— and then go beyond the system, too! One of our favorite sites is *freerice. com*, which has many levels of vocabulary quizzes with multiple choice items and donates rice to people suffering from hunger as you complete quizzes.

There are other online resources, many created by teachers. It would be hard to find a profession whose members are more generous with their knowledge than teachers. In addition to sharing teaching tips and techniques, teachers often share, and sometimes sell, original games, quizzes, lessons, units, and other inventions at places like Pinterest, Quizlet, ESL Café, and Teachers Pay Teachers. If you are already in the language teaching field, you probably know of vast resources already. If not, look around and you will not be disappointed.

QUESTIONS FOR FURTHER STUDY

1. If you had to choose three important ideas from this chapter, which would you choose? How can you apply these ideas to your larger knowledge of teaching English as a new language?

2. What are some ways that input has been made comprehensible in a teaching or learning setting with which you are familiar?

3. The chapter mentions that the order of listening, speaking, reading, and writing is usually considered the general order of SLA. In what ways does this reflect, or not reflect, your own experiences as a learner or teacher of languages? Do you think that order makes sense for all language learning purposes? Why, or why not?

4. Analyze your own foreign language study in terms of the four different kinds of motivation listed in the chapter. How did the presence or absence of motivation affect the success of the language-learning task? What other tasks in your life have been guided by integrative motivation? Instrumental motivation? Intrinsic motivation?

5. Do you think resilience and intrinsic motivation are determined entirely by environment and upbringing, or are they something some people are born with or without? Discuss.

6. Try to think of a time you have modified your speech or writing to create comprehensible input for someone. What techniques did you use to ensure it was comprehensible?

7. Have you seen any examples of the deficit model in action, either as a learner, a parent, or an educator? If so, what did you do about what you observed, if anything? How would you advise others?

8. If you have access to a classroom setting with ELLs, make an inventory of daily activities to see how much time, if any, is devoted to the five

domains of listening, speaking, reading, writing, and communicative competence. Do you think the proportion should change for different age levels? Proficiency levels? Instructional settings?

9. Think about a classroom you know and try to classify its daily activities according to the language-based theory of learning. How much do they teach language, teach about language, or teach content through language? How do you think the time allocated for each area might change for different age levels? Proficiency levels? Instructional settings? From your own experience, which of the functions do you think is most often overlooked in instructional settings?

10. How do you know whether you are introducing children to challenging content? What criteria would you use to know this? Whom would you talk to?

11. Of the overview of best practices at the end of the chapter, which do you think are most similar to best practices for native speakers? Least similar?

12. CHALLENGE QUESTION: What are some ways one might keep track of the development of communicative competence in ELLs? Try to create a rubric or checklist for communicative competence development, and explain how you decided to include certain skills or competencies.

13. CHALLENGE QUESTION: Look at Appendix 1.1 and see if you can plan, or classify, classroom activities according to both the five domains and three functions of language learning assembled together in one chart. Talk about it.

Quick Guide to Including the Five Domains and Three Functions of Language Learning

	Learning language	Learning about language	Learning through language
Listening			
Speaking			
Reading			
Writing			
Communicative competence			

CHAPTER TWO

First-Language Influence in Second-Language Acquisition

New Vocabulary in This Chapter: *contrastive analysis (CA), language acquisition, language learning, interdependence hypothesis, sociocultural theory, compensatory model of second-language reading, hypothetical model of the reading process, world knowledge, language knowledge, cognitive processing strategies, language processing strategies, language distance (linguistic proximity), cognates, orthographic distance, transfer, decoding, cross-linguistic influence, positive cross-linguistic influence (PCI), interference, lingua franca, non-effects, diacritics, metalinguistic awareness, interactive process, bottom-up skills, top-down skills, threshold theory, short-circuit hypothesis, language loss, basic interpersonal communicative skills (BICS), cognitive academic language proficiency (CALP), Teachers of English to Speakers of Other Languages (TESOL), World Class Instructional Design and Assessment (WIDA), Consortium, performance definitions for ELLs*

Although many mysteries remain about how new languages are learned, a good number have now been solved. It doesn't take a book like ours to convince you that learning a new language is not a matter of starting from scratch. Our first language serves as "an already established system of meanings," as the influential Russian educator Lev Vygotsky wrote (1986, p. 197). Some parts of that system of meanings are embedded within the structure of the specific first language, however, while others can be applied directly and indirectly to a new language.

To understand the complex topic of first-language influence on SLA, we think it helps to introduce some of the thinking that predated our current understandings and beliefs. We review several key hypotheses here.

The Contrastive Analysis Hypothesis

The *contrastive analysis (CA)* hypothesis emerged in the 1950s and 1960s when linguists extensively analyzed features shared and not shared by languages. They predicted that learners would have an easier time learning the features of a new language that were similar to features of their first language and a harder time learning features of a new language that differed from their first language. Contrastive analysis was the linguistic basis of the audiolingual method (see Chapter 1), and the result was that materials and lessons were designed around predictions about what patterns of difficulty could be expected in learning the L2.

Since that time, linguists in the field found that the CA hypothesis did not explain many phenomena teachers observed in their students, and that the exercises and drills based on predictions from contrastive analysis only accounted for part of the development of language proficiency. Also, important research, especially that of Dulay and Burt (1974), revealed that English morphemes, such as *-ing* or third-person plural *-s/-es,* were acquired in a certain predictable order, regardless of the first language of the learner. However, the "weak form" of the CA hypothesis, that aspects of L1 systems have explanatory but not predictive power, is still widely accepted because it helps us understand that certain challenges and advantages learners encounter in learning English are directly related to their first-language systems. We discuss the phonological systems further in Chapter 3, the orthographic systems in Chapter 4, and the morphological systems in Chapter 5.

Language as an Innate Human Endowment

During the same time that the CA hypothesis was proposed, the Chomskyian revolution challenged the concept that a first language is "learned" at all. Linguist Noam Chomsky proposed that *language acquisition* is innate, universal, and automatic, a uniquely human endowment (Chomsky, 1965, 1972). Infants are born with the innate capacity to acquire the language or languages that surround them. As people in the second-language teaching field became exposed to Chomsky's theories, they in turn wondered what aspects of second-language learning might also be reframed as "acquisition" rather than "learning." Eventually, a paradigm

shift occurred as new ideas about *language learning* versus language acquisition began to emerge (Krashen, 1982). "Acquisition" was considered
something that occurred effortlessly and automatically, whereas "learning" was considered something that was effortful and conscious. This
deeply affected second-language pedagogy, as described here by Freeman
and Freeman (2004) in an example pertaining to how ELLs attain the
pronunciation of English phonemes.

> Earlier methods of language teaching, based on a learning model, have
> been replaced by current methods that are based on an acquisition
> model. . . . [A premise of the Natural Approach is that] English phonol-
> ogy is simply too complex to be learned through either direct, explicit
> teaching or implicit teaching in the context of carefully sequenced
> drills. Instead, students acquire phonology in the process of develop-
> ing the ability to communicate in a new language. (p. 84)

Although there are many aspects of second-language acquisition versus second-language learning that are of interest, our focus in this chapter and in this book is on literacy, which for the most part is learned.

The Interdependence Hypothesis

The influential *interdependence hypothesis* (Cummins, 1979, 1981) emerged
during this period as well. In examining research about bilingual children in Canada, Cummins proposed that a common underlying proficiency between two languages could help these students achieve high
levels of literacy in PreK–12 settings. Cummins made the case that L1
literacy level closely correlated with L2 literacy level, all other things
being equal. The implication of this hypothesis was that native language
literacy would inherently assist L2 literacy. This hypothesis has provided
strong support for bilingual education and the value of building children's L1 literacy.

The question of first-language influence on second-language development is more nuanced today, and we hope readers of this book will
develop an appreciation for those nuances. Now, there is a recognition
that some aspects of L1 literacy may foster developing the second language, whereas others may not, and learning depends on a wide variety of factors (Birch, 2015; Koda, 2005; Van Gelderen et al., 2007). For
example, learning which words use capital letters in English is specific to
the written conventions of English. However, learning how to make an
inference about a character in a novel, based on the character's speech,
clothing, and accessories, can be done across languages, even though spe-

cific details may differ. We explore these complexities in the remainder of this chapter and throughout the book.

Sociocultural Theory

The field of teaching English as a second language originally focused mainly on teaching English to international college students. Since then, it has converged with the education field, with a focus on teaching children whose families speak a language other than English in the home. As educators have addressed the real-world realities and learning needs of children, new theories with more practical applications have been added to the language teaching field. Key among these theories is the sociocultural theory. *Sociocultural theory* (Lantolf & Thorne, 2006) examines the social nature of language and how people use language to do things in the world. Despite his untimely death in the 1930s, Vygotsky's works (1978, 1986) continue to influence this theory. His powerful writing explores how social interactions through language help to form the child's mind. Sociocultural theorists ask these kinds of questions:

- What does it mean to say one form of language is "correct" or "incorrect"?
- What kinds of language hold power and authority, and which ones are stigmatized (Bourdieu, 1991)?
- Who gets access to the powerful forms and registers of language, and who controls the access?
- What messages are "coded" into different kinds of speech and writing?
- How do the sociocultural functions of language influence its development in a variety of speech communities?

These sorts of questions, asked by sociolinguists and other social scientists, have implications for the learning of new languages. Exploring these sorts of questions engages several academic disciplines in the social sciences. However, those committed to educational access and equity in language education are called to look for ways to support bilingualism and biliteracy and to increase students' "linguistic capital" (Bourdieu, 1991).

L2 Reading Models

The myriad factors that contribute to literacy have made it confoundingly difficult to construct a serviceable model of L2 reading. A good L2 reading model must encompass not only many languages, on both the L1 and L2 sides of the equation, but also account for learners of all ages, all L1 literacy levels, and all socioeconomic groups, along with many individual differences. We have found two models that we consider to be powerful and useful.

Bernhardt's (2011) *compensatory model of second-language reading* (revised) (Figure 2.1) accounts for several of these complexities. Bernhardt examined research about L2 reading by children, adolescents, and adults from a number of first- and second-language combinations in order to construct a model that could explain and predict the development of reading proficiency in a new language. In her model, L1 literacy (alphabetics, vocabulary, text structure, beliefs about word and sentence configuration, etc.) accounts for about 20% of second-language reading proficiency, and L2 language knowledge (grammatical forms, vocabu-

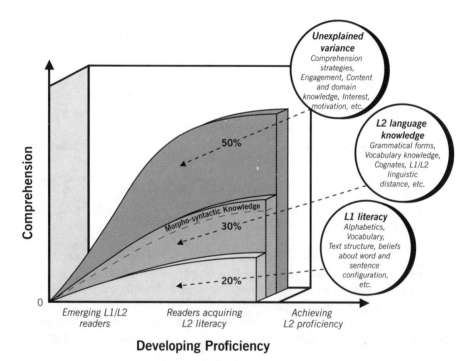

FIGURE 2.1. A compensatory model of second-language reading (revised). From Bernhardt (2011). *Understanding Advanced Second Language Reading.* Copyright © 2011 Taylor and Francis. Reprinted by permission of Routledge, member of the Taylor & Francis Group.

lary knowledge, cognates, L1/L2 linguistic distance, etc.) accounts for another 30%. Beyond those two identifiable areas, another 50%, which she calls "unexplained variance" (comprehension strategies, engagement, content and domain knowledge, interest, motivation, etc.) has yet to be fully explained. In Chapter 1, we point out that many of these unexplained variables contribute to the "syndrome of success." Teacher influence is undoubtedly part of that variance. Bernhardt explains that development within the two known contributors does not have to occur in a fixed order; first-language literacy development may take place before, during, or after second-language grammar development, and learning comprehension strategies, or motivational factors, can kick in at any time. The model is "bidirectional" in nature, so that "as literate individuals process their second language in reading they rely on multiple information sources not a priori determining what is an 'important' source but, rather, bringing whichever sources to bear at an appropriate moment of indecision or insecurity" (2011, p. 37). That is why Bernhardt calls it a "compensatory" model—learners draw from their strong areas of literacy to compensate for their weaker areas, and these areas develop and shift over time. She represents this reciprocal process by means of a two-way arrow between L1 literacy and L2 proficiency and a longer two-way arrow crossing all of the variables.

The second model is Birch's (2015) *hypothetical model of the reading process* (Figure 2.2). Although Birch's model focuses on reading growth within a single language, it seamlessly applies to second-language reading growth. The two large columns, which work in parallel, are the Processing Strategies column (on the left) and the Knowledge Base column (on the right). Each of these comprises two sectors. The two parts of the Knowledge Base column are world knowledge and language knowledge. *World knowledge* (people, places, events, and activities) can be universally attained just by living in the world. However, *language knowledge* (sentences, phrases, words, letters, and sounds) is language specific, is acquired both unconsciously and consciously, and includes literacy. The Processing Strategies column encompasses cognitive processing strategies and language processing strategies. The *cognitive processing strategies* (inferencing, predicting, problem solving, and constructing meaning) are universal in nature. However, the *language processing strategies* (chunking into phrases, accessing word meaning, word identification, and letter recognition) are language specific. These language processing strategies need to be mastered in order for a person to read or write, and they need to be learned for *each language* in which someone wants to read or write.

Now let's look at the model horizontally instead of vertically. If we look across the top of the model, we see cognitive processing strategies

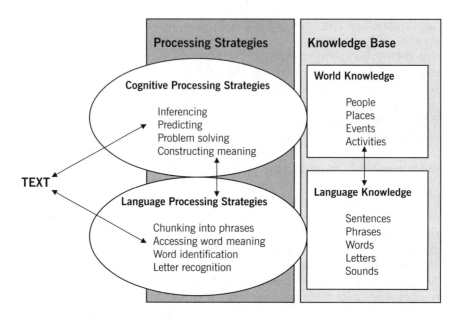

FIGURE 2.2. A hypothetical model of the reading process with some sample processing strategies and types of knowledge. From Birch (2007). Copyright © 2007 by Lawrence Erlbaum Associates, Inc. Reprinted by permission of Routledge, member of the Taylor & Francis Group.

and world knowledge. These are not language specific, and they can be activated in many settings, including many that do not involve reading and writing at all. We use cognitive strategies and world knowledge to know if it's going to rain by looking at the sky or in sensing whether a person likes us from their facial features and body language. We need these skills to function in the world around us and by extension in the classroom. In classroom settings, we can use these skills in a class meeting, for example, to establish a procedure, to choose roles, or to set up a hands-on science experiment. Cognitive processing strategies and world knowledge are necessary mental activities for learning, but they are not sufficient by themselves for reading and writing in any language.

Readers must be able to use the language processing strategies and language knowledge at the bottom half of the model for reading to happen. These skills are specific to each particular language, and without them, reading cannot occur. Just like the Bernhardt model, this model is bidirectional, and the areas are porous. Activity in each area informs the other, and all four areas need to be developed. However, what is too often overlooked is that language processing strategies and language knowledge are indispensable for cracking the code of reading. Moreover, these strategies have to be learned separately for each language.

> *I call the language processing strategies the "dirty little lie about reading." They look so insignificant but they are so decisive. Without those language processing strategies, like chunking text into phrases or accessing word meaning, it doesn't do any good to have the higher-order strategies or world knowledge because reading won't work.*—LEAH

By treating these four areas of the reading process individually, Birch's model helps us understand that language-specific skills need to be learned in a new language, or else the other universal aspects of language cannot be accessed for reading. In brief, without acquiring the nitty-gritty skills of language knowledge and language processing, the higher-order skills just can't be used. Paolo Freire's phrase "Read the word so that you can read the world" might be used as a slogan to represent the way language knowledge unlocks reading (Freire, 1970).

To discuss how first languages influence reading in a new language, it helps to have some precise terms. One of the terms we consider helpful is that of language distance.

Language Distance or Linguistic Proximity

Language distance (Odlin, 2003, p. 443), which is also called *linguistic proximity,* can be thought of as an inventory of how many characteristics two languages share. Language distance or linguistic proximity can be assessed by comparing the phonology, morphology, syntax, and semantics that are built into different languages. In addition, language distance is influenced by the number of *cognates,* or words from different languages that share roots. Languages that are derived from a common origin are more likely to have greater linguistic proximity. You could almost think of it as sharing common "genes" as people do when they come from a closely related ancestry.

As a general rule, the greater the linguistic proximity, the easier it should be for people to learn each other's languages. Of course, many considerations affect the undertaking, including age, motivation, L1 literacy, socioeconomic class, and instructional setting. Still, those languages with a historically close provenance have greater linguistic proximity and make some aspects of language learning easier for those speakers. French, Spanish, and Italian, for example, are "sister languages" that share syntactic patterns, sounds, an alphabet, and many cognates.

My son volunteered on an organic farm in Switzerland with two other guys from Spain and Italy. The Italian guy spoke English and Italian, the Spanish fellow spoke Spanish, Italian, and French, and my son spoke French and English. Each pair had one language in common, and no language was shared by all three. By listening in on the speech of the other two speakers and figuring out unknown words by their similar sounds, they managed to communicate and have a great time!—KRISTIN

At the same time, languages that are similar can cause confusion because a person is not expecting to find a difference. One of the most common areas for potential confusion is that of sounds. For example, English and German are both Germanic languages, with some traits in common, including most of their alphabet, but the letter *j* is pronounced differently in the two languages. L1 German children learning to read in English are likely to pronounce a word such as *joke* with a /y/ at first, like /yowk/, because the letter is pronounced with a *y* sound (/y/) in German, rather than with the English sound /j/. Teachers can help learners notice those differences by providing mini-lessons and giving extra opportunities to practice. Still, common linguistic features of sister languages make them easier to learn.

Orthographic distance is a subset of language distance. It describes the degree of similarity between the orthographies, or writing systems, of two languages. Sometimes, two languages use different writing systems, such as Chinese and English, and a learner must learn the new writing system from scratch. In other cases, a common writing system is used for languages from the same language family, such as the Roman alphabet, which is found in Spanish, Italian, Portuguese, and French. It takes less time for native speakers of one of those languages to learn to read words in the other. However, in still other cases the same writing system may be in use for languages from very different language families, such as English, Swahili, Vietnamese, and Icelandic, all of which use the Roman alphabet, but in dramatically different ways. Although they share an orthography, they are still orthographically distant because the same letters are used in different combinations and represent different sounds. Readers from one of those languages would not have any advantage in trying to read words in another of them even though they share the Roman alphabet. The relationship between the writing systems of two languages can influence how quickly and easily people learn to read and write in a new writing system.

Spanish and English share 26 letters of the Roman alphabet, but Spanish has one additional letter (ñ). Because of the large amount of overlap, it is fairly easy for Spanish ELLs who can read Spanish to recognize the letters of the English alphabet. The Thai alphabet, on the other hand, does not share any letters with the English alphabet, so we can expect Thai ELLs to need more time to learn and use the English alphabet.

The Problem with "Transfer"

Transfer can be defined as "influence resulting from similarities and differences between the target language and any other language that has been previously acquired" (Myles, 2002, p. 7; Odlin, 1989). We prefer not to use the word *transfer* for four reasons.

First, it is too often assumed that any language skill attained in the first language will be automatically available in the second language as well, but that is not always the case. For example, a study of high school-age Spanish-speaking ELLs who were also proficient in English found that the strategies they used to read in Spanish were not the same as the strategies they used to read in English (Pritchard & O'Hara, 2008). The authors conclude, "We cannot assume that proficient readers (much less struggling readers) will automatically transfer the ability to use those strategies from Spanish to English" (p. 637). The process is neither automatic nor inevitable.

The second problem with the word *transfer* is that it implies a facilitating process, but first-language reading knowledge doesn't necessarily make learning to read in English easier, at least not until ELLs master English *decoding*, or identifying written words. Birch (2015) summarizes it thus: "It is true that transfer may facilitate reading in the L2, but it is equally true that it might interfere" (p. 13). In fact, the written system in the L2 might be a seriously complicating factor for learning to decode in English, at least in the short run. The L1 knowledge and skills that pertain to English may be very dependent on features specific to the first language. In Polish, for example, the letter *w* will be pronounced as /v/, and this Polish-specific feature does not transfer to English pronunciation. The name *Sylwia,* for example, is pronounced the same way in Polish and English, as /silviyə/, although the spelling is different.

The third problem with the word *transfer* is that it implies that L1 knowledge is conveyed immediately. Sometimes, an area of potential cross-linguistic influence might lie waiting in the wings, perhaps for years, until it surfaces or can be rendered usable. This issue is discussed in more detail in the upcoming section on the threshold theory.

Finally, Ellis (1997) regrets the use of the word *transfer* for another reason, explaining, "When we transfer money we move it out of one account and into another, so one account gains and the other loses. However, when language transfer takes place there is usually no loss of L1 knowledge" (p. 54).

Cross-Linguistic Influence

Cross-linguistic influence can be defined as the action, conscious or unconscious, of applying features of a first language to the learning of a new language, in this case, English (Koda, 2005; Odlin, 2003). In this book we use this term in lieu of the term "transfer." We prefer a more global concept that includes not only "corresponding or analogous skills, but also metalinguistic or meta-cognitive skills that emerge from competence in the first language" (Genesee, Geva, Dressler, & Kamil, 2006, p. 161). We also refer to the facilitating effects of the first language on second-language literacy as *positive cross-linguistic influence (PCI)* and to obstacles to second-language literacy based on first-language features as *interference*.

Although there are many examples of PCI in action, ironically, it's often easier to spot interference than PCI. That's because the interfering feature stands out—it doesn't look or sound like the target item in the new language. Interference is noticeable, whereas PCI is likely to resemble the production of a native speaker. We can think of PCI and interference like traffic rules while driving. We don't keep track of all the traffic rules we obey perfectly in a day, but when we break a rule, we are very aware of it, especially if it results in a ticket, accident, or other mishap. It's important for teachers to support their learners' use of new forms even when they are imperfect, and to notice not just errors caused by interference.

Examples of PCI

Research supports the assertion that literacy experiences in the first language can benefit the acquisition of a new language. The research covers many of the component areas of reading, including phonological awareness, syntactic awareness, vocabulary knowledge, sentence and discourse processing, text structures, and comprehension. For a thorough review of research into the cross-linguistic relationships that inform learning to read in English as a new language, we recommend Koda's still timely comprehensive review of the research (2005), as well as the literature reviews of August and Shanahan (2006), Bernhardt (2011), and Birch (2015).

Those of us who have taught or learned another language probably know of many examples in which our knowledge of one language helped facilitate learning the other. Most of us can think of English words we know that we can also recognize in spoken or written form in another language. If we learn to write in a language that is written from left to right, we can apply our knowledge of the directionality of English without ever giving it a conscious thought. We may be able to apply the adjective + noun word order of English to languages, such as Dutch, that also place an adjective before a noun. In addition, the influence of English as a worldwide *lingua franca* has introduced English words into many languages, and these borrowed words, as well as cognates, also help with PCI. Teachers who already know or take the time to find out about the mother tongues of their learners will bolster the PCI and English proficiency of their students, while demonstrating respect for their home languages.

In general, the more literacy skills and strategies readers have in their first language, the more they will have available for use in reading in a new language, so long as they are developed in concert with second-language proficiency (Bernhardt, 2011). However, many critical steps must be taken in order to become a good reader, many of which require explicit, language-specific instruction in a wide range of skills and strategies.

Examples of Interference

Interference occurs when structural features of the first language impede acquiring or using a similar feature in the target language. Interference is the opposite of PCI. Not all learner errors constitute interference; they may be due to developmental stages of understanding or to individual interpretations of an item that have nothing to do with the first language. Interference can occur at many levels, including phonological, sound–symbol correspondence, vocabulary, and syntax. The following are examples of each of these levels.

Phonology

Mispronunciation occurs when phonemes and phoneme patterns of a person's L1 are overlaid onto the phonemes and phoneme patterns of a new language. For example, you may have become aware that English has two *th* sounds, and these sounds are not found in many other languages. When students' first languages do not have the two *th* sounds of English, they will be likely to pronounce the English word *this* as *dis*, since the sound /d/ is formed very close in the mouth to the sound /th/, the soft *th* sound found in the word *this*. Similarly, they will be likely to pronounce the English word *thing* as *ting*, since the sound /t/ is formed very close in the mouth to the sound /TH/, the hard *th* sound found in the word *thing*. (If you don't understand the difference, try saying *this* and *think*, and listen to the difference of the sound for the *th* letters.)

Sound–Symbol Correspondence

Conflicting sound–symbol patterns in two languages can be a source of interference even if the languages share an alphabet, such as the example of the German and English pronunciations of the letter *j* mentioned previously. Spelling is also affected by interference. ELLs who have learned to read and write in their first language show spelling errors from patterns in their L1 writing system (Dressler & Kamil, 2006, p. 203). For example, when an L1 Spanish ELL spells the word *beat* as *bit*, he or she is trying to transfer prior knowledge that Spanish represents the vowel sound /iy/ ("long *e*") with the letter *i*. This is a very common spelling error of L1 Spanish ELLs, by the way, and it differs from the developmental spelling of native English speakers (Bear, Templeton, Helman, & Baren, 2003).

Vocabulary

Shared vocabulary can facilitate learning, but it can also be an area of potential interference. Some words sound or look the same in two languages, but have different meanings. These are called false cognates and will be discussed in Chapter 6. In other cases, two or more words combine differently in one language from another, and a word-by-word translation results in a strange utterance. For example, "Tengo veinte años" which means "I'm twenty years old" in Spanish, can be mistranslated as "I have twenty years" in a word-by-word translation. That is one of the reasons it has taken digital translation software so long to work well—it isn't possible to simply pour a set of individual words into one side and have understandable translations come out the other!

There are also cases in which the words are comprehensible, but the cultural meanings differ in the new language, as can be seen in this story from Tenena's early days in the United States.

> *I remember asking for the toilet in the museum, and when the man pointed me to a sign for the rest room, I thought the guy didn't understand what I meant because I wasn't tired. I imagined there was a couch there where you would go and relax after you had walked around. Even though I knew the words, I didn't know the cultural connotation of "rest room."—*TENENA

Syntax

Word order differs among languages, and trying to construct the same sentence in a new language can create errors. For example, the sentence

"The woman who I called her is at home" is a rendering of Arabic word order using English words. Since Arabic doesn't delete the direct object inside a relative clause like English does, there is an extra word, *her*, that sounds non-native to an English speaker. Another example of a word-by-word translation from Spanish is the sentence "No speak English," which means "I don't speak English." Spanish allows deletion of the subject pronoun of a sentence (in this case, *I*) and also does not use an auxiliary verb to indicate the negative in English (*don't*), so in a word-by-word translation, the sentence would be correct.

Non-Effects

Finally, there are features that require attention in one language that are simply irrelevant to another language and are therefore of no effect. For example, Slovak requires learning the placement of diacritical marks, or *diacritics*, such as the three marks in the word *dĺžeň*, which means "accent mark." These small marks are signals that guide the reader in reading, spelling, and pronunciation. However, English has no diacritical marks. Nothing about knowing Slovak diacritical marks "helps" the ELL learner, but nothing about them "hurts" either. It is simply part of the learner's L1 literacy knowledge and as such has positive value.

Those of us in the language teaching profession have come to recognize that there are both PCI and interference effects in our students' learning.

Metalinguistic Awareness Facilitates the Study of New Languages

Metalinguistic awareness is the ability to bring into consciousness, reflect upon, and/or manipulate the forms and functions of language apart from its meaning (Chaney, 1992; Koda, 2005; Pratt & Grieve, 1984). Here are a dozen examples of metalinguistic awareness skills.

1. Distinguish real words from non-words.
2. Hear the phonological error of a mispronounced word and correct it.
3. Recognize a foreign accent.
4. Hear an error in a syntax pattern (word order) and correct it.
5. Segment a spoken phrase into its individual words.
6. Count the syllables in a word.
7. Play with words to make jokes.

8. Create new words or labels for unknown objects or people.
9. Make a mental translation.
10. Recognize cognates or false cognates.
11. Detect structural ambiguities in sentences.
12. Alternate (code-switch) between different registers or dialects of a language.

Some aspects of metalinguistic awareness are a natural byproduct of acquiring one's native language, but others, especially those connected with the written word, emerge through schooling. Metalinguistic awareness goes hand in hand with literacy achievement. In several studies, when children were given training or practice in developing metalinguistic awareness, their reading comprehension increased (Carlisle, Beeman, & Shah, 1996; Pratt & Grieve, 1984; Zipke, 2008). The metalinguistic awareness learners develop in their first language can be a helpful tool when they are introduced to a new language. Moreover, the very process of learning a new language fosters metalinguistic awareness, as new sounds, spellings, syntactic patterns, and words unfold, each with its own peculiarities.

How can we help children develop a sense of metalinguistic awareness in English? Before they are of school age, young children may participate in chants, call and response, jump-rope rhymes, tongue twisters, silly songs, clapping games, and word games. These may be played at home, in child care or day care, or with older siblings, parents, or caregivers. These can enhance the skill before literacy is introduced. When children start school, their metalinguistic awareness moves into literacy activities, as they learn to sort out sounds and letters; listen to poems, stories, songs, and read-alouds; and engage in wordplay and word games. They also learn to understand and tell jokes, such as "knock-knock" jokes (e.g., A: *"Knock knock!"* B: *"Who's there?"* A: *"Boo!"* B: *"Boo who"?* A: *"Why are you crying?"*). Popular children's books, such as the *Amelia Bedelia* series (Parish, 1963–2013), the *Junie B. Jones* series (Park, 1992–2013), Dr. Seuss books, and poems by Shel Silverstein (1964, 1974, 1981) are full of wordplay and quizzical musings about why English is the way it is. For example, Shel Silverstein's poem "Toucan" begins, "Who can catch a toucan? You can!" (Silverstein, 1974). Many classic children's books foster metalinguistic awareness, such as *Who Says a Dog Goes Bow Wow?* (De Zutter, 1993), or books of homophone puns, such as *The King Who Rained* (Gwynne, 1970) or *A Chocolate Moose for Dinner* (Gwynne, 1976). ELLs will come to love the funny misinterpretations of idioms and figurative language as their proficiency increases. Of course, wordplay and metalinguistic awareness can be cultivated in any language. The common feature of wordplay is setting up a "playful but purposeful" word-rich environment.

As you might guess, metalinguistic awareness helps with SLA, and it also works in favor of learning a third language (Clyne, Hunt, & Isaakidis, 2004). Wilga M. Rivers, a famous pioneer in the field of teaching ESL, learned five languages over the course of time. She decided to keep a daily diary of her study of Spanish, her sixth language, and her diary is full of fascinating evidence of her highly developed metalinguistic awareness (Rivers, 1981, pp. 500–515).

Vygotsky (1986) pointed out that studying a foreign language also helps our understanding of our first language. "A foreign language facilitates mastering the higher forms of the native language," he says. "The child learns to see his language as one particular system among many, to view its phenomena under more general categories, and this leads to awareness of linguistic operations" (p. 196). Clearly, metalinguistic awareness helps with language learning in general because it helps us "learn about language"—the third function in Halliday's (1993) language-based theory of learning.

How LI Reading Differs from Reading in a New Language

Reading is an *interactive process* (Birch, 2015; Rumelhart, 1977/1994) that takes place between the text, the reader's processing strategies, and the reader's background knowledge. To read, we need to master the word-level, *bottom-up skills* that allow us to be able to decode connected text. They are represented in the Birch reading model as language processing strategies and language knowledge (see Figure 2.2).

We also need to learn a large set of strategic reading skills, which are the *top-down skills*. Readers use these skills in concert with their background knowledge to construct meaning from text. These are represented in Birch's model as world knowledge and cognitive processing strategies. To summarize, the bottom-up skills refer to the word identification skills that are required for decoding, and the top-down skills refer to the analytical and cognitive processes that we engage in for reading comprehension. You can't have one without the other, but as reading comprehension increases, the bottom-up skills become automatic and unconscious. Even proficient monolingual readers will encounter many kinds of texts and will need to consciously activate bottom-up skills as well as cognitive strategies and background knowledge from time to time as they read. Both skill sets require making many rapid judgments about words and keeping the words in working memory as we form reasonable interpretations about possible meanings.

Surprisingly, it is the bottom-up skills that may cause the greatest hurdles for ELLs even if they are literate in another language. That is because of the effects of interference as well as the peculiar characteristics of English. Teachers of L1 English-speaking children may find this concept counterintuitive. Yet the need for ELLs to master the "nitty gritty" skill of proficient decoding before reading comprehension occurs is one of the big understandings that comes from studying linguistics and its relationship to literacy. Teachers expect L1 English-speaking children to have the bottom-up skills firmly in place by the end of second grade at the latest, or they provide interventions to get those skills in place. Teachers who don't teach at the PreK–2 grade levels may assume that ELLs in their classrooms have the bottom-up skills in place, but this is not necessarily the case. Indeed, ELLs may have these skills in place in their native language, or they may not. However, even if they do, the bottom-up skills are language-specific, and ELL students need to master them at whatever age they begin to study English. Furthermore, the details of English word decoding are exceptionally difficult to learn. In summary, even ELLs who are literate in their L1 need to learn to read twice because they have to crack two different codes, their L1 code and the new code of English.

In addition to the bottom-up skills that students acquire, the top-down comprehension skills that learners hone over many years of schooling require multistep strategies. These include, but are not limited to, predicting, summarizing, inferencing, evaluating, and so on. Readers who are able to use these reading strategies are more likely to enjoy the benefits of PCI because these strategies are less language specific. For example, if Talia knows how to put historical events into a timeline in Hebrew, her first language, it will be much easier for her to put events into a timeline in English.

The top-down strategies cannot be fully activated until the lower-level, language-specific processes are in place. In other words, ELLs will not be able to make use of higher-level reading strategies that cross languages until they are competent in the lower-level skills that are specific to English. The first language of the ELL also makes a difference in the efficacy with which the skills will be learned. These lower-level, bottom-up skills of English are more difficult for students whose L1 has more linguistic distance from English even if the learners are literate in their first language. This, in a nutshell, is the critical way in which the process of reading for an ELL differs from learning to read in English for a native speaker.

Literacy-Related Hypotheses about SLA

In addition to the concept of cross-linguistic influence, two other concepts are important in understanding literacy in a new language: the threshold theory, and the concepts of BICS and CALP.

The Threshold Theory

The *threshold theory* (Alderson, 1984, 2000) asserts that it is second-language proficiency, not first-language literacy, that determines whether or not a second-language learner will become a proficient reader. The implication of Alderson's theory is that ELLs need both the bottom-up, language-specific skills in the second language and its grammar and vocabulary to be successful readers. Until an adequate proficiency level, or "threshold," has been reached in the new language, the benefits of L1 literacy cannot be put to use. According to Grabe (2001), "Few researchers would deny that transfer of literacy skills from the L1 to the L2 occurs, but many researchers believe that positive transfer occurs consistently only after students have had much practice in the L2, have automatized basic L2 language skills, and have been trained to use these potential transfer effects" (p. 32). A summary of reading research from the National Literacy Panel on Language-Minority Children and Youth confirms this observation. "In general, for students with higher second-language proficiency, second-language reading is a function of both second-language proficiency and first-language reading ability, whereas students with lower levels of second-language proficiency are less able to apply their first-language reading skills to reading in a second language" (August & Shanahan, 2006, p. 65). In a comprehensive study, Fitzgerald (1995) also found that the ways ELL readers use reading comprehension strategies in academic tasks look more and more like the strategies of good L1 English readers as they become more proficient.

As Alderson succinctly summarizes, "Second-language knowledge is more important than first-language reading abilities" (2000, p. 39). To give a simple example, even a very skilled reader of English, no matter how literate, cannot read in Chinese until he or she learns the Chinese writing system, its syntax, its grammar, its vocabulary, and more.

The threshold theory helps us understand the development of reading strategies by bilingual children. As these children advance in their literacy development, their dominant language in different domains will shift at different times. Moll, Estrada, Díaz, and Lopez (1997) found that bilingual Spanish–English students demonstrated use of comprehension strategies during Spanish reading but used decoding strategies during their English reading. Seen through the lens of the threshold theory, it appears that the students had not reached the needed threshold level in English to be able to use the comprehension strategies they had achieved in Spanish. They were still working on mastering the bottom-up skills involved in English decoding.

Spelling development is another area in which the cross-linguistic influence evolves over time. Zutell and Allen (1988) found that lower-proficiency L1 Spanish ELLs made spelling errors more related to their native language. However, their higher-proficiency peers made spelling errors that resembled those of their L1 English peers.

Writing proficiency takes much longer to develop in any language, and first-language writing skill is one of several factors contributing to good writing in a new language. However, strong L2 grammar, strong L1 and L2 vocabulary, and good writing instruction in both languages also help to attain proficiency (Garcia, 2000; Grabe, 2001; Yigsaw, 2013). Famed authors such as Joseph Conrad and Vladimir Nabokov created master-pieces in English, although their first languages were not English. These remarkable accomplishments are yet another example of the power of the threshold theory: advanced vocabulary, language knowledge, and gram-mar expertise in a new language make it possible to achieve great writing.

A predecessor of the threshold theory is Clarke's less well-known but very influential *short-circuit hypothesis* (Clarke, 1980). He notes that even successful L1 readers cannot read for comprehension in a new language until they have adequate proficiency in it. Until that proficiency level is reached, their reading process will "short-circuit."

The difficulty, of course, is in deciding exactly what the threshold should be for different learners, in different language domains, at differ-ent ages and proficiency levels, in different content areas, and for differ-ent purposes. Finding thresholds for each learner can be a very fungible process. This problem, along with the costly implications for determin-ing student thresholds and implementing appropriate interventions at a school, may explain why the threshold theory doesn't receive the atten-tion it deserves.

Language Loss

So far, this chapter has been all about the ways to build proficiency in a new language, but it is also possible to lose a language. When children lack the opportunity to study their first language in a school or other organized setting, their L1 skills may plateau or even decline over time. This decline may also lower their PCI and metalinguistic awareness. In addition, a sense of alienation and loneliness can occur if a child gets the direct or indirect message that his or her home language is not valued. These feelings can have profound negative consequences, even rupturing intergenerational relationships that are so important to a child's sense of well-being (Rodriguez, 1982; Wong-Fillmore, 2000). Although L2 profi-ciency affects when and how L1 literacy skills are activated, it is important to achieve and maintain a high level of literacy in one's native language because it is so valuable to a person's identity and sense of self-esteem. Teachers can carry this wisdom into every classroom.

BICS and CALP

Among his many contributions to the language research and teaching field, Cummins is best known for naming the language phenomena of "BICS" and "CALP." He describes BICS as *basic interpersonal communicative skills,* also called "conversational language" (Cummins, 1981), and CALP as *cognitive academic language proficiency,* also called "academic language proficiency" (Cummins, 1979, 1991). BICS and CALP are key constructs in the field of teaching English as a new language. In his research and literature reviews of young second-language learners, Cummins noticed that they often did well in their language classes but had trouble with academic tasks, including reading comprehension, once they entered grade-level classrooms. Similar findings were reported by Skutnabb-Kangas and Toukomaa (1976) with bilingual Finnish children in Sweden, and by Pritchard and O'Hara (2008) in research with Spanish-speaking ELLs in the United States.

Cummins hypothesized that there are two distinct forms of language, whose characteristics we have summarized in Figure 2.3.

BICS, or basic interpersonal communicative skills, consists of a body of simple English that can be acquired in everyday natural settings, without formal instruction. The verb forms are simple, the context makes the message easy to understand, and the conversation takes place in the "here and now." This conversational language is also referred to as "playground language" or "survival language."

CALP, or cognitive academic language proficiency, includes the much larger and more complex academic vocabulary of school. This language, also called academic language, instructional language, or discipline-specific language, is needed for reading and writing, not only in the language arts, but in science, mathematics, and the social sciences (Fang, 2008; Zwiers, 2006, 2007, 2008). CALP language becomes more specialized as students are exposed to higher levels of knowledge in different fields; without extensive CALP language proficiency, ELL students will not be college- and career-ready (Zwiers, 2008) and may not even manage to graduate from high school. CALP language does not provide a great deal of contextual information to aid reading comprehension. It uses more tenses and modes, assumes an unseen audience, and conveys its messages with words alone. CALP language is a prerequisite to academic writing because academic writing requires the ability to address an unseen audience.

The reason that the concepts of BICS and CALP are so critical in teaching ELLs is because ELLs have often been misjudged to have high language proficiency just because they have developed BICS skills; however, it takes years to attain CALP language at a level comparable to that

BICS (context-rich, social, survival) language has some or all of these characteristics	CALP (academic, expository) language has some or all of these characteristics
Utterances are in fragments or memorized chunks.	Utterances and sentences are long and often contain embedded clauses; word order is varied.
Vocabulary consists of high-frequency words with general meanings.	Vocabulary consists of abstract, subject-related content words, often with specialized meanings.
Verb forms are in present tense or progressive aspect.	Verb forms include modal auxiliaries, perfect tenses, and passive voice.
Negative is indicated by the word *no*.	Correct syntax is developed or developing.
Conversation topics are related to the here and now and are context embedded.	Topics focus on subject content and may be context reduced.
Understanding relies on background knowledge.	Understanding depends on language in addition to background knowledge.
Language tends to be conversational, personal, and egalitarian.	Language tends to be distanced, impersonal, and authoritative.

FIGURE 2.3. Some characteristics of BICS and CALP.

of native speakers, and it is a never-ending process (Thomas & Collier, 2002). CALP is needed in any language, not only in English! A good program of bilingual or dual-language instruction includes both BICS and CALP as well. One teacher recalls her own situation as a language learner.

> . . . *[as teachers, we expect] students to know how to read because they know how to speak a language, but this is not true. I personally experienced this. I was fluent in Spanish but did not know how to read it or write it. When I went back to Mexico for 3 years, many teachers just couldn't figure me out. At times they assumed it was laziness because I spoke perfect Spanish but couldn't read or write it. I failed sixth grade and barely passed the second time.*–ROSARIO GOMEZ

Consider the vast range of mental and verbal activities that take place in classrooms over the course of each and every school year. In some classrooms, the CALP language in use will be the language of writing lab reports; in others, it is the language that facilitates oral argumentation; in another, it is the language of math equations and operations. Even producing a definition of a new word is a CALP language skill because the definition is extracted out of its communicative context. Interestingly, the ability to define words is correlated with reading comprehension in ELLs (Carlisle et al., 1996). CALP is the language of the content standards, textbooks, standardized tests, literary genres, and even debates and lectures. It is what the curriculum is all about.

The concepts of BICS and CALP have been very influential in improving the way ELLs are assessed, placed, and exited from programs, as well as the quality of the programs themselves. Before these ideas became well known, ELLs were often wrongly considered "fluent" on the basis of their BICS alone and placed in mainstream classrooms. Now there is widespread understanding that reading and writing skills take much longer to develop in a new language and that proficiency cannot be judged just on the basis of listening and speaking skills. We now understand the necessity of building academic language in programs that support a learner's first language as well. Learners benefit from having access to challenging content in their first language.

Standardized language proficiency tests for ELLs, such as the *ACCESS-ELL2.0* test (The WIDA Consortium, 2016) measure ELL language proficiency in the four domains of listening, speaking, reading, and writing on a yearly basis. ELLs are able to exit programs only when they reach a satisfactory level of social and academic English proficiency. Even so, the composite exit scores have been raised more than once in several states, as states found that children needed more time in support programs and longer follow-up than originally believed. This development affirms the value of the threshold theory in language policies that benefit ELL students.

As we evaluate our own experiences in learning new languages, we can analyze our knowledge of BICS and CALP and clearly see how that knowledge influences what we are able to do in those languages.

We have observed some common misunderstandings about the notions of BICS and CALP as we have come to understand them, and we describe them briefly in Table 2.1.

Here is an example of how one kindergarten teacher builds CALP in her classroom.

CALP skills can be incorporated into the listening and speaking aspects of any lesson. I will often rephrase student responses from BICS to CALP orally in conversation and sometimes have students repeat them. Another example is that during attendance I play a role and

TABLE 2.1. Fallacies and Realities about BICS and CALP

Fallacy	Reality
BICS is oral and CALP is written.	BICS is usually oral, but could be written, too: it consists of high-frequency words and phrases that are highly contextualized through visual and contextual clues. For example, an illustrated menu could be considered a BICS text even though the items are written down because the words can be easily accessed on the spot. CALP can also be oral, such as a college lecture that requires a listener to carefully follow a topic.
BICS will take care of itself; all attention must be paid to CALP.	If children have learned English as a foreign language in a non-English-speaking country and then immigrate to the United States, they may have acquired some academic English because of the method in which they studied English, but lack conversational English or communicative competence. Older children with strong formal education in their native language will also have more CALP skills to transfer from their L1, but may need help acquiring BICS, especially if they are very self-conscious. It should never be assumed communicative language will take care of itself. If ELLs don't have conversational abilities in English, they will be isolated from their peers, and school will be an unpleasant experience for them.
Teachers should wait until BICS is in place before beginning CALP.	Exactly the opposite is true. It is never too early to introduce CALP language and skills, even when students are not totally proficient in BICS, and even if they are not fluent decoders. CALP skills can involve oral analysis and listening vocabulary as well as written words.
BICS and CALP transfer automatically between languages.	This book is devoted to laying out some of the complexities of the landscape for developing English reading proficiency. Although some skills can be used automatically or easily in a new language, others are language specific and require care and conscious attention

students have to respond appropriately to that person. So, today I was the Queen of England, which meant my students could not say "Wuz Up!" to me when I called their names as they had been doing the day before when I was their big brother. Instead they had to say, "So nice to meet you, Your Majesty." I also use CALP language during instruction to normalize and familiarize my students with it. For example, in my kindergarten math lessons we use either the words digit *or* quantity *instead of the generic* number, *and we say* equation *rather than* number sentence.–JOANNE LOVAGLIA

Although the concepts of BICS and CALP are descriptive and not definitive, they are unquestionably a powerful "shorthand" to help millions of educators understand that social functions take less time to grasp than the complex academic functions of education.

Before leaving this topic, we note that the BICS skills are extremely important too, and should never be taken for granted! Having daily conversational exchanges is indispensable, especially for very young learners. Practicing conversational skills, listening to narrative spoken forms, and taking part in problem-solving strategies form the very foundation of the young child's learning experience (Epstein, 2007). This also holds true for children of any age.

Performance Definitions for ELLs

How do we describe what an ELL in grades PreK–12 is able to do? This used to be a daunting task because there were no standards against which to judge performance. As a result, it was impossible to compare the criteria used in one ESL program with another. An "advanced" learner in an ESL or bilingual program, once exited, might still be performing below grade level in a classroom of native speakers or in a different program of instruction. This situation has changed for the better. Now, *Teachers of English to Speakers of Other Languages (TESOL)*, the field's premier professional organization, in conjunction with the *World Class Instructional Design and Assessment (WIDA)* Consortium, a multistate working group, has created PreK–12 language proficiency standards that describe *performance definitions for ELLs* (Gottlieb, 2006; Teachers of English to Speakers of Other Languages, 2016; The WIDA Consortium, 2016). The overall performance definitions of the six English proficiency levels can be found in Appendix 2.1. The standards are valuable because they focus on the language needed to perform both social and academic tasks in each of the content areas, in each language domain, and in each grade range. Included in these standards is a set of

Early English Language Standards and Spanish Standards for children ages 2.5–5.5 in dual-language programs. The WIDA standards consist of a set of five standards for grades K–12, but the Early English Language Standards include an additional standard for physical development (Pre-K–12 English Language Proficiency Standards, 2016). The creation of these standards is a major accomplishment for the English language teaching field.

The field of ESL teaching changed dramatically when the No Child Left Behind (NCLB) Act of 2002 required schools to demonstrate that ELLs were making adequate yearly progress toward English language proficiency. Combined with greater knowledge of how languages are learned, sociocultural theory of language, and a set of academic standards in each discipline, the teaching of ELLs has come of age. Now academic language is part of the curriculum, raising the expectations for ELL achievement, and all three functions of Halliday's language-based theory of learning are in use: learning language, learning through language, and learning about language.

HOW DOES THIS LOOK IN THE CLASSROOM?

As mentioned in Joanne Lovaglia's example on pages 49 and 51 of using the "Queen's English" in kindergarten, using academic language in daily dialogue will help students get accustomed to hearing CALP and using such language in reading and writing. When teachers feel comfortable talking in an academic English register, it gives ELLs repeated exposure to the words they need to know. A teacher might say to young ELLs, "You sang that so well—can we replicate that performance in the assembly later on today?" *Replicate* is one of the verbs in the formative assessments of the WIDA standards.

Reading both stories and nonfiction books aloud is also a natural way to expand academic vocabulary. Books have vastly more vocabulary than even the most eloquent spoken language (Krashen, 2004). To encourage written CALP use, it helps to display CALP vocabulary words in the room and to provide positive reinforcement when students try to use them.

QUESTIONS FOR FURTHER STUDY

1. If you had to choose three important ideas from this chapter, which would you choose? How can you apply these ideas to your larger knowledge of teaching English as a new language?

2. How would you appraise your own metalinguistic awareness? What are some examples of it? Do you think that there is an optimal age at which to develop this awareness? If possible, discuss with a partner.

3. Try to find three examples of PCI, three examples of interference, and three examples of non-effect from your own language teaching or foreign language study. Which examples were easiest for you to find?

4. Look at the dozen examples of metalinguistic awareness in the chapter (pp. 41–42). Which of them do you think can be introduced at lower levels of English proficiency? Which ones might require a higher level of proficiency or a higher grade level? What ways can you think of to build metalinguistic awareness in your own teaching setting?

5. Sometimes ELLs who come to the United States or Canada in mid- or late adolescence have strong CALP skills in their L1, but lack any English BICS. Think of some ways to build BICS skills for these older students.

6. Lesson plans often account for CALP skills in the domains of reading and writing. What ways can you think of to support building CALP skills in practicing listening and speaking?

7. Thinking about the language(s) you have studied or acquired, evaluate your own BICS and CALP skills in them. Using the instructional models introduced in Chapter 1, (pp. 13–17) what kinds of teaching methods do you think encourage the development of BICS? of CALP?

8. When we understand that a first language can be stronger, or weaker, than the new language in each of the domains, how can ESL instructors incorporate some of the understandings of the threshold theory when creating assessments for ELLs?

9. What successful experiences have you observed or taken part in that treat children's home languages as a resource?

10. CHALLENGE QUESTION: Look closely at the compensatory model (Figure 2.1, p. 32 and create some classroom scenarios for a specific unit of study in which L1 literacy, L2 proficiency, and unknown factors interact with each other in a dynamic way.

Performance Definitions for the Levels of English Language Proficiency

At the given level of English language proficiency, ELLs will process, understand, produce, or use:

6—Reaching	• specialized or technical language reflective of the content areas at grade level • a variety of sentence lengths of varying linguistic complexity in extended oral or written discourse as required by the specified grade level • oral or written communication in English comparable to proficient English peers
5—Bridging	• specialized or technical language of the content areas • a variety of sentence lengths of varying linguistic complexity in extended oral or written discourse, including stories, essays, or reports • oral or written language approaching comparability to that of proficient English peers when presented with grade-level material
4—Expanding	• specific and some technical language of the content areas • a variety of sentence lengths of varying linguistic complexity in oral discourse or multiple related sentences or paragraphs • oral or written language with minimal phonological, syntactic, or semantic errors that do not impede the overall meaning of the communication when presented with oral or written connected discourse with sensory, graphic, or interactive support
3—Developing	• general and some specific language of the content areas • expanded sentences in oral interaction or written paragraphs • oral or written language with phonological, syntactic, or semantic errors that may impede the communication, but retain much of its meaning, when presented with oral or written, narrative, or expository descriptions with sensory, graphic, or interactive support
2—Beginning	• general language related to the content areas • phrases or short sentences • oral or written language with phonological, syntactic, or semantic errors that often impede the meaning of the communication when presented with one- to multiple-step commands, directions, questions, or a series of statements with sensory, graphic, or interactive support
1—Entering	• pictorial or graphic representation of the language of the content areas • words, phrases, or chunks of language when presented with one-step commands, directions, WH-, choice or yes/no questions, or statements with sensory, graphic, or interactive support

Note. From Teachers of English to Speakers of Other Languages (2016). Copyright © 2016 Teachers of English to Speakers of Other Languages, Inc. All rights reserved. Reprinted by permission.

CHAPTER THREE

ELL Oracy

Listening Comprehension
and Oral Language Development

New Vocabulary in This Chapter: *oracy, literacy, listening comprehension, oral text, phonological awareness, onset and rime, phoneme segmentation, concept of word, stress patterns, content word, function word, contrastive stress, intonation patterns, paralinguistic features or cues, probabilistic reasoning, auding, gist, proposition, listening vocabulary, simple view of reading (SVR), ellipsis, discourse markers, context-reduced oral language, auditory comprehension, oral proficiency, silent period, intensive listening activities, dictation, cloze, extensive listening activities, total physical response (TPR), interactive read-alouds (IR), story grammar*

In this chapter we talk about comprehending and using spoken English, which is composed of listening comprehension and oral language production. Together these two skills lay the groundwork for the emergence of reading and writing. Sticht and James (1984) refer to the listening and speaking level reached by native speakers before they learn to read as their "reading potential" and refer to the combined skills as *oracy*. They chose the term *oracy* to serve as a parallel to the term *literacy*, which had been considered at that time to consist of only reading and writing. To some extent, current views of literacy encompass oracy, which is sometimes referred to as "oral language proficiency," but we prefer the term *oracy* because we believe listening skills are too easily overlooked. Students with strong oracy in English are more likely to develop strong literacy levels in English as well.

Oracy develops in ELLs in different ways than it does for children acquiring their native language. To explore those ways, we begin with a discussion of the nature of listening comprehension, how it develops in ELLs, and its role in reading. Then we look at how speaking skills develop in ELLs and how they interact with reading development. Finally, we look at how teachers can support developing strong ELL oracy in the classroom setting as a path to literacy and competence in English as a new language.

Listening Comprehension in English as a New Language

The first of the two oracy skills is listening comprehension. Listening is one of the primary modes through which we learn about our world; if listening is weak, overall comprehension suffers. *Listening comprehension* is the ability to understand spoken language, or *oral text*, and, in this case, the spoken language of English. That might seem self-evident, but it isn't. The listening comprehension we acquire more or less unconsciously in our native language, just by being around and interacting with people who speak it, encompasses many different complex skills we don't even realize we have mastered. Children learn very early on which speech sounds to ignore and which to attend to as they interact with caregivers. All children with normal abilities acquire the set of sounds that make up their native language, and will learn to use them, so long as they are exposed to speakers of the language and have opportunities to interact with them. The ability to acquire the sounds and rhythms of one's native language occurs in literate and nonliterate societies and is part of the "hard-wiring" of the human brain. This differentiation process, which sorts out the specific sound patterns of the language(s) an infant hears, occurs between 6 and 10 months of age (Conboy & Kuhl, 2011; Pinker, 2007).

However, there are other listening skills that are language specific and need to be cultivated or taught as part of a bridge to literacy. Here are some of them.

Phonological Awareness

Phonological awareness is the ability to recognize the sounds of a language. It is considered one of the most important skills for reading. Young children develop phonological awareness through interacting with caregivers, nursery rhymes, wordplay, rhyming games, and songs. When children begin their schooling, at most schools in North America, they will further refine their phonological awareness. By the beginning of kindergarten, the focus of phonological awareness will shift from children understanding words they hear to manipulating the sounds in words they are going to learn to read. Children learn to recognize the order of sounds within a word gradually, moving from bigger parts of a word to individual sounds.

English-speaking children gain phonological awareness in developmental steps that lead toward literacy (Caravolas & Bruck, 1993). First, they are able to identify the sounds of a word, beginning with its consonants. Then, they manipulate the syllables of a word, often through rhymes. For example, they can recognize that *snow* rhymes with *go* in the nursery rhyme "Mary Had a Little Lamb," and they can learn to supply the missing rhyme. In the next step, after hearing the rhyming words, they are able to break down an English syllable into its "onset + rime" pattern. Onsets and rimes are a way of looking at English syllable structure by separating the *onset*, the beginning sound(s) of the syllable, from the *rime*, the remaining sounds of the syllable. For example, the rime *-at* can be combined with the onsets of *b-, c-, s-*, etc., to form the words *bat, cat*, or *sat*. Analyzing words in this way, children can learn to identify and supply the onsets that can go with a rime in a syllable.

Finally, children learn to manipulate the *phonemes*, or individual sounds, of a word. For example, they can look at pictures of a *cat* and a *cap* and point to the picture that matches the sounds they hear, indicating that they can hear the closing consonant. They can also look at pictures for a *ship* and a *sheep* and point to the picture of the word they hear, indicating that they can hear the difference in the two vowel sounds. When children get to the point that they are able to break down the individual phonemes of a word (called "segmenting") or put them back together (called "blending"), they have achieved *phoneme segmentation*. Phoneme segmentation is considered an important step toward learning to read in English.

Phonological awareness is one of the strongest predictors of reading comprehension in L1 English-speaking children (Geva, 2006) and ELL children. It is also important in learning to read in other first languages. Of course, the various written forms of languages affect how phonological awareness comes into play (more on this in Chapter 4).

To summarize, phonological awareness helps ELL learners in three distinct ways:

1. They imitate the sounds and thereby learn to pronounce and say the word.
2. They recognize the word when they hear it because the sequence of sounds is stored in their long-term memory and becomes part of their listening vocabulary.

3. Once they begin to read and write, their phonological awareness, and in particular their ability to do phoneme segmentation,
will greatly assist ELLs with decoding, writing, and spelling new,
unknown words in English.

Concept of Word

As we acquire a language, we learn to perceive the boundaries between
words even though they blend together in spoken form. The ability to
distinguish word boundaries within the flowing stream of speech is called
concept of word (Morris, 1993). When we hear people animatedly speaking
a language we do not know, we hear it as a torrent of connected sound
without form or meaning. However, once we know a language, we can
tell where one word ends and the next begins, and how the words taken
together have meaning. One of the benefits of having literacy in a first language is that the concept of word will be taken for granted in the new language—although the language-specific word boundaries will have to be
learned. Concept of word can also extend to recognizing short phrases,
such as "Stand up."

Stress Patterns

Stress patterns are audible differences in how long and how loudly a
speaker pronounces a word or group of words. Stress patterns follow a
complex set of rules that are part of the deep structure of each language
and are unconsciously known to native speakers of the language. *Syllable
stress* rules tell us how to assign stress to individual words, and *sentence
stress* rules tell us how to assign stress to phrases and sentences. Although
native speakers pick up these rules unconsciously as part of their native
speaker advantage, for ELLs, as you might guess, some of these unconscious rules may need to be unpacked and taught explicitly.

Syllable Stress

As we become proficient in a new language, we learn to recognize the
stress patterns of syllables within a word. Every multisyllable English word
has a stress pattern, and matching these stress patterns with words is one
of the subskills that allows us to recognize a spoken word. In addition,
some words in English can have more than one stress pattern according
to the part of speech they occupy. For example:

Lettuce is in the produce section of the store. (produce is an adjective)
Bees produce honey by pollinating flowers. (produce is a verb)

or

> *I feel con<u>tent</u> when I'm with my family.* (*content* is an adjective)
> *The <u>con</u>tent of this chapter is difficult!* (*content* is a noun)

Sentence Stress

In English, the *content words* in a phrase or sentence (the nouns, verbs, adjectives, or adverbs) receive the strong stress, whereas the *function words* (the prepositions, pronouns, conjunctions, or articles) do not. For example, in this sentence, the stress is on the final content word *game*.

> *I went to the <u>game</u>.*

We can teach the listening strategy that the last content word of a sentence is important even if learners miss some of the previous, shorter words. When listeners catch strong-stressed content words in the final position of a sentence, it helps them capture key points, even if the message is degraded somehow by background noise or other interference.

> *When my class learned the listening comprehension strategy that the last content word of a spoken sentence can serve as a "hook" to the larger meaning of the sentence, one of my ESL students, remembering an idiom we had covered, said excitedly, "In other words, we save the best till last, right?"*—KRISTIN

Contrastive Stress

In addition to learning to recognize the stress patterns of English, proficient listeners also develop an "ear" for nuances of meaning when speakers alter regular stress patterns. For example, look at the differences in meaning when the sentence stress changes in this sentence.

> *I hid the <u>keys</u>.* (normal stress is on *keys*)
> <u>*I*</u> *hid the keys.* (emphasis is on *who* hid the keys)
> *I <u>hid</u> the keys.* (emphasis is on *what you did*)

Contrastive stress patterns occur when speakers change normal stress patterns to emphasize a particular part of a message. Playing with contrastive stress patterns of a sentence in a classroom can be a fun activity to encourage predictions for listening comprehension, whether with ELLs or L1 English speakers.

Intonation Patterns

Intonation patterns are vocal changes of pitch that occur in the normal course of speaking. They differ according to many factors, including the speaker's region, dialect, gender, age, speech community, and individual personality. Intonation patterns vary among the many dialects of English and are not necessarily shared by native speakers from different regions of the same country. Native English speakers may have difficulty understanding each other when they are from different English-speaking countries, which is partly due to differing intonation patterns. Part of the skill of listening comprehension is being able to tell that two sentences with the same words can have completely different meanings based solely upon their intonation. For example:

> *The power went out.* (a declarative statement)
>
> versus
>
> *The power went out?* (trying to confirm whether the power went out)

In the second sentence, our voice rises at the end to signal that it is a yes/no question. Understanding the meanings of intonation patterns is a subtle and complex process, and learners need to train themselves to pick them up over time. This is not only a listening skill, but also part of the domain of communicative competence. Good teachers may not be able to predict when these types of utterances occur, so they may need to teach intonation patterns on the fly as examples of them come up in class. In particular, because intonation can signal differences in "tone," many teachers of ELLs have noted that it takes extra effort to help ELL students learn to identify sarcasm and irony when listening to oral speech. For example, when a person says this sentence with normal intonation or with exaggerated intonation, it alters the meaning completely.

> *The student followed all the rules.* (and the outcome was positive)
>
> or
>
> *The student followed all the rules. . . .* (but still got in trouble, unfairly).

Paralinguistic Features

Another related ability is knowing the meanings of gestures, body language, and facial expressions that accompany speech. Gestures and body language are not universal; like sounds, spelling patterns, phrases, and syntax, they are specific to language and culture. *Paralinguistic features* are nonverbal cues made by the human body. Although they are not part of listening comprehension per se, they do contribute significantly to meaning. In fact, robots that were programmed to use iconic hand gestures were able to be understood as well as human speakers, once those hand gestures were coded in (Bremner & Leonards, 2016). It's no wonder that so many film fans bonded with the *Star Wars* robot C-3PO, with his polite British intonation and elegant hand gestures. Paralinguistic features work in concert with the oral text to help us understand the meaning of the words.

The TESOL and WIDA standards, as well as the Early English Language Standards and Spanish WIDA Standards, help teachers identify the listening comprehension skills needed by learners at various ages and proficiency levels, as discussed in Chapter 2 (Gottlieb, Katz, & Ernst-Slavit, 2009; Teachers of English to Speakers of Other Languages, 2016; The WIDA Consortium, 2016).

Probabilistic Reasoning

Probabilistic reasoning is the cognitive strategy of recognizing patterns and applying that knowledge to predicting "what comes next." It is developed through conscious or unconscious practice and through repetition. The term *probabilistic reasoning* comes from the fields of computer science and cognitive science, and it is now widely applied in the field of artificial intelligence (Birch, 2015; Pearl, 2014). The ability to recognize patterns and make predictions from them is part of the human endowment and part of human learning. Probabilistic reasoning is a core concept that infuses the rest of this book.

Probabilistic reasoning comes into play in oracy, as seen in the following three examples. First, we use probabilistic reasoning in listening comprehension to predict the next word people are going to say. For example, when we hear someone start a sentence with the words *what kind*, we know, without consciously realizing it, that the next word will be *of* because we know that *what kind of* is a common and predictable English phrase. Second, we also use probabilistic reasoning for understanding the meaning of intonation patterns. If someone says, "You lost your cell phone?" with rising intonation, we know that it is a question, even though the words are not in the correct word order for a yes/no question in English (which would be "Did you lose your cell phone?"). Finally, if we look into a classroom from a hallway, we might be able to predict what kind of interaction is taking place solely from paralinguistic cues we get by watching the teacher. This would include his or her body language, hand gestures, and facial expressions, which come through even if we can't hear a word. (Children learn to read the body language of their teacher sometimes even before they can understand all of the words.) These skills can and must become part of a second-language learner's toolkit over time. We can be more effective teachers of ELLs when we understand, and systematically "unpack," some of the assumptions native speakers are able to make using their probabilistic reasoning and make them part of our curriculum.

The Active Nature of Listening Comprehension

Once we understand the components of listening comprehension, we realize why listening must be considered an active process. Like reading, however, it is sometimes wrongly labeled as a "receptive" skill, as if acquiring it were a passive process. If listening didn't require active engagement, we could understand speech when we weren't paying any attention to it, by osmosis, like a plant receives and processes sunlight. Remarkably, native speakers of a language are so proficient that they can often keep track of some of the drift of spoken language even when they are not concentrating on it, such as hearing the news on a radio from a different room. However, only the most proficient L2 learners have that luxury. Comprehending oral text in a new language requires constant attention.

In fact, comprehending oral text in a new language is such hard work that it can be downright exhausting (Igoa, 1995). Active listening is an intense mental workout—it's no wonder many children listening to a new language all day feel fatigued. It's even possible that the inattention or behavior problems some ELLs exhibit are related to listening fatigue. Here is how author Francisco Jimenez (1997) describes his first attempts to understand spoken English in his first-grade classroom, in the book *The Circuit*.

> Miss Scalapino started speaking to the class and I did not understand a word she was saying. The more she spoke, the more anxious I became. By the end of the day, I was very tired of hearing Miss Scalapino talk because the sounds made no sense to me. I thought that perhaps by paying close attention I would begin to understand, but I did not. I only got a headache, and that night, when I went to bed, I heard her voice in my head.
>
> For days I got headaches from trying to listen, until I learned a way out. When my head began to hurt, I let my mind wander . . . but when I daydreamed, I continued to look at the teacher and pretend I was paying attention because Papa told me it was disrespectful not to pay attention, especially to grownups. (pp. 17–18)

Auding: A Way to Describe Listening Comprehension

Auding is a word coined by Brown (1950) and subsequently adopted by Carver (1981) to describe not just hearing, but active listening. During auding, a person actively constructs meaning from an oral text similarly to the way a reader actively constructs meaning from a written text. Auding does not require literacy, but the two skills develop hand in hand. We like this term because it reminds us of the interactive nature of listening comprehension. Auding is an interaction between active listeners and spoken language as listeners rapidly process oral texts through their mental systems. These systems include all the listening skills presented earlier in this chapter, as well as the listener's background knowledge, the setting, and cultural and emotional filters. Moreover, the listening is happening in "real time."

As we perform these complex maneuvers, we also hold the message in short-term memory and later store it in long-term memory so that it can be retrieved for future use. In auding, we do not remember the exact form in which a text was conveyed to us, unless there was something very striking about the words themselves or about their delivery. Instead, we remember the main idea, or *gist*. Richards (1983) described the concept in the following way: "The basic unit of meaning in oral communication is the proposition or idea" (in O'Malley & Valdez-Pierce, 1996, p. 58). *Propositions* are the means through which the brain processes input and stores it in memory in condensed form. A mental proposition comprises the predicate, or verb, of the message and the information attached to it. When we are trying to get the gist of an oral message, however, we may miss the critical details, due to missing or misunderstanding part of the message. Those critical details are also likely to be missed in a new language, as demonstrated in this anecdote from an ESL teacher traveling in Taipei after studying Chinese.

> *As a newly arrived student in Taipei, I had studied Chinese for only 2 years and had very limited experience listening to normal-speed speech. In addition, the local accent was different from the accent of the teacher I had primarily studied under. During my first week, I got lost trying to find my college and asked directions of someone on the street. He understood my carefully rehearsed question, which clearly made me sound more capable than I actually was. He gave me rapid directions, which I in turn thought I understood. Unfortunately, the speed of his speech caused me to fail to remember a few essential steps. I got the gist, but for following directions around a city that just isn't enough. I ended up far from home, even more lost, and having to sacrifice my very limited funds to take a cab back. I finally found the college the next day, when I made sure to have written directions.—*JANIS MARA MICHAEL

Although listening for the content words is a good strategy, research into the listening processes of ELLs has shown that they are likely to hear content words and miss some of the shorter function words (Field, 2008).

Those little, unstressed words which seem to be merely "details," such as prepositions, articles, pronouns, and conjunctions, can actually be the pivots for comprehension. Since they are unstressed words, they are spoken more quickly and in a softer voice than content words. It takes a long time to learn to hear them in context. As we have seen in the previous anecdote, a wrong preposition can literally set a person off "in the wrong direction."

When we consider all the complex skills of listening comprehension, think about all the compromised environments in which we are asked to listen and understand, and further realize that these tasks occur in real time, without benefit of any kind of "instant replay," we can gain a new appreciation of how remarkable it is that we can process oral texts as fast and as well as we do. It's even more remarkable when it occurs in a new language!

Similarities between Comprehension in Listening and Reading

There are striking similarities between the comprehension processes involved in listening and reading, as summarized in Table 3.1. Listening involves learning how to make "reasonable interpretations" of an oral text (Brown & Yule, 1983, p. 57), and reading involves the same process for a written text. There are other similarities as well. Listening comprehension includes all of the content of a language—its vocabulary, syntax, meanings—that can be borne by the oral text alone, whereas literacy situates all of that language within a written system. Oracy acts as the bridge between a natural language process, which is listening, and an unnatural process, which is reading.

All of us learn to listen in our native language, and the habit of listening comprehension becomes automatic and unconscious by the time we begin school. Once we begin to learn content in school, however, even native speakers need to develop their auding skills in order to learn new content, and the listening comprehension we take for granted is no longer completely automatic. There are two areas in which all learners must be active listeners in an academic setting:

1. *Increasing listening vocabulary.* When we hear new words or words we are not sure about, we need to perk up to listen to how they are contextualized in order to understand them. Here are some examples.

I heard a politician say, "That's a bunch of malarkey," and I didn't know the word. I thought it might be Malachi *from the Bible, but it didn't make sense. I had to ask somebody about it.*—TENENA

I had to whisper curmudgeon *to myself and then look it up when I first heard it in a British drama. Now I hear it all the time and don't have to stop anymore.*—LEAH

When I heard my colleague say, "We have to perform triage," in a meeting at school, I had no idea what triage *meant, but as she continued, I figured out that it must mean to "sort" students. I got it completely from context.*—KRISTIN

The three examples here show three different strategies we used to disambiguate new words: asking a friend, subvocalizing a word to remember it and then looking it up, and figuring out the word's meaning from context.

2. *Following sustained academic content.* Students need to learn how to actively listen to sustained academic discourse in the classroom. The academic demands of listening to content increase as students move up in school, and apply to native speakers and ELL students alike.

TABLE 3.1. Similarities between the Listening and Reading Processes

1. Both require active construction of meaning, with interaction between the text (oral or written) and the person.
2. For both reading and listening, text is remembered as the "gist," not as the exact words.
3. Both listening and reading require phonological awareness.
4. Both the reading and listening processes benefit from larger vocabularies.
5. Reading and listening comprehension require having the concept of word (as a unit of meaning that can be manipulated).
6. English has many similar-looking and similar-sounding words, and these can be confusing.
7. Longer words are harder to store, retain, and retrieve from memory.
8. When context is stripped away, comprehension becomes much more difficult.
9. Automaticity facilitates the ability to construct meaning for both listening and reading, and this can be developed.
10. Learners need to become familiar with different genres and what can be expected from the structure of the genres.
11. Listening or reading tasks vary according to different purposes, different texts, and different contexts.
12. Both intensive and extensive practice are needed to improve listening and reading levels.
13. Both listening and reading require knowledge of English syntax patterns in order to make good guesses about what is coming next.

ELLs and Listening Vocabulary

By the time they start school, native speakers have a large storehouse of listening vocabulary: an estimated 5,000–7,000 words (Grabe & Stoller, 2002). ELLs, however, do not have this *listening vocabulary,* or storehouse of known English words. Although they have undergone the same universal processes of acquiring their native language that L1 English speakers have, the set of words, sounds, and patterns is not the same. Therefore, the features that would allow a smooth bridge from oracy to literacy, such as those in Table 3.1, do not apply to transitioning to reading a new language because ELLs don't have the English listening vocabulary yet. Until the English listening vocabulary of an ELL is well established, the skills that they can import from listening into reading cannot come into play. They simply don't have the threshold of listening vocabulary (Alderson, 1984, 2000) to allow a bridge to reading in English. For this very reason, newcomer programs begin with a period of building listening comprehension before any literacy is introduced.

The Simple View of Reading

The *simple view of reading (SVR)* (Gough & Tunmer, 1986) considers reading comprehension to be the product of listening comprehension and decoding. In other words, in the SVR framework, reading comprehension consists of everything that remains when decoding is not a factor, leaving listening comprehension or what can be called *language comprehension.* This includes all of the listening skills mentioned earlier in the chapter, our listening vocabulary, and probabilistic reasoning. Robust research supports the idea that listening comprehension is a decisive factor in reading comprehension (e.g., Biemiller, 1999; Dymock, 1993; Garcia & Cain, 2014; Gough & Tunmer, 1986; Stanovich, 1996). In a metastudy of 110 studies examining the relationship between decoding and reading comprehension, Garcia and Cain (2014) found that listening comprehension had a significant positive effect on reading comprehension, confirming SVR. Their literature review notes, "Readers with poor listening comprehension skills are likely to have poor reading comprehension" (p. 76). It should be noted, however, that only studies of native English-speaking children were included in the metastudy.

When Dymock (1993) studied L1 English middle school students with good decoding but poor comprehension skills, she also found that poor comprehenders had poor scores on listening comprehension, leading her to conclude that "once a child has become a good decoder, differences in reading ability will reflect differences in listening ability" (p. 90).

Biemiller (1999) points out that it is important to continue to build a strong listening vocabulary even as students begin to decode because a strong listening vocabulary will allow students to recognize many words once their decoding catches up with their listening vocabulary. Royer and Carlo (1991) found that Spanish ELLs' English listening comprehension, assessed in fifth grade, was one of the strongest predictors of their English reading comprehension in sixth grade. Carlisle et al. (1996) documented that English listening comprehension and quality of vocabulary definitions could account for 50% of the variance in reading comprehension scores of teenage Mexican ELLs. This kind of evidence makes SVR intriguing to those in the field of SLA.

The simple view of reading implicitly accepts the idea that oracy is the foundation for literacy. It also helps explain why ELLs need to have a good foundation of English listening vocabulary in place before they can comprehend text.

The Grammar of Oral Language

The grammar used in spoken English differs from that of written grammar. Native speakers of a language do not, typically, use full sentences when speaking. Spoken language usually uses less specific vocabulary, looser syntax, pronouns instead of nouns, and a lot of *ellipsis* (omitted words that can be understood from context), because the setting and the interaction provide many clues to meaning. Spoken language also has a large variety of *discourse markers*, such as conversational fillers and other sounds, as well as the paralinguistic cues mentioned earlier, in order to help listeners keep track of where in the course of an utterance the speaker is at a particular moment (Brown & Yule, 1983). These fillers, such as "uh huh," "hmmmm," or the word *like* serve as an informal kind of "oral punctuation." Brazil calls this real-time process a "step-by-step assembly of a spoken utterance" (Brazil, 1995, p. 17).

Slang and idioms particular to a time and place abound in spoken language. In addition, pronunciation may be less precise. Because oral language happens in real time, it can afford to be somewhat fragmentary because there are other cueing systems available to the listener. However, *context-reduced oral language* (Cummins, 1996), such as language exchanged during telephone conversations or when the other speaker is not visible, lacks the extra cueing systems that we use to compensate when our *auditory comprehension* breaks down. Context-reduced listening tasks can be especially stressful for ELLs, even when their proficiency in other areas is high. Unfortunately, context-reduced listening tasks are exactly the kinds of tests some ELL students receive these days, such as those that assess an ELL's conversational skills online, through an unseen online interviewer.

Oral language contains many forms. It may be informal, BICS language, such as conversation between two friends on a public bus, or more formal, CALP language, such as lectures, in-depth news reports, speeches, or technical trainings. The level of difficulty and the purpose for listening change from task to task, and these changes require flexibility and strategic listening. There are at least three ways in which listening comprehension can fail: first, the percentage of unknown words is too high or the syntax of the sentences is too complex; second, the sheer quantity of spoken words is too great; and third, the listener cannot maintain concentration because the duration of the listening task is too long. When the spoken language is beyond the learner's zone of proximal development (ZPD; Vygotsky, 1986), the input is no longer comprehensible. This can result in full-scale frustration, mental shutdown, and a resulting lack of academic progress.

When students are placed in listening situations in which the context cues are reduced, the listening task gets harder because the words alone must convey the meaning. Here is one account by a second-grade ESL teacher that captures the nature of the challenge, not only for these students but also for their instructors.

> *I speak Spanish, but would by no means call myself bilingual. However, I often have to speak Spanish in my school with both students and parents. If I am called upon to make a phone call in Spanish, I tend to panic because I cannot see the person talking to me and therefore do not have any body language to interpret, or anything visual, for that matter. I also translate for conferences, and by the time the night is over, I am mentally exhausted. And when analyzing why, I think that listening to the parents and making sure I am understanding what exactly they are saying is pretty stressful. And then to translate that to the teachers, then translate back to the parents is really tiring. People can "zone out" while someone is speaking their native language and still get the gist of what they are saying, but to do that in a person's second language is just not possible.—VICKI MUSIAL*

All of these factors—the fleeting nature of spoken words, the fragmentary nature of oral grammar, the casual pronunciation of words, idiomatic vocabulary, different purposes and difficulty levels for listening tasks, and cultural factors—combine to make it challenging for ELLs to achieve a high level of listening comprehension. Because listening remains effortful for ELLs for a long time, it is important to practice it with them often, in manageable amounts and at the appropriate level.

Oral Proficiency in English as a New Language

The second component of oracy is *oral proficiency*, sometimes called the speaking skill. Although being able to speak a language well does confer many benefits, oral proficiency in itself doesn't predict reading proficiency (August, Calderon, & Carlo, 2002; Geva, 2006). For ELLs, reading proficiency is more affected by the core decoding skills, which include phonological awareness, letter identification, word recognition, and knowledge of English grammar (Bernhardt & Kamil, 1995), in addition to the listening comprehension described previously. Geva's (2006) literature review of second-language literacy research concludes, "having well-developed oral language proficiency in English is associated with well-developed reading comprehension skills in English" (p. 135).

It is important for ELLs to learn to take part in instructional conversation and interactive dialogue (Saunders & Goldenberg, 1999; Tharp et al., 2003; Waxman & Téllez, 2002). Instructional conversation can be defined as "planned, goal-directed conversations on an academic topic between a teacher and a small group of students" (Tharp et al., 2003, para. 6).

ELLs need daily opportunities to engage in instructional conversation in English. For example, learners may use instructional conversation to explain the steps of a mathematical process, or express their opinion about a current topic in an informal debate, or present a project to the rest of the class. English instructional conversation can take place in pairs, in a small group, or in a teacher-directed large group, but small groups give the richest opportunities for students to practice and flex their speaking skills.

There are three major benefits to instructional conversation. First, when ELLs engage in probing conversations about instructional topics with peers and expert others, including teachers, they improve their academic skills through conveying information, discussing, analyzing, inferring, debating, summarizing, evaluating, and synthesizing (Zwiers, 2008). Second, when students engage in instructional conversation, they also build communicative competence by practicing vital social and emotional skills, such as taking turns and expanding on their classmates' ideas. Finally, instructional conversation provides authentic practice of paralinguistic skills like vocal intonations and body language. These three aspects can be seen in the oracy skills framework (Mercer, 2014; see Table 3.2), developed and used at Oxford University.

As children advance in grade level, more and more CALP language is used in the instructional conversation of the classroom. The pedagogical implication is that all teachers, even at the PreK level, need to provide

TABLE 3.2. Oracy Skills Framework

<u>Physical</u>

Voice	• Fluency and pace of speech • Tonal variation • Clarity of pronunciation • Voice projection
Body language	• Gesture and posture • Facial expression • Eye contact

<u>Linguistic</u>

Vocabulary	• Appropriate vocabulary choice
Language variety	• Register • Grammar
Structure	• Structure and organization of talk
Rhetorical techniques	• Rhetorical techniques (e.g., metaphor, humor, irony, mimicry)

<u>Cognitive</u>

Content	• Choice of content to convey meaning and intention • Building on the views of others
Clarifying and summarizing	• Seeking information and clarification through questions • Summarizing
Self-regulation	• Maintaining focus on task • Time management
Reasoning	• Giving reasons to support views • Critically examining ideas and views expressed
Audience awareness	• Taking account of the level of understanding of the audience

<u>Social and Emotional</u>

Working with others	• Guiding or managing the interaction • Turn taking
Listening and responding	• Listening actively and responding appropriately
Confidence in speaking	• Self-assurance • Liveliness and flair

Note. Adapted from Mercer (2014). Copyright © The Faculty of Education, University of Cambridge. Adapted by permission.

early opportunities to engage in instructional conversation in class. It is all too tempting for teachers of ELLs to simplify speech, becoming inadvertent "enablers" of lowered expectations and not giving ELLs the CALP "workout" they deserve (Zwiers, 2007, p. 107). When teachers finish a sentence for the student, affirm too quickly, or oversimplify, students pay the price. Students benefit most when teachers ask focused questions, provide sufficient wait time (Rowe, 1986), and pay attention to the thinking process of the students without supplying answers or steering them toward a "correct" answer.

Oral Language Development in ELLs

Children learning their first language produce speech in roughly the same order no matter what their native language is: they start with nouns, followed by verbs, then adjectives (National Institute of Child Health and Human Development, 2004). ELLs go through somewhat analogous stages of oral language development, moving from single-word production all the way to complex sentences, and gradually incorporating their growing unconscious mastery of English deep structures (Dulay & Burt, 1974; Krashen, 1977). The TESOL/WIDA standards include descriptions of the oral language stages, along with suggested activities for ELLs at different grade levels (Gottlieb et al., 2009; Teachers of English to Speakers of Other Languages, 2016; The WIDA Consortium, 2016). ELL oral language development may reach a native-speaker level for English BICS language in the space of about 3 years (Thomas & Collier, 2002), but this is certainly not a "one-size-fits-all" metric. Development is influenced by such factors as the age at which the learner begins to learn English, L1 oracy and literacy, prior schooling, the presence of English-speaking siblings, motivation, learning style, and related factors. Of course, progress is also affected by teachers and the instructional setting.

One of the phenomena in the stages of oral language development that every teacher of ELLs must be aware of is the preproduction or *silent period*. Not all ELLs experience this stage, but many do, and it is not only young children who have a silent period. During the silent period, which may last as long as a year, the learner focuses on the listening load of spoken English and may not produce any oral language. The silent period is similar to the prespeech period of infants in their native language, but it can occur at any age for ELLs. Although it may appear on the surface as if no learning is occurring, the silent period is very dynamic. During this period, ELLs are actively gaining knowledge of the sounds and patterns of English, and teachers can have full confidence that learning is taking place. At the same time, while respecting that children may not be ready to speak, teachers need to continue to actively include and engage such students. This can be done by asking them to point or gesture, perform motor activities, manipulate objects, act, pantomime, or create some kind of visual art to show what they have understood. Clear speaking and expressive oral reading by the teacher are important sources of linguistic modeling for students during this period.

> *I have witnessed an extreme example of the silent period in a seventh-grade student whose first language was Chinese. She was in an ESL class, and although her father, a bilingual Chinese–English speaker, went over the English lessons with her every night, she wouldn't say a word in class. For 9 months she was mute, and the district was getting ready to test her for a learning disability, but then summer came. Although she spoke only Chinese during the summer, she came back the following fall and, after a week in school, was speaking full sentences and carrying on conversations in English, like a native speaker, with no accent or anything.*—LEAH

Of course, we need to be careful not to mistake a silent period for a student as just "tuning out" or resisting instruction when they are adolescents. Teachers might think older newcomers and refugees are tired, resentful, or resistant, but this is simply how the silent period might look at the adolescent level. Students at this age need just as much support and latitude as children at younger ages. Teachers need to make sure not to leave older children "out of the loop" but to include them in activities. In one study, teachers claimed they were allowing an extended silent period for new ELLs, but to observers, "the students seemed neglected" (Mohr & Mohr, 2007, p. 443).

Assessing Oracy

Assessing a student's listening skills is key to their academic and social success. Notwithstanding its importance, the listening comprehension level of ELLs is often hard to assess. Because listening comprehension cannot be easily seen, teachers may have a false sense of how much an ELL understands. On the one hand, if students' oral language has not reached a threshold that allows them to produce connected sentences, they may comprehend but not be able to demonstrate their comprehension verbally. On the other hand, students may signal that they understand, even when they don't, because they simply don't want to call attention to their confusion. Whenever possible, listening assessments should include an opportunity for ELLs to hear the text and the prompt more than once.

Assessing a student's speaking skills may seem easier, but it's important to keep the affective filter low. Students need adequate processing time when they are being assessed for oral activities. Timed tests may not provide a fair measure of what ELLs may be able to do. Speaking assessment should focus on progress in communicative competence and recognize the developmental nature of oracy.

Oracy Development for School Success

Research shows that children who come to school with strong oracy are at an advantage, and those with limited oracy are more likely to have difficulty learning to read (Scarborough, 2001; Tracey & Morrow, 2002). Early delays in oracy development can be reflected in low levels of reading comprehension, which in turn can lead to lack of academic success (Biemiller, 1970). Thanks to the inborn proclivity of children to acquire language, children who are learning English can easily develop oral vocabulary. In fact, at least one study has indicated that kindergarten-age ELLs learned more English vocabulary in a classroom than their English-only counterparts did (Silverman, 2007). Children who speak a home language other than English also benefit from developing strong oracy in their first language. When their L1 oracy is strong, they will bring more vocabulary, background knowledge, listening skills, speaking skills, and self-confidence to the English-learning endeavor.

For all of these considerations, developing ELLs' oracy to a high level is an important ingredient in their syndrome of success.

HOW DOES THIS LOOK IN THE CLASSROOM?

To boost listening skills, we suggest alternating *intensive* and *extensive* practice activities.

Intensive Activities

Intensive listening gives students a chance to focus on discrete features of the sounds of English in a controlled setting in which they can hear the oral text more than once and analyze its features and sound combinations. The insights gained from intensive listening can be applied to other listening experiences. Intensive activities can be embedded within extensive activities.

Three intensive listening activities—dictation, transcribing, and using subtitles and captions—can help build listening comprehension.

Dictation

Dictation is a great way to practice phonological awareness and concept of word, two of the key components of listening comprehension. There are several ways to use dictation.

1. Choose a short text to read aloud, saying the words and punctuation, and ask students to write down all the words (and the punctuation) they hear.
2. Choose a set of sentences and read them aloud, pausing at the phrase and clause breaks. By increasing the number of words in the sentences over time, students become proficient at holding more words in working memory. It is a great way to spot-check development of ELLs' syntax, and it provides spelling awareness at the same time.
3. Use a prerecorded text by preparing stopping places in advance and pausing the audio track.
4. For math practice, create a dictation for numbers, equations, and operations. Students can write the dictated math on paper and read back what they wrote, which is good speaking practice.
5. Many in the language teaching field use *cloze* dictations, sometimes called gap fills or fill-in-the-blank activities. In a cloze dictation, some of the words are provided and others are left out. To practice listening comprehension, a teacher can read sentences or a paragraph to help students recognize the words they hear in casual speech. This activity requires the students to have a proficient level of English reading and writing already. By listening to these items, students can listen to features of American English pronunciation. For example, in American English, when one word ends with /t/ and the following pronoun begins with a /y/, we normally produce a "ch" sound between the words, such as /downchuw/ for *don't you*. Once that is explained and demonstrated, that pronunciation feature can be practiced through cloze exercises. For example, when a student hears the sentence "Wouldn't you like to sit down?" they understand that the sounds /wudnchuw/ should be written as *wouldn't* + *you*.

Transcribing

Transcribing a text while listening to it is really a variation of dictation, but the text isn't designed to be a dictation or cloze dictation. Rather, it is an existing text. The best and most logical texts for transcribing are song lyrics. Students already seek out lyrics to their favorite songs online, so this activity should be familiar to them. Choose a song with words that are slow enough, and few enough, to be transcribed in a few listens. A simple folk song or pop tune with a repeating chorus works best. Split the class into small groups and assign each group to transcribe one verse of the song, then play it. After hearing it twice, members of each group huddle together to write the best version of their verse, and then write it on the board for the rest of the class to see. When all the verses are written on the board, play the song one more time, to see if any corrections need to be made. Finally, supply copies of the complete lyrics, and let students check their work against the correct lyrics. Plan to assign the chorus of the song to a group that has less listening proficiency because the chorus repeats several times.

This tried-and-true method of building listening comprehension is entertaining, motivating, and can create great discussions about the meanings and spellings of words, while also introducing students to a song that may be new to them. One of us, Kristin, has had great success using the song "Que Sera Sera" on YouTube, as sung by Doris Day.

Using Subtitles and Captions

Using subtitles and captions is a natural choice for helping students connect the ways words look with the way they sound. Many videos contain captions or subtitles and can be played with captions as the video plays, allowing ELLs to read along as they listen. Old TV sitcoms, movies, and videos include closed-captioning options as well. DVD formats allow students to see subtitles in the language of the film, so they can see the English words as they hear them. (Be careful, however; the subtitles are not all of the words, but a condensed version of the meanings, and they can sometimes make listening more, rather than less, complicated!) The DVD can also be stopped to point out specific features. This dual pathway to language, using both sounds and written words, is an incredible resource for improving listening comprehension inside and outside the classroom.

Extensive Activities

Three *extensive listening activities*—total physical response, guest speakers, and interactive read-aloud—work well in giving students practice in getting the gist of an utterance as they develop strategic listening skills in authentic but low-stress contexts.

Total Physical Response

Total physical response (TPR) is a popular ESL teaching technique in which students act out a word, sentence, or scenario (Asher, 1988), demonstrating their listening comprehension. It works well for the earliest learners who cannot write or speak English yet but can indicate comprehension through movement. A classic example is that of preschool students performing the song "Head, Shoulders, Knees, and Toes," showing they know the part of the body they are singing about by touching it as they sing.

Sam Willingmyre uses TPR in her second-grade math class for the game Geometry Simon Says, a variation of the old children's game Simon Says. Students learn different arm movements that visually represent geometric concepts, such as "line" (both arms extended), "ray" (one arm ends in a fist), and "line segment" (both arms end in fists), among others. After teaching the arm movements, Sam calls out the different geometry terms at the front of the class. When she precedes them with the phrase "geometry says," the students must perform the actions, but when the phrase is omitted, students must stand still or else they have to sit down. It's uproariously fun, and it helps students remember abstract geometry concepts using "muscle memory."

TPR can also work with older learners. The game In the Manner of the Word, for example, can be used to show an understanding of subtle qualities of characters in literature in a language arts class. After having learned a list of adverbs in previous classes, students are given a piece of paper with an adverb not known to the rest of the class. The student then reads a folk- or fairytale "in the manner of the word." Students try to guess the adverb from their classmate's tone of voice and body language. For example, when the slip of paper says "sarcastically," the student reads "Little Red Riding Hood" using intonation dripping with sarcasm. It is important to choose adverbs that are easy to act out, not ones that are too abstract. *Slowly*, for example, works better than a subtle word like *quizzically*.

Guest Speakers or Videos

The second method for increasing extensive listening is inviting a guest speaker to class. If students are highly proficient, they can combine their listening with note taking or by filling in a graphic organizer that has been prepared in advance by the teacher or the speaker. Bringing guest speakers to class is also a great way to get children used to hearing different speaking voices and to add to their background knowledge.

Teachers can also invite family members to share their talents, occupations, or stories about their own childhoods. This taps into ELL students' funds of knowledge (Moll, Amanti, Neff, & Gonzalez, 1992). Although they are less immediately exciting than a "live" visitor, lively and exciting videos and webcasts are also available. One of our favorite kinds is short interviews with children's book authors.

Interactive Read-Aloud

The third method is a core literacy technique especially effective for learners in the early primary grades. In *interactive read-aloud (IR)*, teachers read a book or a story to children without displaying the written text. IR is usually used with picture books. First, the teacher directs students to the title and author on the cover of the book, and they use probabilistic reasoning to guess what the book might be about. Then the teacher might also mention its literary genre, such as biography or mystery. Next, the teacher does a "picture walk," turning the pages of the book, as students "read" the pictures and use words to make observations about the story. Now, the teacher expressively reads the story, stopping at key points selected in advance to generate interest in the plot or the characters, and to make personal connections. At this point, the teacher might ask students to draw or write a response to something in the book. It might be based on a prompt, such as "Draw your favorite part of the book." For ELL children, an IR can occur over the better part of a week because the repetition gives them increasing confidence in understanding the story line and knowing and using the vocabulary.

Samar Abousalem talks about a challenge of using a three-day IR with her first-grade ELLs, and how she addresses it.

> One challenge that is easy to encounter when using IRs with ELLs is difficulty maintaining students' interest for very long on the third day. They sometimes feel they've answered all the questions they want to answer. For this reason, I caution against spending too much time asking questions. Ask fewer questions, yet strive for questions that require higher-level thinking. However, therein lies another challenge: finding higher-level questions that will elicit answers that the students are able to produce. The best solution for this is a well thought out lesson plan so that the two previous days leading up to the third day set the foundation for making deeper connections and inferences. (Lems & Abousalem, 2014, p. 14)

In addition to fostering oracy, IRs build crucial background knowledge of people, places, and events ELLs need to know. As ELLs hear more stories, they develop a sense of *story grammar*, the probable sequence of events that a listener or reader can expect over the normal course of a story. Learning story grammar helps children develop probabilistic reasoning, which they can later use in their reading and writing.

It is also possible to use informational text in IR, such as short articles from *Time for Kids* or articles from *National Geographic* children's books. This helps develop world knowledge as well as an understanding of literary genres, which will serve ELLs for both reading and writing.

L1 English-speaking students benefit from read-alouds even through eighth grade (Biemiller, 1999; Chall, 1996), and ELLs can benefit from IRs at any grade level. Teachers can also read chapter books aloud on a regular basis, which helps students build skills in text analysis as well as increasing listening vocabulary all the way up through the grades. The many accounts of classroom engagement by children who have taken part in Harry Potter read-alouds and marathons are a testament to the excitement that can be generated at any grade level using oral reading.

For the Youngest Learners

Barb Prohaska, a preschool teacher of many ELLs, confirms that children can get very fatigued from listening tasks that are too long. She has these suggestions for keeping children alert and fresh.

- Working in groups works best when children have a task, such as finding out information and reporting back.
- Giving children an idea of what they are supposed to be listening for is helpful so that they aren't just listening to listen.
- Playing I Spy with My Little Eye, and building clues to help then home in on what the object is. They may not know all the clues, but some of the clues can help them determine the object.
- Making up a short story as students listen and draw the different scenes. I have done this individually and with small groups so they can help each other. This way they are taking part in active listening and making sense of the story.

Barb also describes the following activities, which she recommends for improving oral language and learning to use and understand body language.

- We do an oral dictation activity in which I begin writing on chart paper a 3- or 4-word sentence, such as "The rabbit ran." Then the kids continue adding words as I write, such as "The rabbit ran fast." "The rabbit ran fast across the green grass." I prompt the kids to use describing words and stretch out the sentence. We practice this same prompt for a couple days, and believe it or not, they remember the content of the sentence.
- We do a lot of pantomime too, especially when we do our unit on "feelings." I know that gestures and body language are not universal, and I see that when I talk to my Chinese ELL students. They are very quiet and frequently look down when I am trying to talk to them.

Teachers can support language growth through the kinds of questions they use in class. Although teachers need to check comprehension of important facts, good questions should move from the fact-based kind to those requiring higher-order critical thinking. Like other academic skills, the ability to engage with meaningful questions does not happen overnight but has to be practiced regularly. Good questions help with instructional conversation and cognitive skills. Like all students, ELLs need to be held to high academic expectations (Swain, 2005; Zwiers, 2008).

QUESTIONS FOR FURTHER STUDY

1. If you had to choose three important ideas from this chapter, which would you choose? How can you apply these ideas to your larger knowledge of teaching English as a new language?

2. Can you think of something someone said to you that you remember exactly, with a great deal of detail? What do you think was so striking about the words? Why do you think we remember some words we hear exactly, but most only for their gist?

3. Have you had any experience, either as a teacher or a language learner, in which someone seemed to understand an oral text until it was shown that he or she did not? What, if anything, were you able to do about it? Describe it.

4. Think of a recent example in which you engaged in instructional conversation. With whom did you share it? What were some of its characteristics?

5. With a partner or alone, think of some "meaning-bearing" gestures and body language commonly used by teachers in schools. Talk about ways those gestures could be taught to ELLs. If you have the opportunity to ask ELLs about this, you may find that they have perceived gestures that adults have missed!

6. If you are familiar with another culture, can you describe the differences in paralinguistic cues, such as body language, hand gestures, or facial features between that culture and the one in which you now live? How could you address those differences in a classroom of learners from that culture?

7. Do you think probabilistic reasoning takes place in species other than humans? When forming your position, give examples.

8. We often hear the lyrics of a song but interpret them completely differently, changing the meaning of the song to our own skewed interpretation. Do you have any memories of this phenomenon in your own life? Do you think songs have a "right" or "wrong" meaning? Share your thoughts with others.

9. Can you think of any words that you tend to mispronounce? Try to analyze what it is that makes these words tricky.

10. When you look at a TV show or movie without sound, what do you catch and what do you wonder about? How does it compare with hearing a TV from another room when you cannot see the picture? Have you ever

looked at a TV show or movie in a language you didn't know, with no subtitles? What can you figure out from the vocal inflections and body language?

11. Looking at the similarities between the listening and reading processes in Table 3.1 on p. 65, talk about which similarities between listening and reading you had realized before reading this chapter, and which ones were new to you. Can you think of any others?

12. Look at the oracy skills framework in Table 3.2 on p. 70. In which areas do you feel you are already strong? In which areas do you feel you could use some improvement? Which areas of the framework do you think are important to learn about in teacher preparation programs, and which are not?

13. CHALLENGE QUESTION: Think about ways that a person's paralinguistic cues, or body language, might reveal as much or more about them than their words. How do we respond when body language and words give contrary messages? Try to design a lesson or set of guidelines to help ELLs develop communicative competence about "reading" paralinguistic cues as part of their communicative competence.

14. CHALLENGE QUESTION: Make a table or chart of the characteristics of ELL students you teach that demonstrates their listening comprehension. What does it look like? What does it sound like? What kinds of interactions occur between students and the teacher? Among students?

CHAPTER FOUR

Learning to Read, Write, and Spell Words in English as a New Language

New Vocabulary in This Chapter: *phonemes, graphemes, word recognition, decodable words, sight words, recoding, phonics, reasoning by analogy, alphabetic orthography, alphabet, consonantal alphabet, syllabic writing system, syllabary, logographic writing system, logograms, generative, orthographic transparency or depth, transparent/shallow orthographies, deep/opaque orthographies, opacity, orthographic depth hypothesis, transparency, word calling, digraph, pinyin, alphabetic/letter name spelling, numeric spelling, numeracy, emojis, morphemes, invented spelling*

In this chapter we discuss how learning to read is influenced by the orthography of the target language, in this case, English. Each written language in the world has an *orthography*, or writing system, and English uses the Roman alphabet. The way words are represented in the English writing system affects the way everyone, including ELLs, learns to read in English. The experiences ELLs have with the English alphabet can be influenced by the writing system of their first language and its orthographic distance from the English writing system. There are many positive aspects to first-language literacy, and knowing a writing system is a definite advantage that provides PCI for the learner, as we discussed earlier. However, learning the English writing system can be challenging and is too often overlooked in designing instruction for ELLs.

We begin by discussing how native speakers of English learn to recognize words and decode text.

How Word Recognition Occurs in English

To read English words, we learn to match their *phonemes,* or sounds, with their *graphemes,* or letters. When we learn to read English words, we learn to perform several steps very rapidly. First, we identify the first letter(s) of the word and try to find a matching phoneme. Then, working left to right, we quickly "sample" the rest of the graphemes and phonemes of the word. Holding the sounds in our working memory, we recombine them to form a mental representation that we attempt to match with a word from our listening vocabulary. Once that lightning-fast process occurs, we can access its meaning. Of course, there are other strategies involved if we are reading out loud or if we don't already know the word. Goodman (1970) refers to this complex process as a "psycholinguistic guessing game."

Accessing and recognizing individual words is called *word recognition,* and accessing and recognizing words in connected text is what we call *decoding.* There are two broad categories of words in English: those with easy-to-match phonemes and graphemes, called *decodable words,* and those that have to be learned as whole words, called *sight words.* Decoding and sight-word recognition are the primary word-attack skills for English word recognition. There are good reasons that English word recognition is taught through both phonological decoding and whole word memorization, which will become clear as we proceed through this chapter.

The process is somewhat different when we want to represent words in written form, which is called *recoding* (sometimes referred to as *encoding*). We retrieve the desired word from our listening vocabulary and try to write the letters that represent the sounds of the word, proceeding in order from left to right. Recoding words in English proceeds in two possible ways. It proceeds by putting letters in order, for easily decodable words, or by learning how to write some words by memorizing them, in the case of sight words.

Although some of the shortest and most common English words are sight words, overall the great majority of English words are decodable and recodable. Learning to decode and recode is necessary in order to read and write in English.

When learners decode English words, they start with the letter symbols and match them with the sounds, and when they write English words, they start with the sounds and match them with the letter symbols. No matter which end we start from, both processes involve matching the English sounds and letter symbol combinations. The skill involved in matching sounds and letter symbols is called *phonics*. Phonics knowledge requires an understanding of how the English sound system and writing system map onto each other. In order to help learners develop the phonics skill, teachers need to understand how the phonemes and graphemes of English work together in the English writing system. At the same time, a teacher of ELLs also needs to appreciate how the orthographies of ELLs' first languages affect the ways they will learn to read and write in English. Exploring these similarities and differences is the principal purpose of this chapter.

For a native speaker of English, the process of learning to read and write words usually begins before or in kindergarten and continues until it is firmly in place, normally before third grade. This is a lengthy and often laborious process, and must be accomplished before the focus of reading can change from "learning to read" to "reading to learn." Learners of English as a new language need to go through this process just like native speakers do, but the process might occur at any age or grade level, depending on when ELLs begin to learn English. The phonics skills, or "bottom-up" skills, are critical to cracking the code for reading and writing English and must be accounted for in any comprehensive instructional program. As Calderon (2006) nicely summarizes, "Whatever the grade level, teachers with ELLs will eventually have students who need instruction in these basic skills, before they can comprehend a text" (p. 131).

Probabilistic Reasoning for Reading

We introduced the concept of probabilistic reasoning in Chapter 3 to talk about the advantage native speakers might have in figuring out the messages of spoken English. When probabilistic reasoning is applied to learning to decode, however, native speakers of English have less of a natural advantage. That's because English sounds do not predict English spelling patterns with a high degree of consistency so, in some ways, decoding is more of a level playing field. However, the big advantage for native English speakers is that they have a larger listening vocabulary, so it will help their probabilistic reasoning as they try to decode the sounds of an unknown word. However, we want to reiterate that learning to read and spell in English is not an easy task for either native speakers or ELLs. It is a tough job!

Even though the relationship between phonemes and graphemes is not consistent in the English writing system, L1 English readers can come to predict that when a consonant or vowel occurs next to certain other letters, it is likely to be pronounced in a specific way. For example, when they see the word *pride,* even if they don't know its meaning, they can unconsciously compare it to other English words they know, such as *side,* and say to themselves, "This word is probably pronounced like *side,* a word I already know."

Probabilistic reasoning is honed through the stages of reading development and can be called *reasoning by analogy* (Goswami, 2013). *Reasoning by analogy* is the development of the ability to predict the meaning of unknown words through familiarity with the frames that surround the unknown element. As young readers have more experiences with print, they become better and better at predicting what the next letter of a word is likely to be and how it is likely to sound. When we become really proficient readers, we can even compensate for missing letters or missing words when the message is compromised somehow. The game show *Wheel of Fortune* is a contest that tests the probabilistic reasoning skills of contestants who try to be the first to guess a hidden phrase with the fewest letters revealed. McGuinness describes the process as when brains "actively resonate with regularities in the input, and automatically keep score of the probabilities of recurring patterns" (McGuinness, 2004, p. 47).

Probabilistic reasoning is embedded in many digital devices. Search engines "guess" how we want to complete a word or phrase as we type in the first couple of letters. If a person starts a Google search with the letters *st,* for example, the search brings up the most high-frequency letter string beginning with *st,* and it is often *Starbucks.* The same phenomenon occurs when a person starts a question or keyword search in Google, and Google bring up the most common ending to the string of words. Spellcheck programs and apps also predict the word we were trying to spell based on the most common misspellings of the word.

Once we realize that we are talking about the brain's ability to make guesses based on its assessment of probabilities, we also realize that what we call "rules" are really just highly probable events, and "exceptions" are just less probable events. Seen that way, we can approach English decoding and recoding from a different perspective. English words don't "break spelling rules" but are instead less probable ways to represent the sounds of the word.

Let's look at how different writing systems are organized in order to better understand how sound and letter combinations work in English.

Major Kinds of Writing Systems

Over time, human beings have developed many kinds of orthographies. All of them are attempts to capture and preserve the information contained in speech. The way an orthographic system represents spoken language influences how people learn to read in that language. Orthographies can be classified into three large systems: alphabetic, syllabic, and logographic (Birch, 2015; Perfetti & Dunlap, 2008). The major difference between these three systems is in the size of the unit the word is made up of. An alphabetic system uses a letter or letters to represent the sounds of a word; a syllabic system uses a syllable as the smallest unit to represent a word's sounds, and a logographic system uses a whole word as the unit for representing a word, giving less detail about its sounds. "The defining feature of a writing system is its mapping principle—graph to phoneme (alphabetic), graph to syllable (syllabic), and graph to word or morpheme (logosyllabic)" (Perfetti & Dunlap, 2008, p. 15). Within each of these large systems, there are many individual orthographies belonging to different languages. Moreover, each of these kinds of writing systems is well represented in the languages of immigrant groups to the United States and Canada.

When we learn to read in a new language, we need to learn its orthographic system. If we are literate in our first language, we also retain the knowledge of its orthographic system.

Alphabetic Writing Systems

An *alphabetic orthography* represents each sound with a symbol or symbols. The set of all of the symbols that can make up words is called an *alphabet*. Many languages use alphabetic orthographies. These include English, Russian, Spanish, Arabic, and many more. Within alphabetic orthographies, however, there are many different alphabets. English uses the Roman alphabet, and so do many other languages; however, the relationship between the letters and the sounds they represent differs from language to language. For example, the letters *ch* represent the /ch/ sound in English, as in the word *church,* but the /sh/ sound in French, as in the word *chateau.*

In addition to the Roman alphabet, the Cyrillic alphabet is a widely used alphabet for languages, including Russian, Ukrainian, Mongolian, and Bulgarian. A few of the letters are shared with the Roman alphabet, but most do not map to the same sounds, which means readers of those alphabets will experience initial interference in trying to read English words.

Arabic is another widely adopted alphabet. It is called a *consonantal alphabet* because only some of the vowel sounds are written out. The Arabic alphabet is used not only for Arabic, but for Urdu, Persian, Malay, and other languages spoken by many ELLs. It is written and read from right to left, and it also uses a different numbering system from English. In addition, each Arabic letter can take three forms according to whether it is at the beginning, middle, or end of a word, but Arabic does not use capital letters. When L1 Arabic speakers are learning English, they need extra practice in learning how to say and write the myriad vowel sounds in English. In addition, they need practice in writing English numbers, using capital and small letters, and reading and writing from left to right as well as turning pages in that direction.

One of our students notes the fact that Arabic readers of English "rely heavily on the consonants when attempting to recognize English words" (Birch, 2015, pp. 40–41) and comments:

> *We know that this strategy is not very effective and can really cause problems for Arabic speakers trying to learn and pronounce similar sounding words in English. A perfect example of this is Hassan, my Arabic-speaking husband's frequently mixing up the name of my father, Gene, with my best friend's mother, Jan, and two of our good friends, Jenn and Jane. The fact that he has so much trouble hearing the differences between these tense and lax vowels has been the cause of confusion multiple times.*—LEAH COOPER

Generally, ELLs whose first language is represented by an alphabetic script will have an advantage in learning to decode English words because they already understand the notion that the letters of the alphabet represent sounds. In addition, ELLs whose languages use the Roman alphabet have the added advantage of knowing some of the letters and numbers of English from the start.

Syllabic Writing Systems

The *syllabic writing system* uses a consonant–vowel combination as the smallest unit to represent sounds. Each symbol cannot be broken down further (Comrie, Matthews, & Polinsky, 1996). Languages that use syllabic orthographies include Japanese Hiragana and Katakana, Khmer, Hmong, Bengali, Gujarati, and Cherokee. Words in syllabic writing systems consist of a sequence of syllables, and the complete set of syllables in the language is called a *syllabary*. The disadvantage of a syllabic writing system is that words are often very long since the syllable is the smallest possible unit, and these long words can become unwieldy. Figure 4.1 shows a primer used to teach the syllables of Gujarati. Each of the symbols represents a whole syllable, and the whole word written under each illustration includes the syllable.

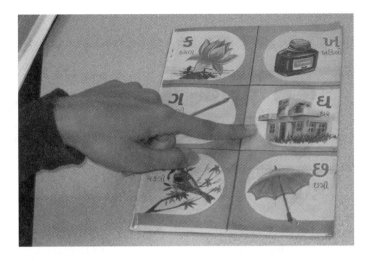

FIGURE 4.1. Learning the syllables of Gujarati.

Logographic Writing Systems

No writing system in the world is devoid of a phonological element. However, those that use a *logographic writing system* have less phonological information than alphabets and syllabaries. Chinese (Mandarin) has the best known logographic writing system. A Chinese word is composed of a radical that contains semantic information and a phonetic component, which is not always apparent. Chinese has about 2,500 *logograms* that can combine into many thousands of words (Yule, 2006). Because the smallest phonological unit is a word, reading Chinese involves less phonological processing but more semantic processing (analyzing of meaning). Nonetheless, it has been shown that phonological awareness, an important building block of reading, affects reading ability in Chinese as well (Pang & Kamil, 2003; Perfetti & Dunlap, 2008).

It takes a long time to acquire a complete set of logograms (McGuinness, 2004). However, there are two major advantages for logographic orthographies. First, they provide a direct pathway to meaning, allowing people to read and write "what they mean," not just "what they say" (Ellis et al., 2004, p. 438), and second, since logograms carry less phonological information, they can be understood by a wide range of regional language and dialect speakers who cannot speak with each other but can understand each other's writing.

Of the three orthographic systems, alphabetic systems have the added advantage of being the most *generative,* because a limited number of letters and sounds can be combined to generate an astronomical number of words. The elegance and economy of an alphabetic system has convinced many societies to adopt them, as we shall see presently.

Although English uses an alphabetic writing system, it also contains logograms. These symbols, which include numbers, do not contain phonological information, but they form an integral part of the writing system. These logograms can be found on the standard keyboard. Examples of English logograms include $, &, @, ?, and so forth. As students begin working in the content areas, they will be exposed to more and more logograms, especially in such fields as mathematics, chemistry, music, and computer science. These symbols need to be memorized and understood as whole units, just like other logograms.

The differences children experience in learning literacy through these writing systems are profound, but proficient readers emerge through the medium of all of these writing systems. For a detailed inventory of the world's writing systems, we recommend *Omniglot,* an online encyclopedia of writing systems and languages of the world (Omniglot, 2017).

Some of the diverse orthographies used by members of immigrant and ethnic communities in Chicago are featured in the photo essay Chicago Orthographies (Figure 4.2).

Orthographic Transparency and Depth

An important concept that describes how predictably writing systems represent the sounds of words is called *orthographic transparency or depth.* A writing system's orthographic transparency describes how closely its sounds and symbols correspond to each other. *Transparent (or shallow) orthographies* are writing systems that have a close match between their sounds (phonemes) and symbols (graphemes). These orthographies are also referred to as "phonetic," "consistent," or "reliable" in different academic sources, and they include such languages as Italian, Spanish, Czech, Turkish, Korean, and Dutch.

Opaque (or deep) orthographies, on the other hand, have symbols that do not match consistently with their phonemes. These languages include Chinese, French, Lao, Japanese Kanji, and most important, English. Languages that have kept the same written form for a long time are naturally more opaque because written language changes more slowly than spoken language does. Over time, the gap between the two forms widens. Another reason is that when a region or country is occupied or colonized, the central governmental authority may insist upon the use of a common writing system for convenience or national unity. For these and other reasons, languages with deep orthographies generally take longer to learn to read and write.

Amharic sign
on an Ethiopian restaurant.

Georgian store with Georgian
and Russian orthographies.

Chinese soybean seller
in a new Chinatown neighborhood.

Skokie Public Library
welcomes its residents
in many orthographies.

Bilingual sign in
Vietnamese and Chinese.

FIGURE 4.2. Orthographies found on signage in the Chicago area.

Korean signs adorn stores
in many Chicago
and suburban neighborhoods.

Neon sign in "Greektown."

Arabic adorns all the panels
of the door at this center.

Russian sign
for a hearing aid company.

English/Hebrew sign.

Hindi sign on a restaurant.

FIGURE 4.2. (*continued*)

Because English has an opaque orthography, many English words cannot be identified by sounding out the letters across the word. There are 40-plus phonemes in English (Ellis et al., 2004; Venezky, 1970), but only 26 letters to represent them; therefore, the alphabet letters must be used in a variety of combinations in order to represent English sounds (McGuinness, 2004). The letters *ough,* for example, have four different pronunciations in English, /uf/ for *tough,* /uw/ for *through,* /ow/ for *bough,* and /awf/ for *cough.* The pronunciations can only be learned by rote, not by decoding. English has such an extreme discrepancy between its sounds and letters that it has been called "the least consistent of any alphabetic orthography" (Caravolas et al., 2012, p. 679), and can even be considered an "outlier orthography" (Caravolas et al., p. 678).

Historical Features Contributing to the Opacity of English

English has an opaque writing system because of at least three historical factors that have had a significant impact. The first of these was the Christianization of England, in which new writing systems were adopted by the indigenous peoples who lived there. The second factor was the various foreign invasions that occurred, most notably the Norman Conquest in 1066, which infused spoken and written English with thousands of new French words. The Norman Conquest introduced a second word for many words that already existed in English, but they took on different nuances, with the French words having a higher status. Examples of parallel Old English and French words still found in English include *pig* and *pork, cattle* and *beef, sheep* and *mutton,* and *deer* and *venison.* The third factor is the effect of the wide diffusion of written materials that resulted from the invention of the printing press. Printed materials codified the spellings of some words and distributed them widely. All of these factors have contributed to the *opacity* of the English spelling system.

The opacity of English explains why not only ELLs but also native speakers of English have so much trouble with spelling. For example, both will have to figure out if the letter *c* is pronounced with a /k/ sound, as in *coat,* or with an /s/ sound, as in *city.* Some words even have silent letters, as in *comb* or *sign,* and these must be learned one by one, as sight words.

Chinese is also opaque because, although Chinese characters contain some phonological information (Li, 2002), the characters cannot be separated into a linear sequence of sounds. Like English, Chinese orthography is a writing system that has changed more slowly than its spoken forms, so its symbols are pronounced in many different ways. Because of its opacity, readers of Chinese employ a reading strategy that includes looking at the semantic element of a word more than its pronunciation clues. Recognition of the difficulty in learning to read Chinese has led

Chinese-speaking countries to adopt writing system reform, which will be discussed further on.

The Effect of Orthography on Learning to Read and Write

Katz and Frost (1992) proposed the *orthographic depth hypothesis* to address how different writing systems influence the ways children learn to read. They hypothesized that it would be easier for children whose orthographies were transparent to learn to decode and spell than it is for children whose orthographies were opaque, and that children whose languages had transparent orthographies would use more phonologically based strategies to identify words. The hypothesis has been confirmed by a number of studies, including one that examined children learning to read in alphabetic, syllabic, and logographic orthographies (Ellis et al., 2004). The children from transparent orthographies learned to read more quickly, read longer words more slowly, and were more likely to substitute non-words or nonsense words when they made reading mistakes. Children from more opaque orthographies, on the other hand, took a longer time to learn to read, did not read longer words more slowly, and were more likely to substitute other real words when they made reading errors. In addition, they were more likely to skip words.

These and comparable results have confirmed that readers from backgrounds with different orthographies enact different processes in learning to read. Readers whose writing systems have transparent orthographies read across the sounds of a word, which is why it takes them longer to read a longer word. In addition, the fact that readers in transparent orthographies are more likely to substitute nonsense words when reading aloud suggests that some may not be reading for meaning, at least initially. Clearly, this is the downside of the *transparency* advantage. *Word calling*, or decoding without comprehension, is possible because the ease of decoding allows the reader to focus on the sounds without analyzing the meaning of the words being decoded (Paulesu et al., 2000). Decoding is not really reading if it doesn't include comprehension. This statement is from an L1 reader of Korean, which is one of the most transparent orthographies.

> *When I read out loud in Korean in my school days, I often found myself decoding words without thinking about any meanings of the sentences, and now I understand what the reason might be. Also, I noticed that when I started learning to decode words in English, I couldn't comprehend much while reading aloud either because I mostly focused on decoding the words correctly.*—SEUNG-HEE HA

Readers whose writing systems have opaque orthographies, on the other hand, go through different kinds of strategies as they learn to decode. Although phonological decoding is surely one strategy, they also engage in phonemic segmentation, whole-word recognition, probabilistic reasoning, and generalizing from syllable patterns found in short words, using *onset* and *rime*. As discussed in Chapter 3, an *onset* is the beginning sound of a syllable, and the *rime* is the remaining sounds of the syllable. The Ellis et al. (2004) study showing that readers from opaque orthographies make real-word substitutions when they read aloud suggests that they are probably using a different set of compensating strategies to read for meaning as they learn to decode.

Languages with opaque orthographies take a longer time to learn, and reading problems are more common for readers in those languages. A longitudinal study of children learning Welsh (a transparent orthography) and English in a dual-language setting found that after 3 years of instruction, no learners were still struggling to read in Welsh, but a number of learners were still struggling to read in English. The researchers concluded that "in the long term the detrimental effects of an opaque orthography are most damaging to the poorest readers" (Hanley, Masterson, Spencer, & Evans, 2004). Another downside to learning to read in an opaque orthography like English is that it takes a toll on the overall curriculum. Cloud (2016) summarizes it well: "There are places in the world where kids study architecture because there's space in the curriculum for that because they've already learned to read. We're very bogged down in the United States with the teaching of reading, and it cramps the curriculum, and in some cases it dominates the curriculum in very negative ways because it's taking away other subjects that the students might have enjoyed learning about."

Orthographic transparency and depth is one major factor related to the ease of learning to read and write. There are also three other issues related to writing systems. The first is the visual complexity of the writing system, the second is the closeness of the written language to the spoken form of the language, and the third is lack of access to L1 literacy.

Visual Complexity

In addition to its transparency, the visual complexity of a writing system affects how easily it can be learned. For example, Czech and Polish are two transparent orthographies, and they are moderately visually complex. In Czech, children must learn the complex consonant onsets found at the beginning of syllables (Caravolas & Bruck, 1993), but once they do, Czech is predictable. Polish has consonant *digraphs*, which can appear side by side in a word (such as *cz* and *sz*, in the word for the Polish city *Szczecin*), but once this is learned, Polish too is elegantly decodable. However, some consistent orthographies are very complex, and take a long time to learn, and one of these is Modern Standard Arabic. Before it can be decoded, the learner has to master the wide range of symbols and sounds of the Arabic alphabet. It includes symbols for subtle vocal features such as glottal stops and consonant lengthening. As a result of this visual complexity, learning to decode Arabic will take a long time (Abdelhadi, Ibrahim, & Eviatar, 2011). Japanese, too, has a visually complex orthography, drawing upon four different writing systems, each of which is applied according to the specific text being read or written.

The "script," or visual representation of a writing system, can also increase its visual complexity. A writing system may take several forms, including handwritten forms such as cursive, upper and lower case letters, and different fonts. Learners must be able to recognize a range of visual presentations of a writing system—and that includes the handwriting of the teacher, both on the board and on student assignments. Teachers cannot take for granted that their students can read their writing, especially if they are ELLs!

The Distance between Written and Spoken Language

Another important issue in mastering the written code of a language is how closely it corresponds to the learners' spoken code. If students speak a version of the language that diverges greatly from its written form, they will have greater difficulty in recognizing the written forms of the words, because the words, and possibly some of the sounds, are not in their listening vocabulary. This is a concern for Chinese speakers whose first language is far from the spoken form of Mandarin that most closely matches written Mandarin. The distance between written and spoken forms is also a concern for those who speak a version of Arabic that is greatly different from Modern Standard Arabic. The same holds true for English dialect speakers in the United States. Of course, many groups of people grow up speaking a home language that is not represented in their school system at all, and that includes children in the United States who are placed in immersion situations. All of these discrepancies affect the ease of transition into reading and writing.

Lack of Access to L1 Literacy

Some students have not had prior access to literacy in their L1 for a variety of reasons. They may have had limited or no access to education, or their exposure may have been fragmented. Children from nonliterate families might include refugee children, the children of seasonal workers, or children who have not been to preschool. For these children, learning English orthography will be their first exposure to an orthographic system, so all of the assumptions we can make about connecting sound to symbols must be unpacked and clearly presented. A child without prior literacy exposure needs to learn that the sounds they hear can be broken down sound by sound and represented with letters, that these letters form words, that these individual words have meanings, and that words can be strung together to represent thoughts. All of these understandings are not intuitively obvious, are not universal, and must be learned.

Writing System Creation and Reforms

When writing systems are created or reformed, the result can be an explosion of literacy. We give a few examples in the following accounts.

In 1819, after 10 years of labor, Seqouyah, a Cherokee man with an English father, created a writing system for Cherokee, which is a southern Iroquoian language. The phonetically regular, syllable-based orthography Sequoyah created was easy enough to learn that "within a few years after its invention, a high level of literacy had been achieved within the Cherokee community" (Comrie et al., 1996, p. 207), even surpassing the literacy rates of their European neighbors, according to historical records of the time (Wilford, 2009). This achievement was followed shortly after by the establishment of a bilingual Cherokee/English newspaper. Social studies teachers might well highlight this man's remarkable achievement as part of the study of American history and culture. A simple Google search will uncover rich historical material about Sequoyah.

Other spoken languages have been codified into written forms recently. For example, since national independence, some postcolonial African countries have adopted local languages for use in instruction. The language policy of Nigeria states that Yoruba, Igbo, and Hausa, the major languages spoken in Nigeria, for example, be incorporated in the school curriculum, along with English and Arabic. Kiswahili (Swahili), an amalgam of several languages, has been adopted as the national language of Tanzania, where it is now the sole language of primary school instruction (Mohammad, 2015). Closer to home, the Navajo language is taught in the Puente de Hózhó Trilingual Magnet School in Flagstaff, Arizona, which has two-way immersion programs in Spanish/English and Navajo/English (Puente de Hózhó Trilingual Magnet School, 2016). These efforts help close the gap between the mother tongue and the written language children are expected to use in their schooling.

Writing system reforms have also made a difference in literacy levels. An important reformer was Mustafa Kemal Atatürk (1881–1938), the founder of modern Turkey. He reformed Turkish orthography by adopting the Roman alphabet in lieu of the Arabic alphabet, which had been used for centuries during the Ottoman Empire. The Arabic symbols were not a close match with Turkish sounds, resulting in an opaque writing system that was difficult for Turks to learn to read and write. Modern Turkish script more closely matches Turkish sounds and is an easy alphabet to learn. Emel Gokçen describes the change in her own family that occurred when Atatürk introduced alphabet reform to Turkey.

> When Atatürk changed the alphabet] my father immediately had a teacher come to teach my mother the new Turkish, the new alphabet. My mother could write in the old ways. She had been schooled enough to write her own letters. But she told me that the old Turkish writing, the Arabic alphabet, was so difficult that it took years to learn, whereas the new one was not only easy to read and write but very easy to pronounce. It is much easier to read than French or English because it is like Italian. You don't have to know the language. It was phonetically clear, very easy to learn. So all the grandmothers started reading books and learning. . . . Reading spread like wildfire all over Anatolia, and it reduced the tremendous ignorance of the population—the workers out in the fields and so forth; they could take part in a better government. (in Cherry, 2008, p. 25)

Other languages have adopted the Roman alphabet as part of their writing system reform, too, but the most far-reaching reform is certainly the introduction of the *pinyin* system for learning Chinese. Pinyin is a phonetically based alphabetic system that uses the Roman alphabet along with extra diacritics to represent the Chinese tonal system. Pinyin is used more or less as a "learner alphabet" to be coupled with learning Chinese logographs. It has made a great difference in access to literacy and has been incorporated in schools as a system of support. However, computer-based pinyin shortcuts, which are typed like alphabet letters instead of written by hand using Chinese calligraphy, have been shown to have negative effects on the reading of Chinese children who use it (Tan, Xu, Chang, & Siok, 2013).

Over all, it is much easier to learn to read in a transparent writing system. Some call transparent orthographies "learner-friendly orthographies." They are also easier to read aloud because there are no unpleasant surprises.

Research published in *Nature Neuroscience* revealed that Italians were considerably faster in reading words aloud in Italian than English speakers were when they read English words. Positron emission tomography (PET) scans, which show which portions of the brain are in use while a person performs certain tasks, revealed that the portion of the brain accessing phonological information was in greater use for the Italians than for the English speakers. Conversely, the portion of the brain used for naming objects and processing the meaning of words was used more for the English speakers (Paulesu et al., 2000). Greek children acquire decoding skills earlier than their English counterparts due to the transparent orthography of Greek (Tafa & Manolitsis, 2008). The benefits of learning to decode early on, however, do not necessarily translate into long-term superiority in reading comprehension (Ellis et al., 2004), because reading is so much more than decoding.

> *To me, learning to read in an opaque writing system is like learning to drive a car with standard transmission: it takes longer to learn, and there are more subskills involved, but once you've got it, it's just as smooth a ride. A driver learning to drive with automatic transmission is like a reader from a transparent orthography–he or she learns faster, but they may not have quite as good an understanding of how the car goes forward since it works just fine by pressing the pedal!*—KRISTIN

Another advantage of transparent orthographies is that learners don't need to spend so much time on spelling as compared with learners from opaque orthographies.

> *A Mexican elementary school teacher in one of my classes said, "In Mexico there's no subject called 'spelling' like you have in America. That's because Spanish spelling, at least for most words, pretty much takes care of itself. When students start to write words in Spanish, they are easier to read than the invented spelling of kids in English."*—LEAH

Many children have trouble learning to spell in languages with opaque orthographies, such as English, even if they can read well. When school systems place correct (often called "proper") spelling at a premium, a lot of students may believe that they can't write at all simply because they can't spell well, and this type of thinking can set in motion a syndrome of failure.

For an opaque orthography like French, on the other hand, spelling is elevated to the level of an important subject. Classes in "Orthographe," or spelling, are part of a French learner's language study, just as spelling study is, and needs to be, a part of language arts in schools in English-dominant countries, such as the United States and Australia.

Spelling is taught best as a reasoning activity, not just as a "hit-or-miss," rote activity. If a child writes the word *goal* as "gole," for example, it's an indication that the child hears the long-*o* sound and knows that some words with a long *o* can be spelled with a silent *e*, such as the words *pole* or *role.* The spelling miscue demonstrates phonological awareness of the vowel sound as well as knowledge of the English spelling pattern of long vowels in words with silent *e* at the end. This is a good example of probabilistic reasoning in use.

The Strange Case of Proper Nouns and Names

The area where decoding and spelling hits the wall is with proper nouns, especially place names and last names. Often, they are cemented into a fixed spelling pattern even if their pronunciation has changed over time. Kids may need to learn to recognize and write place names as whole words, rather than sound-by-sound or letter-by-letter.

> *My mother's first name was Bengta, a Scandinavian name, and her last name was Disdier, a French name. These were both names that were hard to pronounce and spell. We lived in Bannock County, in Pocatello, Idaho. I learned how to spell all of those names very early by rote, through sheer necessity. My mom's name was not decodable at all, and neither was her personality.*—LEAH

Table 4.1 gives a rough view of how easy or difficult it is for various L1 learners to attain literacy in their first language. The table applies to L1 learners only and considers the three levels of orthographic difficulty discussed previously: opacity, visual complexity, and closeness to the spoken language. As you can see, for L1 English learners, attaining literacy is difficult, whereas attaining literacy in Spanish or Russian as a first language is not as hard. Later, when ELLs undertake to learn English as a new language, they will find that some of the ease they might have had in achieving literacy in their first language does not carry over to learning to read and write in English. These three criteria do not include many other factors that contribute to literacy. As noted, the table's rankings apply only to native speakers of a language and do not imply that someone learning any of these languages as a new language will find the task easier or harder. The table illustrates how much orthography influences first-language literacy.

If the students you teach are from an unfamiliar language background, it's easy to find out how opaque their language is simply by asking the adults of their family two questions: "Is it hard to learn to read in your language?" and "Is it hard to learn to spell in your language?" If they attended school using that language, they should have a ready answer.

English sounds can be represented in a number of different ways, so spelling takes a long time to learn, and many people never learn to

TABLE 4.I. Difficulty Ranking for Selected L1 Orthographies

Orthography	Opacity (closeness of symbol to sound and sound to symbol)[a]	Visual complexity (phonological or graphemic features in the orthography)[a]	Closeness to a spoken language[b]	Total score[c]
English	3	3	2–3	8–9
Arabic	3	3	1–3	7–9
Japanese	2–3, several orthographies used in combination, some more transparent than others	3	1	6–7
Spanish	1	1	1	3
Mandarin (Chinese)	3, without pinyin; 2, with pinyin	3	Native speakers of Mandarin dialect, 1; other dialects, 2–3	6–9
Persian	3	2	1	6
French	3	3	1	7
Turkish	1	1	1	3
Korean	1	1	1	3
Welsh	1	2	1	4
Russian	1	2	1	3

[a]1 (easiest) to 3 (hardest).

[b]1 (close to the spoken language) to 2–3 (for dialect groups depending on the distance from the spoken language).

[c]3 (easiest) to 9 (hardest).

spell very well. The trickiest part of English spelling is usually found in its vowels. The sound /ay/, or the long-*i* vowel, for example, can be spelled in at least five different ways: *buy* (/bay/), *try* (/tray/), *sigh* (/say/), *height* (/hayt/), and *lie* (/lay/). Also, the vowels of unstressed syllables in English are usually pronounced with the schwa sound /ə/, so it is impossible to "hear" the correct vowel even with good phonological awareness. The word constant, for example, is pronounced with a schwa sound /ə/ for the letter *a,* and, based on sound alone, it would be just as logical to write *constunt* or *constynt* as it is to write *constant.* There are thousands of English words with reduced vowels in unstressed syllables—we can't hear which vowel the reduced vowel is supposed to represent. That's where probabilistic reasoning comes in—we spell better when we know from reading that a sound pattern is more likely to be spelled a certain way, and in this case -*ant* is a more likely spelling pattern for those sounds than -*unt* or -*ynt*.

In addition, English has a larger variety of vowel sounds than many other languages, and these vowel sounds have multiple spellings. To spell a word, ELLs must first develop the phonological awareness to perceive the (often subtle) differences in vowel sounds. As the earlier anecdote about Arabic (p. 86) indicates, this is a challenge in itself. Then, using probabilistic reasoning, they must try to match the sounds with the grapheme(s) that seem most likely to represent the sound. Vowel sounds are the most malleable sounds of a language because they consist of air passing through the mouth, with the tongue and lips held in certain positions, and they are not tethered to the other organs of speech. Just think of the subtle differences between the sound of the vowels in *book* and *buck*, for example. Think, too, of how differently vowels are pronounced by people from different areas within the English-speaking world. Because it is hard to differentiate the sounds of English vowels to begin with, it is no wonder that it's hard to spell them.

> *When I first arrived in the United States, a friend was supposed to meet me at the airport. I waited in vain; he never showed up. After about 3 hours of waiting, I decided to take a cab. I told the driver that I was going to "Queen" Street. We drove around and around for another 3 hours looking for "Queen" Street. After a long drive around town, the cabdriver asked me if I had the address on a piece of paper. I said yes, and pulled it out from my folder and showed it to him. He went, "What are you talking about, man?" It was Quinn Street; we had passed it again and again, and I didn't pay any attention to it. I was too busy telling him to look for "Queen Street."*—TENENA

Spelling Changes Due to New Technologies

Text messaging is having a profound effect on the way words are spelled, not only in English but in many other languages. Although learning to read and spell the full forms of words is still imperative in the classroom setting, informal messages increasingly use a combination of traditional spelling and alphabetic or numeric spelling of words. *Alphabetic spelling,* sometimes called *letter name spelling,* occurs when an alphabet letter is written with the expectation it will be pronounced by its letter name. The most common example is using the letter *u* to represent the word *you. Numeric spelling* is the same principle applied to numbers; a number name is included in a word or sentence with the expectation that it will be pronounced by its number name. An example is *gr8* to mean *great*. These hybrid words are becoming more and more common in the literacy practices of young people and in advertising. Figure 4.3 shows some examples of alphabetic, numeric, and simplified spelling.

> *When I was a kid, we had autograph books, and everyone wanted to write a message that used alphabetic and numeric spelling. In my book, my best friend wrote "U R A QT. G I N V U." As you can see, I still remember it to this day.*—KRISTIN

Two wonderful books by New Yorker cartoonist William Steig play with alphabetic spelling in a delightful way. They are called *CDB!* (1987) and *CDC?* (2003). The books consist of Steig's cartoons with captions created entirely of alphabet letters making whole sentences.

Implications for Teaching

ELLs who study English have home languages which have have all kinds of different orthographies, with varying degrees of transparency. This requires that instruction in using the English alphabet should be differentiated according to the characteristics of the ELL's L1 orthography. If students have already learned to read and write in a transparent orthography, they may be good at phonological decoding, but may not notice when they read a real word as a nonsense word. In addition, they have to be taught to read for meaning. It is important to teach ELLs a number of strategies that L1 English readers use to decode and recode printed words. These include recognizing onsets and rimes, breaking a word down into its individual sounds, and practicing making guesses from context, among other strategies. An implication of *orthographic depth* is that children learning to read in a deep orthography need more training in phonological awareness and phonics (De Jong & van der Leij, 2002) because there are so many spelling patterns that can occur for each of the phonemes.

ELLs from languages with transparent orthographies that do not share the Roman alphabet with English, such as Bulgarian, will need to learn not only how to read for meaning, but also the details of the English alphabet and phonics system. As mentioned earlier, Arabic requires changing the directionality of reading and writing, as well as learning a new numbering system when learning English. ELLs who read Chinese will need extensive guidance and practice with phonological awareness as well as with the English phonics system. For these students, phonological

Simplified spelling.

We don't miss the *E* in HLP
because the consonants guide us.

Simplified spelling.

A mix of standard and alphabetic spelling.

Simplified spelling.

A mix of numeric spelling and simplified
spelling by vowel removal.

FIGURE 4.3. Use of alphabetic, numeric, and simplified spellings.

Simplified spelling on an awning.

Alphabetic spelling of *you* in a wordplay.

When *dough* changes to *do*, we lose the morpheme telling us it's made of dough.

FIGURE 4.3. (*continued*)

awareness will really bear fruit because it is the way they will be able to learn to decode unknown words.

We have summarized possible pedagogical directions for readers and writers from different L1 orthographies in Table 4.2. Of course, the amount of L1 literacy and prior educational experiences will influence the instructional focus as well. Table 4.2 can be used more or less as a checklist.

TABLE 4.2. Early Reading Instruction for ELLs Literate in Different Kinds of Orthographies

L1 orthographic system	Example languages	Spend more time on:	Spend less time on:
Transparent Roman alphabet with some similarities to English	Spanish Polish Turkish Welsh	English phonics (focusing on differences from L1), reading for meaning, learning sight words	Phonological awareness, phonics for sounds/letters shared with L1
Opaque Roman alphabet with limited similarities to English	French Portuguese	Phonological awareness, English phonics, learning sight words	Reading for meaning
Transparent alphabet or syllabary other than Roman alphabet	Ukrainian Arabic Korean Gujarati	Reading for meaning (for transparent), English phonics, learning sight words	Phonological awareness
Opaque alphabet or syllabary other than Roman alphabet	Mongolian	Phonological awareness, English phonics, learning sight words	Reading for meaning
Opaque orthographies that do not use an alphabet	Chinese Japanese Kanji	Learning the concept of an alphabet (representing sounds through symbols), phonological awareness, English phonics, learning sight words	Reading for meaning
Nonliterate	Any	All of these through a balanced literacy program	None

Numeracy: Also Not Universal

We expect to find different writing systems in the backgrounds of our ELLs, but we may not be as prepared for their different numbering systems as well. If you have ever tried to decipher the Roman numerals on a monument or a sports championship trophy, you can understand the frustration of looking at a numbering system you can't access automatically. Ironically, English uses the Roman alphabet and Arabic numerals, but the numerals used with the Arabic alphabet are not "Arabic numerals"! They originate from earlier languages, Sanskrit and Hindi. Here are the numerals from 0 to 10 in Arabic orthography and their English equivalents.

٠	١	٢	٣	۴	۵	۶	٧	٨	٩	١٠
0	1	2	3	4	5	6	7	8	9	10

As you can see, some of the numerals look just similar enough to other symbols in English that they can be confused. For example, the 0 resembles a period (although it is placed higher above the line than the period, and the period is also used in Arabic). Math teachers in particular should factor in extra practice time for learners who have been taught math in a different numbering system. Like new languages, new number systems take time to learn.

In addition to numbers, punctuation symbols and math symbols differ among languages. These include the "hollow" periods used by Korean writers, the use of dashes in place of quotation marks, and commas in place of decimal points in many European languages. In addition, "upside down" exclamation marks and question marks frame Spanish sentences on two ends of the sentence. Some of these are non-effects and are not obstacles, but the more teachers know about their learners' L1 written language systems, the better they can meet their students' needs.

Emojis: A Writing System?

The changes resulting from the digital revolution include changes to written systems. A telling example is the choice of *emoji* as *The Oxford English Dictionary's* 2015 Word of the Year (Oxford Dictionaries, 2016). The "word" they chose is actually not the word *emoji*, but rather the ever-expanding set of images that can be inserted into texts to express emotions, attitudes, or situations. Emojis are a byproduct of improved keyboards and number pads, which are now better able to represent shapes and symbols. Emojis can be "spoken" in any language and do not contain any fixed phonological information of their own. Since they cannot be broken down further, they most resemble logographic orthographies. Emojis are emerging as a new shorthand for conveying information quickly. However, using them does not enable language learners to practice the skills of decoding, handwriting, pronunciation, or spelling, and using them does not give the learner practice in becoming a better reader or writer.

Orthography Is Not Destiny . . . but It's Important

When we discover how different orthographies influence the way students learn to read, write, and spell in their L1, it explains a lot about the way they learn English. However, we add a word of caution: L1 orthography is only one factor in the vast array of factors that determines how ELLs learn English as a new language. Wang and Koda (2007) summarize it well:

> L2 readers with different L1 orthographic backgrounds engage in both universal and language-specific processes. On the one hand, properties of the L2 writing system affect L2 processing similarly across learners irrespective of L1 backgrounds. On the other hand, L1 reading experiences also come into play in L2 reading. . . . The properties of both L1 and L2 interact with one another, jointly contributing to L2 reading processes. (p. 201)

HOW DOES THIS LOOK IN THE CLASSROOM?

Through lively implementation of engaging explicit instruction, guided practice, and communicative opportunities, we can help ELL students internalize the regular and consistent patterns of English graphemes and phonemes and learn the irregular, inconsistent words by heart, regardless of their complexity.

Identifying Logograms of English

Children can become familiar with identifying and using the logograms of English as they interact with them. Some of these are common punctuation marks, such as a period (.) or quotation marks ("), and we want students to be able to recognize the logograms in context and identify or write them. Other logograms can be understood without being able to say the name commonly associated with them, such as "&," which is named *ampersand* but functions to mean *and*. Children can create an illustrated book of logograms and the ways they are used in equations and sentences. Although we have never seen it, a "logogram wall" could be a fun way to call attention to their properties and give support for the "mechanics" of writing.

Using Morphemes in Opaque Writing Systems

Languages with *deep orthography* make up for their phonetic inconsistencies by conveying semantic information through their morphemes. *Morphemes* are the smallest units of meaning of a word, and they are the focus of Chapter 5. We can often figure out a word's meaning by examining its morphemes. For example, *highlight* is not an easily decodable word because of its two silent *gh* letters, but learners can get a clue to its meaning if they can identify the two morphemes *high* and *light* in the word.

Phonological Awareness and Phonics

Phonological awareness and phonics skills can be developed through many enjoyable activities that increase metalinguistic awareness. Word sorts that use words from the day's lessons are one way to do this. Students simply write the new words on index cards and sort them by sounds or letter patterns. In a class of mixed ELLs and native English speakers, this might be best done in pairs. Another way to sort words is through word walls. Word walls can be organized by phonemes, not only by first letters of words. For example, students can classify words on the word wall according to their different vowel sounds.

Invented Spelling and Spelling Practice

In 1975 and thereafter, Read (1975) discovered that children learning to read and write in English go through predictable stages of spelling development (Peregoy & Boyle, 2005, pp. 195–199). In the first stage, the prephonetic level, children learn to hold writing instruments and move them across the page in "squiggles." In the second stage, the phonetic level, children grasp the idea that letters represent sounds and that words can be separated into sounds and letters. At this stage, learners begin to represent the sounds they hear with the letters they know. In the third stage, called transitional spelling, they begin to apply their knowledge of both decodable words and sight words and write words using some of the patterns of English; finally, the fourth stage is conventional spelling, in which learners correctly represent the letters of an English word, whether it is a decodable or a sight word. Development through these stages can be slow, and specific instruction, as well as prior literacy experiences, can greatly influence how students progress.

The stages of English spelling development and error patterns may look different when children have learned to read and write in a different language. For children who have learned to read their language in a Roman alphabet, such as Spanish, for example, their spelling development may reflect Spanish phonological influence, such as using the letter *i* for words with the long-*e* sound (e.g., writing the word *seat* as "sit"). Children reading in a logographic orthography, such as Chinese, on the other hand, may remember the letters making up a word, but not the order of their appearance because reading Chinese characters does not require identifying sounds in sequence. Therefore, early learners may write the word *table* as "tbale" until phonological segmenting is firmly in place. These kinds of developmental manifestations are not learning disabilities, but stages of English language development.

Understanding the stages of *invented spelling* allows reading specialists to focus on exactly where an individual student might need help. At the same time, it enables early childhood educators to be able to read the invented spelling of the early writing of children they work with. Because developing proficient English spelling takes a long time, having regular spelling lessons and quizzes makes sense. However, an integrated approach works better. "Make sure that encoding (spelling) and decoding (reading) are connected at every level of instruction via looking (visual memory), listening (auditory memory), and writing (kinesthetic memory)," suggests McGuinness (2004, p. 38). These lessons can begin with high-frequency decodable words and move toward less common, less decodable words, including sight words. Students can also take turns reading the week's spelling words for the other students, giving them oral practice.

Here are a few possible ideas that give students a chance to practice spelling words based on specific sound and letter patterns.

1. Draw a picture that contains things with the letters *sh*. See who could draw the most items.
2. List five words that end with the sound /t/. (Remember, they might not end with the letter *t*!).
3. Make a list of items in the classroom that have a long vowel sound.
4. Make a list of animals and sort the names by the number of syllables each animal name contains.
5. Write one sentence that includes a word ending with a silent *e*.

Celebrating Different Writing Systems

Celebrating writing systems in schools and classroom helps students and their families gain an appreciation of the remarkable ways humans have devised to put words down in print. An innovative third-grade teacher, Theresa Kubasak, does this by organizing an annual Hangul Day Festival at her school. Hangul Day, which takes place on October 9, is a Korean holiday celebrating the invention of the Korean alphabet in 1444. It is touted as the most elegantly transparent alphabet in the world, both easy to read and easy to spell. At the all-school festival, parents from L1 languages with different orthographies are invited to share their way of writing with children and other families. Children and their families circulate among the classrooms and learn how to write their own names in Arabic, Chinese, Devanagari, Cyrillic, and other scripts. Each language station uses different materials to write, such as black ink painted on rice paper for Japanese, silver pens on black construction paper for Arabic, and fine-tip pens for Cyrillic. Theresa adds, "Also we splashed the room with environmental print from the various alphabets, which is easy to obtain in Chicago through menus, posters, newspaper ads, and wedding announcements. It is an amazing day in a classroom." Celebrating Hangul Day helps all learners become more metalinguistic as they internalize the understanding that writing systems are widely varied, invented, and arbitrary, and that all of them are ways to represent speech.

Exploring past and present writing systems, such as hieroglyphics, codes, and secret languages such as *nushü*, a Chinese writing system developed in one part of China for "women only," adds even more luster to the learning of English orthography.

QUESTIONS FOR FURTHER STUDY

1. If you had to choose three important ideas from this chapter, which would you choose? How can you apply these ideas to your larger knowledge of teaching English as a new language?

2. Besides the probabilistic reasoning used in email programs, spellcheck, and cell phones, what are some other examples of probabilistic reasoning in the tools you use every day?

3. Look at the sign in Figure 4.4. Based on the analysis of writing systems in this chapter, what do you suppose the L1 writing system of the person who wrote this sign might have been? Why?

4. How do you make your handwriting accessible to the students in your classroom? How do you ensure that they can read the comments you write on their papers? Is this something you might want to work on?

FIGURE 4.4. Sign on a fuel pump.

5. In what ways do you consider emojis to be a writing system? In what ways could they be used to help students build an understanding of written systems?

6. In what ways do you consider yourself to be a strong decoder (reader) or recoder (speller) in English? Do you remember how you were taught these things, and do you think the teaching was effective? Why or why not?

7. A 20-year-old immigrant from El Salvador never had the benefit of formal education. Now he wants to learn to read and write at a community college night school that offers a Spanish or English GED. His first language is Spanish, but he speaks some English. Would you advise him to learn to read and write first in Spanish, or in English? Why?

8. A Chinese ELL administrative assistant is typing names into a database and comes across a handwritten last name she cannot read. She types exactly what she sees: Sctubert. What do you think the name actually was? What is your guess based on? Explain this anecdote in terms of probabilistic reasoning. How could you help a Chinese ELL develop the kind of reasoning you applied to solve the unreadable name problem?

9. What experiences have you had trying to read another writing system? If you have done this, what kind of writing system was it? What strategies did you use to try to decipher it? Which strategies helped, if any?

10. Reflect on ways a teacher with a classroom of mixed-language ELLs can differentiate instruction so that children from backgrounds with different orthographies from the Roman alphabet can get the extra practice needed in decoding the Roman alphabet and developing reading comprehension skills.

11. A quipu is a set of knotted strings that was used as a writing system during the Inca Empire to keep track of inventories and convey news about the Empire (see a quipu in Figure 4.5). The knotting system was learned by select members of the court. The quipu was taken to the king by a runner, sometimes as far as 1,200 kilometers away, and "read" there. In what way can a quipu be considered an orthography? In what ways is it not?

FIGURE 4.5. Quipu from Peru. Reprinted with permission from Frank Salomon.

12. CHALLENGE QUESTION: Make a short list of place names, last names, and other proper nouns with which you are familiar. Then try to classify them into two groups: decodable, and whole words/sight words. What can you generalize from this, if anything, for the teaching of reading and spelling proper nouns?

13. CHALLENGE QUESTION: What are some more examples of logograms in English? What kinds of lessons can be created to teach them? Write a possible lesson plan using logograms that are common in English, and if possible, try it out in a classroom. Reflect on what you learned.

CHAPTER FIVE

Using Morphemes
to Learn Vocabulary

New Vocabulary in This Chapter: *morphophonemic, etymology, grammatical category, root, affix (prefix/suffix), bound root, free morpheme, bound morpheme, lexical morpheme, functional morpheme, derivational morpheme, inflectional morpheme, open class, lexicon, modal auxiliary verb, closed class, phrasal verb, syllable*

Think for a moment about all the varied ways a person can "know" a word. We can recognize it when it's spoken by others. We can pick it out from a word list. We can understand its meaning when it appears in a sentence of a text. We can recognize it as part of a phrase or idiom, or see it as part of a figure of speech. We can know how to pronounce it. We can use it in different social settings, we can make puns with it, we can spell it, and we can include it in our writing. Learning these many levels of word knowledge can be daunting in a first language—but it becomes truly frightening in a new language! Nevertheless, it is the ability to learn thousands of new words in a new language that, more than anything else, determines a learner's success, both academic and social.

In Chapter 3, we talked about the *phonemic* aspect of words—how words sound and how ELLs can build a listening and speaking vocabulary that readies them for literacy in English. In Chapter 4, we discussed the *graphemic* aspects of words: how words look in different writing systems, how readers and writers process text in different languages, and how the decodability of words affects learning to read in English. In this chapter, we focus on *morphemes,* the smallest linguistic units of meaning. We look at the ways they combine within and across words, and look at the ways they can help ELLs learn English vocabulary. Understanding English morphemes will greatly add to the toolkit of ELL students and contribute to their syndrome of success.

Morphemes: The Building Blocks of Words

A morpheme consists of words and word parts and can be defined as "a minimal unit of meaning or grammatical function" (Yule, 2006, p. 246). ELLs who can separate words into smaller parts and make connections between words that have the same morphemes have increased vocabulary growth (Kieffer & Lesaux, 2009; Prince, 2009). As we described in Chapter 1, all languages have four universals (phonology, morphology, syntax, and semantics). All languages have morphemes, and all words are made up of morphemes. Morphemes are the units of meaning that make up the words of a language and the ways those units of meaning can be combined. It is through morphology that we obtain our knowledge of the meanings of a language. Analyzing the morphemes of any language is a tricky business, but the kinds of forces that influence word meanings in English are unusually complicated. Freeman and Freeman (2014) describe three forces: *phonological* (changes in pronunciation over time), *semantic* (changes in meaning over time), and *etymological* (retention of spellings from earlier versions of a word even when their pronunciations have changed) (pp. 161–162). There are also strong sociopolitical forces that can further affect any language. With so many complex factors at play, morphological study deserves explicit classroom study, but ironically, it receives little or none in the typical American classroom. Many teachers are expected to learn about morphemes "on the fly," and this undertaking can be daunting for busy teachers.

English, a Morphophonemic Language

There are many kinds of languages in the world, and they are structured in many different ways. In the case of English, the words are morphophonemic in nature. A *morphophonemic* language is one in which words contain both phonemic and morphological information, affected by its *etymology,* or the history of the word. A morpheme may be pronounced differently in different words because of the sounds of the letters around it. A morpheme may also be spelled differently in different words because of the sounds around it as well as its underlying etymology. For example, the morpheme *medic* derives from the Latin word *medicus,* which means "physician" and its root, *mederi,* "to heal" (Online Etymology Dictionary, 2016). The morpheme has three different pronunciations in the three words *medical, medicine,* and *medication.* Saying the words aloud, one hears that the word stress and the pronunciation of the letter *c* sound differ in the three environments, due to the influence of the sounds of the letters that surround the morpheme. Even though the neighboring sounds change their pronunciations, all three words contain the same morpheme, which carries the same meaning. The spelling of the three words gives us a clue about their meanings.

Recognizing the relationship between words that share morphemes is a key strategy for ELLs as they work to acquire academic English. When students rely mainly on their BICS language, which is delivered mostly in oral form, they may not identify words with shared morphemes because the morphemes may sound different in different words.

> *After hearing the word* electricity, *my ELL students did not recognize its connection with the word* electric *because the* c *was pronounced differently and the word stress changed. It was pronounced still another way in the word* electrician. *Once the three words were written on the board, however, their resemblance was very clear, and students began to grasp the morphophonemic nature of English–that neighboring sounds can influence the way a morpheme is pronounced, but its meaning is preserved.*—KRISTIN

Here are two key ideas about morphemes that teachers can incorporate in their instruction.

1. Morphemes may be pronounced differently but still bear the same meaning.
2. Spelling patterns in English give us information about both morphemes and phonemes.

Once learners grasp these abstract ideas, they will find that they are able to recognize the morphemes and therefore use probabilistic reasoning to understand many new words.

The Morphemes *-s/-es* and *-ed/-d*

Two dramatic examples of the morphophonemic nature of English can be found in the morphemes *-s/-es* and *-ed/-d.*

There are three distinct pronunciations of the *-s/-es* morphemes, which are word endings in English. This morpheme suffix gives information about the *grammatical category* of the words they are part of. We add the letters *-s/-es* to the ends of many words for three different processes.

1. To indicate a plural (e.g., *book* → *books, dish* → *dishes*).
2. To indicate the third-person singular form of a present tense verb (e.g., *play* → *plays, go* → *goes*).
3. To indicate noun possession, including names (e.g., *Leah's cat, students' desks*).

Table 5.1 shows the three distinct pronunciations of the morphemes *-s/-es* at the end of a word. Say the words in the table and pay attention to the last sound (phoneme). If the last sound is an unvoiced consonant (the larynx doesn't vibrate), the pronunciation of the *-s/-es* will also be unvoiced. If the last sound is a voiced consonant (the larynx vibrates) or any vowel, the *-s/-es* will also be voiced. If the last sound is a fricative (its sound creates friction in two parts of the mouth), we add a syllable with a /z/ sound at the end of the syllable. The *-s/-es* endings are very common in English because third-person singular verbs, plural forms of nouns, and noun possessive forms all use them.

The second example is the morpheme suffix spelled as *-ed/-d*, which is added to the end of words for three processes.

1. To indicate the past tense form of regular verbs (e.g., *watch* → *watched, live* → *lived, donate* → *donated*).
2. To indicate the past participle of regular verbs (e.g., *watch* → *has watched, live* → *has lived, donate* → *has donated*).
3. To indicate adjective endings derived from regular verbs (e.g., *shocked, pleased, interested*).

Table 5.2 shows the three pronunciations of the *-ed/-d* endings. Say the words in the table and pay attention to the last sound (phoneme). If the last sound is an unvoiced consonant (the larynx doesn't vibrate), the pronunciation of the *-ed/-d* will also be unvoiced. If the last sound is a voiced consonant (the larynx vibrates) or any vowel, the *-ed/-d* will also be voiced. If the last sound is either /t/ or /d/ (called alveolar stops), we add an extra syllable with the sounds /əd/. These *-ed/-d* endings are very common in English because regular past tense, regular past participles, and adjectives derived from regular past tense verbs all use them.

You may have realized that these very common endings are not always pronounced the same way, but never understood the reason for this phenomenon. The reason is that the sounds that precede the morphemes influence the pronunciation of the morphemes.

TABLE 5.1. Pronunciation of -s/-es Endings

Last sound of base word	Pronunciation of -s or -es
Voiceless consonants	Voiceless endings (/s/ sound added)
/p/ tap	/ps/ taps
/t/ get	/ts/ gets
/k/ take	/ks/ takes
/f/ laugh	/fs/ laughs
/TH/ booth	/THs/ booths
Voiced consonants	Voiced endings (/z/ sound added)
/b/ grab	/bz/ grabs
/d/ bid	/dz/ bids
/g/ tug	/gz/ tugs
/m/ hum	/mz/ hums
/n/ gain	/nz/ gains
/ng/ sing	/ngz/ sings
/l/ pull	/lz/ pulls
/r/ stair	/rz/ stairs
/v/ love	/vz/ loves
/th/ soothe	/thz/ soothes
/ey/ day	/eyz/ days
/iy/ see	/iyz/ sees
/ay/ try	/ayz/ tries
/ow/ go	/owz/ goes
/uw/ clue	/uwz/ clues
All fricatives	Long ending—Extra syllable (/əz/ syllable added)
/s/ place	/səz/ places
/z/ size	/zəz/ sizes
/sh/ wash	/shəz/ washes
/ch/ touch	/chəz/ touches
/zh/ garage	/zhəz/ garages
/j/ judge	/jəz/ judges

ELLs might be more likely to pay attention to those "pesky" word endings in their writing and speaking when they learn to recognize the meaning of the morphemes and realize that morphemes aren't always going to be pronounced the same way in every word.

Along with changes in pronunciation, just to complicate matters, morphemes may also have variations in spelling. For example, the Latin prefix *in-*, meaning *into*, can be spelled in four distinct ways, due to the sound that comes after the prefix:

in-	*inflame, incur*
im-	*imbibe, impress*
en-	*engrave, engorge*
em-	*embolden, emblazon*

Although the spelling of the prefix changes, the morpheme giving the idea of "into" can be reflected in many words, using all four of those

TABLE 5.2. Pronunciation of -d/-ed Endings

Last sound of base word	Pronunciation of *-d or -ed*
Voiceless consonants	Voiceless endings (/t/ sound added)
/p/ sto*p*	/pt/ sto*pped*
/k/ ki*ck*	/kt/ ki*cked*
/f/ lau*gh*	/ft/ lau*ghed*
/s/ ki*ss*	/st/ ki*ssed*
/sh/ wa*sh*	/sht/ wa*shed*
/ch/ wat*ch*	/cht/ wat*ched*
/TH/ too*th*	/THt/ too*thed*
Voiced consonants	Voiced endings (/d/ sound added)
/b/ gra*b*	/bd/ gra*bbed*
/g/ tu*g*	/gd/ tu*gged*
/m/ hu*m*	/md/ hu*mmed*
/n/ gai*n*	/nd/ gai*ned*
/ng/ ba*ng*	/ng/ ba*nged*
/l/ pu*ll*	/ld/ pu*lled*
/r/ sti*r*	/rd/ sti*rred*
/v/ lo*ve*	/vd/ lo*ved*
/th/ ba*the*	/thd/ ba*thed*
/z/ surpri*se*	/zd/ surpri*sed*
/j/ ju*dge*	/jd/ ju*dged*
/zh/ assua*ge*	/zhd/ assua*ged*
Vowels	Vowels
/ey/ sta*y*	/eyd/ sta*yed*
/iy/ agr*ee*	/iyd/ agr*eed*
/ay/ tr*y*	/ayd/ tr*ied*
/ou/ fl*ow*	/owd/fl*owed*
/uw/ s*ue*	/uwd/ s*ued*
Last sound /t/ or /d/	Long ending—extra syllable (/əd/ syllable added, last sound changes to a flap sound)
/t/ wai*t*	/ɨəd/ wai*ted*
/d/ loa*d*	/ɨəd/ loa*ded*

spellings. Spelling reflects modifications in pronunciation made by speech communities. Speakers of all languages generally pronounce words in the easiest possible way while still preserving a word's identity. When we can learn to identify the morphemes in words, we won't be misled by spelling or pronunciation, and we can use them as powerful tools to figure out word meanings.

In the previous chapter we looked at the opaque nature of English orthography and the fact that its sounds and letters do not "map" neatly onto each other. Sometimes words don't "sound like they look" or "look like they sound." Now we can see that the same idea can be applied to morphemes: morphemes do not necessarily "map" neatly onto their pronunciations or spellings. Nevertheless, the morpheme retains its meaning even when it has variations in pronunciation or spelling. This linguistic insight applies to English and, indeed, to all languages. Any users of English can benefit from this linguistic insight.

Morphemes through Different Lenses

We can look at morphemes through two lenses: through a "microscope," to see how they make up parts of words, or with a "telescope," to see how they function in larger units of language. Let's look first with a "microscope," to see how morphemes make up individual words.

The Microscope: Roots and Affixes

When we examine words "up close" through a microscope, we see that words are composed of two kinds of morphemes: roots and affixes. *Roots* are morphemes that contain the primary meaning of a word. They "cannot be cut up into any smaller parts" (Pinker, 2007, p. 128). A root may form a complete word, such as *plant*, or *fly*, or it may be combined with other morphemes in order to form a word. The second category is affixes. *Affixes* attach to roots. They are called *prefixes* when they are attached to the beginning of a word and *suffixes* when they are attached to the end of a word. Affixes are morphemes, but they are not words, and they cannot stand on their own. They can also be "coupled" like train cars: many words contain several affixes.

As we move forward in our understanding of morphemes, it will serve us well to remember the complex origins of English morphemes. English etymology includes many Old English or Germanic roots and many more recent words with Latin roots, in addition to words from many other language sources. Some older words of Old English origin, such as *sparrow* or *father*, have two syllables but only a single root morpheme that cannot be broken into smaller units. Another example of a very old word is *goodbye*, which consists of a single root that has been contracted over time from what was once four separate words, *God be with ye.* One more example might be the word *fulfill*, which has a single root meaning "to complete" and can no longer be separated into two morphemes. We're including these two-syllable, one-morpheme words to point out that many high-frequency words from Old English have single roots even though they consist of two syllables. They are still among the most high-frequency words of English.

In addition to roots that have two syllables, there is also a small group of very old roots that no longer have any identifiable meaning on their own but can be part of a larger word. They are called *bound roots* and will be discussed later in the chapter.

The Telescope: Lexical and Functional Morphemes

In examining words "from afar," through a telescope, we find that morphemes also provide information about the grammatical roles of words in a sentence. Now we will look through the "telescope" to view morphemes in terms of the roles they play within and among words in a sentence. This perspective uses a different, distinct classification system from the one used in the "microscope" analysis.

Two Major Categories of English Morphemes

Linguists have placed English morphemes into two major categories. The first category is *free morphemes,* which are words. Free morphemes are composed of two subcategories: lexical morphemes and functional morphemes. The second category is *bound morphemes,* which form parts of words and cannot stand on their own. Bound morphemes are composed of two subcategories: derivational and inflectional morphemes. The inverted morphemes pyramid (Figure 5.1) allows us to see the distribution of these categories at a glance.

As you can see, the top two portions of the pyramid are the free morphemes, which represent words. The vast majority of words are *lexical morphemes.* The second category of words is that of *functional morphemes,* and it is much smaller. There are more than 100 functional morphemes. The lower levels of the pyramid are called *bound morphemes,* which consist of two groups, *derivational morphemes* and *inflectional morphemes.* They are not words, but combine with other morphemes to make words. Let's examine each of these four categories and see how they fit into the structures of English sentences.

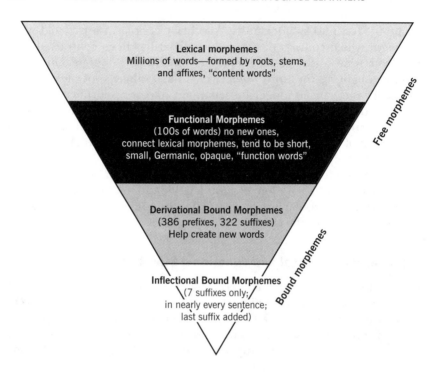

FIGURE 5.1. Inverted morphemes pyramid. From Lems (2008). Reprinted with permission from Kristin Lems.

Free Morphemes

Free morphemes are words. They may consist of one or more roots and affixes. We can subdivide free morphemes into two categories: *lexical* and *functional*.

Lexical Morphemes: The "Vital Organs"

Lexical morphemes comprise the vast majority of the words of a language. Also referred to as the more commonly understood term *content words*, lexical morphemes include nouns, verbs, adjectives, adverbs, and some prepositions. We can think of them as the "important" meaning-bearing words of a sentence. Lexical morphemes range from high-frequency words like *run, spinach, around,* or *quickly,* to academic language, such as *ecology, angle,* or *migration,* to abstract words such as *love, concept,* or *form.* These content words can be considered the "vital organs" of the body of language. Linguists call lexical morphemes an *open class* category because new words can always be added. That is exactly what is happening every day as people stretch and mold language to fit their needs. No wonder there are so many English words! Not coincidentally, *lexicon* is the word usually used to mean "all the words in a language."

Lexical morphemes encompass both BICS and CALP vocabulary, and they become more difficult to learn as the curriculum content becomes more advanced and abstract. Lexical morphemes help ELLs develop that all-important academic vocabulary of the content areas, and they are rightfully at the center of most ELL vocabulary study.

Functional Morphemes: The "Connective Tissue"

Functional morphemes, on the other hand, include prepositions, articles, pronouns, conjunctions, modals, and auxiliary verbs. They are often referred to as *function words.* Examples of functional morphemes include *of, the, and, she, modal auxiliary verbs* such as *can,* and auxiliary verbs such as *is.* Functional morphemes define the relationships among the content words around them. For example, they can stand in for a content word in the case of pronouns, or they can provide the meaning of a sentence by using a different modal verb, such as in the two sentences "she might study" or "she should study." Linguists call functional morphemes a *closed class* category because, unlike content words, no new functional words can be added. For example, the feminist movement of the 1970s and 1980s tried to create new gender-neutral pronouns, such as *hesh, tey,* or others (Pinker, 2007, p. 46), but these pronouns never took hold. Functional morphemes can be considered the "connective tissue" in the body of language.

What's more, additional morphemes cannot be added on to function words. They are what they are! For example, we can't put *-ed* at the end of the word *below.* Another characteristic of functional morphemes is that they are bound by the rules of English syntax, or word order. As sentences become longer and more complex, they can be difficult to understand or to produce. For instance, ELLs need to be considerably advanced to understand, or correctly produce, a sentence like this: "I wouldn't have eaten if I had known you were going to feed me." A comprehensive explanation of function words can be found in Freeman and Freeman (2004, pp. 177–179).

The number of functional morphemes is small, but they are used frequently. Function words abound in English and are found in nearly every sentence. Of the top 10 most common American English words, 8 are function words, and the other 2 (*be* and *have*) double as both auxiliary verbs (function words) and main verbs (content words) (Word Frequency Data, 2016). In fact, we can scarcely find a sentence of more than two or three words without a function word! Without function words, English wouldn't make sense because the relationships among the words couldn't be expressed. For a list of the 50 most common English words, see Appendix 5.1.

The Trouble with Function Words

The focus of vocabulary learning in schools is usually on learning lexical morphemes (content words), but functional morphemes are equally important for ELLs. It should not be taken for granted that ELLs know these all-important functional morphemes. In fact, despite their frequency, they are harder to learn than content words, for the following three reasons:

1. *Function words are opaque.* Because function words have been in the language for a long time, their spelling is more likely to be opaque, that is, not decodable. This feature makes them harder to read, spell, and pronounce. Think about how hard it is to read or spell the function words *of, could,* and *though.* In addition to not looking the way they sound, some function words are homophones (*to, two, too; there* and *their*). Moreover, some of the most common function words look and sound bafflingly alike to beginning readers and writers. Examples of exasperating opaque function words are those with the "silent h," or letter combination *th,* found in such function words as *when, the, then,* and *them* (Hiebert, Brown, Taitague, Fisher, & Adler, 2004). Beginning ELLs also have trouble spelling common function words with a silent *l,* such as *would, could,* and *should* and those with silent letters that are spelled with a *g* or *gh,* such as *through* or *although.* Because these older, high-frequency words have less decodable spelling and pronunciation, they are considered "sight words" and must be memorized as a whole rather than decoded.

2. *Function words are not cognates with Latinate languages.* The second reason, related to the first one, is that English function words tend to be of Old English or Germanic origin and are not cognates of words in Latin-based languages such as Spanish. (Cognates are words that share a common root and meaning across languages.) That means that these words will not look or sound like words familiar to ELLs from Latinate languages such as Spanish.

When my kids and I were visiting my Dutch family, we could hardly recognize any Dutch content words, but a number of function words, such as en *for the English word* and, dis *for the word* this, *and* bij *for the words* by *or* near *were easy for us to pick out. Due to the Germanic*

*roots Dutch and English share, we were able to experience the strange
sensation of not knowing the topic of a sentence, but being able to tell
more or less where the sentence was going.*—KRISTIN

3. *Function words can cause interference.* The third and most important
difficulty with English function words for ELLs, however, is that the way
they combine with verbs in particular is English-specific. Native speakers of English use thousands of combinations of verbs-plus-prepositions
(called *phrasal verbs*) in their everyday speaking and writing. Those particular word combinations are not the same in other languages. For example, in French the preposition *de* is used in the verb *se souvenir de,* which
means *to remember.* A French ELL might be likely to say "I remember from
her" instead of "I remember her" because the word *de* in French might
seem to be equivalent to the word *from* in English. Unfortunately, these
small but important differences in the distribution of prepositions must
be learned one by one in a new language, and the facilitating effect of PCI
on the process is very limited. Interference from function word distribution patterns in another language can cause considerable problems in
learning to read, write, listen, and speak in English.

To further complicate matters, the native languages of some ELLs
use no function words at all! These languages, such as Polish or Arabic,
are called "case-ending" languages. The relationships between the content words is established through suffixes put at the end of words rather
than by function words such as those used in English. For students whose
L1 is a case-ending language, the very "function of function words" as
well as the words themselves may need to be taught explicitly, through
mini-lessons. If you have these ELLs in your classroom, we suggest that
you make sure to design lessons and practices for phrasal verbs and other
sentence parts that use functional morphemes.

Function words deserve attention in the ESL classroom. Figuring out
how function words work within phrases and sentences can be a revela-
tion to ELLs who can understand the content words around them but get
tripped up by the "little words" in between.

The Dangers of Analyzing Words by Syllables

The *syllables* of English are the set of allowable consonant–vowel patterns.
They are based on a word's sound. Sometimes syllables consist of a single
morpheme, but often they don't. Although analyzing words by syllables is
useful when young learners are developing phonological awareness, analyzing words by written syllables is more problematic in English because
it is so opaque. For example, the word "played" is pronounced as only

one syllable, but it contains two distinct morphemes, *play* and *-ed*. If we analyze it only by syllables, we will lose the information provided by the two morphemes, the root *play*, and the inflectional morpheme *-ed*, which indicates the past tense. Focusing on the syllable overlooks the morphophonemic nature of English and misses information that assists in both reading and spelling words.

Once ELLs are no longer at the Entering or Beginning levels of English and are beginning to read connected text, focusing on morphemes, instead of syllables, is more useful. In fact, using a syllable-based decoding strategy may conceivably contribute to "word calling," a concern discussed in Chapter 7. When the phonemes and graphemes of a word get all the focus, rather than its morphemes, it is possible that words may be pronounced correctly, but their meanings overlooked.

Some teachers ask students to look for words that can be made from letters in other words, such as finding the letters to make the word *bear* in the word *bread*. This activity is less valuable than one in which learners are asked to look for morphemes within a word because morphemes are more than letter combinations; they carry meanings.

When morpheme analysis is used as a tool for word attack, ELLs are more likely to pay attention to the meanings of words as they read. In the Harry Potter books and movies, for example, the family of the main antagonists has the last name *Malfoy*. When ELLs learn the Latin root *mal*, meaning bad or evil, they will recognize it not only in that name, but also as a root in many words they will encounter in the future, such as *malodorous, malefactor, malaria, maladjusted,* and *malfeasance.*

In oral reading, focusing on morphemes may create pronunciation miscues in the short run, but it will pay off in the added attention students pay to comprehension. For example, if an ELL student pronounces the word *musician* as /myuwzikiən/, with a "hard *k*" as in the morpheme *music,* it indicates that the reader recognizes the morpheme *music* in the word. Although the student mispronounced the word, this kind of morpheme recognition is something we want to encourage. When ELLs make pronunciation miscues that signal their recognition of a morpheme, teachers should be reassured that the student does recognize the morpheme, and therefore is accessing part of the word's meaning.

There are other hazards of syllable-based analysis. If we separate the word *antifreeze* into syllables, for example, we see three morphemes. One of them, *freeze,* is a free morpheme that carries a meaning all by itself. The other two syllables, *an* and *ti,* do not retain any meaning when they are split up; however, when we see them as a single morpheme instead of as two syllables, we see *anti-,* a prefix that means "against" or "opposite." Viewed as three syllables, we can't grasp the meaning of the word, but viewing two morphemes instead, we can derive a meaning of "against freezing," the purpose for putting antifreeze in a car. Here is a similar example from a grades 1–2 bilingual teacher.

> *In my class last week, one of my ELLs broke up the word* altogether *into "all to get her." He said with excitement, "All the words are on the word wall!" And they were. But they have no relationship to the meaning of the word. I realized I needed to help them understand that some words can't be broken into smaller words—they are inseparable.*
> —MARGARITA (MARGIE) JAIME

The most striking example of the danger of dividing words into syllables instead of morphemes is the classic joke about the word *therapist*. It makes sense broken into its morphemes—*therap* from the Greek word "to treat medically," and *-ist*, a bound morpheme meaning "one who practices." However, if *therapist* is divided into syllables instead of morphemes, the word can also look like *the rapist*!

Bound Morphemes

Bound morphemes are the other major category of morphemes. As noted earlier, there are two kinds of bound morphemes, *derivational* and *inflectional*. Unlike free morphemes, a bound morpheme alone cannot be a word. Bound morphemes need to be attached to free morphemes in order to make a word. Examples of bound morphemes are *pre-, -s, -ed, un-, -ment,* or *-ist.* On the pyramid in Figure 5.1 (see page 120), they occupy the two smallest parts of the pyramid shape.

Derivational Morphemes

Derivational morphemes can be either prefixes or suffixes in English. Derivational morphemes are dynamic and rich. They are one of the devices that grant English its remarkable ability to generate so many new words, as we discuss in the following chapter on word formation processes. Derivational morphemes not only allow many new words to be formed, but they also change the grammatical category, or part of speech, of a word, such as adding *-ful* to *thought,* thus changing it from a noun to the adjective *thoughtful.*

Derivational morphemes operate in three powerful ways within words.

1. They can create words when added to a root (e.g., *pay* + *ment, progress* + *ive*), or a bound root (e.g., *ex* + *pel,* with *-pel* being a bound root).
2. They can change the meaning of an existing word. Examples

include adding the derivational morpheme *non-* to the word *dairy,* creating *nondairy,* which means that a food does not contain dairy products, or adding *dis-* to *respect,* meaning not to respect.

3. They can change a word's grammatical category and therefore its meaning. For example, the noun or verb *respect* can be changed to its opposite meaning, *disrespect,* and can change to an adjective by adding the suffix *-ful,* to make *disrespectful.* Knowing common adjective suffixes alone, such as *-ious, -able,* and *-ful,* we can unlock the meanings of thousands of unknown words.

Inflectional Morphemes

The last category consists of inflectional morphemes, the bottom of the pyramid. There are seven *inflectional morphemes,* and they serve as grammar markers that show the categories of tense, number (singular/plural), possession, or comparison. (Linguists disagree about how inflectional morphemes are counted, and the number may vary between 7 and 11.) Table 5.3 depicts the seven inflectional morphemes and their functions.

Inflectional morphemes are distinguished by a few distinct characteristics.

1. Unlike derivational morphemes, they cannot create new words.
2. All inflectional morphemes are suffixes.
3. The inflectional morphemes are very short—the longest is only three letters long (*-est* and *-ing*). Thus they are easy to overlook in both reading and writing, but they serve a key role in the meaning of sentences.
4. They are attached to the end of a word, after all other morphemes.

Although insignificant in terms of letters, inflectional morphemes are both very common and very important in conveying grammatical information about English words. Furthermore, an inflectional morpheme at the end of a word may have several pronunciations and confuse early readers and spellers. Inflectional morphemes can be found at the end of most plurals (*tree/trees*), possessive nouns (*fox/fox's tail*), and verbs (*run/runs*).

A Special Category: Bound Roots

Sometimes, we don't find understandable morphemes when we break a word apart. This is because, over time, the meanings of some morphemes have become lost to the speakers of the language. These "orphan" morphemes, which seem to have no meaning of their own, are called *bound*

TABLE 5.3. The Seven Inflectional Morphemes of English

Inflectional morpheme	Grammatical function	Part of speech inflectional morpheme is added to	Example
-s or -es	Noun plurals	Noun	*apples, buses*
	Third person singular in present tense	Verb	*makes, goes*
's or s'	Possessive for singular or uncountable nouns	Noun	*the book's, oil's*
	Possessive for plural nouns	Noun	*the students'*
-ed	Regular form of past tense	Verb	*talked, tried*
	Regular form of past participle	Verb	*(have) talked, (has) tried*
-en (left over from Old English)	Some plurals	Noun	*oxen, children*
	Some past participles	Verb	*written, given*
	Derivation from noun	Verb	*strengthen, threaten*
	Derivation from noun	Adjective	*golden, silken*
-er	Comparative form of adjectives and adverbs	Adjective	*friendlier*
		Adverb	*faster*
-est	Superlative form of adjectives and adverbs	Adjective	*friendliest*
		Adverb	*fastest*
-ing	Derivation from verb	Noun (gerund)	*swimming*
	Present continuous (present progressive)	Verb	*going, trying*

roots. A bound root has no identifiable meaning until it is combined with another root or affix to create a single morpheme. For example, the words *lukewarm, overwhelm,* and *cranberry* look like they have two morphemes in them because they have more than one syllable, and one of the other parts of the word has meaning. The free morpheme *warm* can be found in the word *lukewarm,* the word *over* can be found in *overwhelm,* and the word *berry* within *cranberry.* However, the other half of these words, *luke, whelm,* and *cran,* are not morphemes and do not have any meaning on their own—they are bound roots.

In addition to words with a free morpheme and a bound root, there are words that have a prefix followed by a bound root. Examples of these words are *defunct, receive,* and *inane.* When we remove the prefixes *de-, re-,* and *in-,* the remaining parts of the word, *-funct, -ceive,* and *-ane,* have no recognizable meaning. Other examples of bound roots can be found in the words *reduce, conceive, impeach,* and *repeat.*

Earlier in this chapter, we pointed out that some old two-syllable words, such as *father,* contain only one morpheme and cannot be broken down further. The same is true for words with bound roots. They may appear to have two morphemes, but one of them has no meaning on its own and is dependent on the complete morpheme for meaning. When we encourage ELL students to take apart new vocabulary words to find meaning in their morphemes, it's important to be aware that some bound roots will crop up. Here are the takeaway ideas to convey to students.

- Some multisyllable words are composed of only one morpheme and can't be reduced any further.
- Although all morphemes carry meaning, not every meaning of every English morpheme can be figured out due to the history of English words.
- The vast majority of English words can be separated into morphemes, and doing so is a great strategy for word learning.

Morpheme Study in the Classroom

Because English is derived from two big streams, Old English/Germanic and Latin/Greek, some English words are more decodable than others. The same holds true for morpheme study; words from the Latin/Greek backgrounds, which dominate the vocabulary of the advanced content areas, are most useful to understand from a morphological perspective. Looking at words from Greek and Latin roots will yield better results than trying to take apart the older Germanic or Old English words whose morphemes have become "cemented" into a single root or a bound root.

To Aid in Spelling

From time to time, writers call for "simplifying" English spelling to make it more phonetic. Freeman and Freeman (2004) see reform proposals as humorous and not to be taken seriously. In their opinion,

What many reformers don't realize is that the current system is a good compromise. Writing systems are designed to serve two different groups of people: writers and readers. Changes that would make writing easier would make reading more difficult, and changes that make reading easier would make writing harder. Most reforms are aimed at simplifying the task of spelling words by making spellings more closely correspond to sounds. That is, the reforms favor writers. But most people read a great deal more than they write, so these changes would not be beneficial. (p. 106)

If spelling were simplified, we would lose morphemic information that helps us read in English. Homophones, such as *two, to,* and *too* would become indistinguishable. English spellings do not just represent the sounds of a word; they also point to its meanings and in some circumstances its origins.

Because English is a morphophonemic writing system, information may be contained in the visual display of a word that cannot be heard in its pronunciation. For example, in the word *cupboard,* the *p* isn't pronounced, and the morpheme *board* is reduced to a syllable that sounds like the word *bird,* but if we examine the word, we can get a clue about its historical meaning: it has something to do with a place where cups are stored.

Sometimes students will find a string of letters that looks like a morpheme but simply isn't one. Teachers can encourage students to develop an "eye" for finding morphemes even though some attempts will lead to a dead end. For example, a student found the word *meter* in the word *cemetery,* but analyzed the meaning of the word and quickly realized that *meter* was not a morpheme in that word—just a letter string!

Using L1 Morpheme Study as a Resource

Studying morphemes in students' native language helps them to become more metalinguistic and to increase L1 vocabulary. Comparing morphemes of words in an L1 and L2 can also highlight differences in the way a word's meaning is shared between two languages. A good example is the Spanish word for birthday, *cumpleaños,* which is derived from two Spanish morphemes meaning *complete* and *year.* Thus, a birthday is the "completion of a year." In English, on the other hand, the word *birthday* comes from the Germanic roots *birth* and *day,* a commemoration of the first day of a child's life. In a bilingual or dual-language Spanish/English classroom, pointing out the morphemes for the Spanish word can help students recognize that when they "turn 10," 10 years of life have been completed on their birthday, and that is a useful mathematical concept. In Korean culture, moreover, a person's age is calculated by taking the current calendar year, subtracting their year of birth, and adding one. Learning other languages exposes learners not only to new words, but also to the new concepts found within those words.

Morpheme study can be a messy business due to the complicated paths words can take before and after they enter the English language. For that reason, we don't advise using morphemes as a target of study until children are in the elementary school grades. However, morpheme recognition as a word-learning strategy brings great benefits for students and teachers alike.

HOW DOES THIS LOOK IN THE CLASSROOM?

Studying Etymology

Etymology is a great history project, and it's also a lot of fun. While learning about content, students can also explore the etymology of words that relate to that content and talk about how those words are created. For example, what is the origin of the word *bankrupt,* and what morphemes can be seen in it? Students can easily research the origins of words they are learning and share them with the class. For example, if we look at the two morphemes of *breakfast, break* and *fast,* we find added meaning in the idea that we are not only eating the first meal of the day, but "breaking our fast" from the night before. Thanks to the digital revolution, there are now good sources for finding word origins. *Etymology Online* is an increasingly useful source for capturing some of the histories of words. Older unabridged dictionaries are also still a great source of word histories and etymology.

Morpheme Word Walls

ELLs benefit greatly from morpheme analysis at every grade and proficiency level (Kieffer & Lesaux, 2008, 2009). Charts, word walls, word banks, and binders can be organized not just by sounds or words, but by morphemes. Figure 5.2 shows a morpheme word wall in a seventh-grade science classroom in Elgin, Illinois.

Rob Schoonveld, an eighth-grade science teacher who has a class of mixed ELLs and native speakers, puts up large cards with common science morphemes around his classroom and refers to them regularly. He finds that the visual reminder of the morphemes helps students feel more confident with new science vocabulary. The morphemes, which are a combination of roots and affixes, can also be found in science words in a number of other languages, which provides substantial PCI for ELLs from those language backgrounds. Some common science morphemes and other key content morphemes are listed in Appendix 5.2 at the end of this chapter.

FIGURE 5.2. Morpheme word wall in a seventh-grade science classroom. The teacher writes the meaning of each morpheme next to it and color codes the morphemes by science unit.

Five Good Morpheme Games

Word List Contest

It's possible to learn a lot of new words by listing them by prefixes, suffixes, and roots. First, teachers put students in small groups, and a secretary is chosen by the group. Next, the teacher writes or calls out a prefix, such as *pro-*, or a suffix, such as *-ment*. The groups have 5 minutes to generate as many words as they can that use the prefix or the suffix—no cheating with a smartphone! After the time is up, the groups take turns reading them out loud. Any word shared by other groups is crossed out by all the groups. The group that has the largest number of words the other groups did not find wins the round.

This game can also be played using roots, but it is harder because the spelling of roots can change in different environments due to the morphophonemic features of English. We would suggest differentiating this activity for more advanced ELLs. Teachers can use the content-focused morpheme charts in Appendix 5.2 or others connected to their course's content area. For example, the root *digitus,* the Latin word for *finger,* is found in many words connected to numbers, such as *digitize, digital, three-digit numbers,* or *prestidigitation.* Talking about how people "count on their fingers" is a good way to help students see the relationship between these words. The list of words based on their roots can be kept up and added to as students encounter new words in reading and speaking. Incidentally, this activity builds metacognitive awareness in L1 English learners, too.

The Compound Noun Game

Reena Patel, an ESL teacher in a second-grade Chicago public school, created a game for ELLs based on the theme of recognizing and creating compound nouns. The game has two parts. She created cardboard tiles with pictures of lexical morphemes that can be used to create compound nouns. She gives one tile to each student in the class. The students walk around the room and find the partner whose tile allows them to create a real compound noun. For example, one student had an image of a book, and another had an image of a bag. Together they formed the compound noun *bookbag*. Then, she re-collects the tiles, shuffles them, and lets each pair choose four tiles from the box. With the four tiles, all consisting of high-frequency nouns, she asks students to form at least two possible new words, create a definition for them, and share them with the class. For example, students in her class created the new compound noun *dream shelf,* a "place to put objects that will bring you happy dreams."

Animal Compound Game

Reena also compiled a list of compound nouns that are used in many animal names, such as *mole rat, butterfly, anteater,* and *muskrat.* She made separate cards for each of these words and asks students to combine them to create names for new imaginary animals, which they then illustrate and share with the class. It creates a wonderful menagerie of morphemes, and lots of laughs! For a set of game cards and full instructions for both of the games, see Appendix 5.3.

Compound Noun Chain Game

In this classroom activity, a teacher splits the class into small groups and gives the whole class a free morpheme. The class should be given 3–5 minutes to come up with as many other compound nouns as they can by adding another noun in either direction. Then each group reads its words. If another group shares the word, cross it out. The group with the most words not thought of by other groups wins. For example, *pot* can form part of compound nouns such as *flowerpot, teapot, crackpot, potholder,* or *potbelly.* Some other nouns that combine with many other words include *moon, home, stop,* and *ground.* A variation of the game is to generate not only compound nouns but also phrasal verbs, listemes, and idioms from the word. We'll provide more examples of word combinations in Chapter 6.

Words from Content Morphemes

Appendix 5.2 has a list of key morphemes used in four different content areas. Take the most appropriate list and note how many word lists students can generate from the morphemes in each content area. You can also add your own morphemes specific to the topic in use at the time.

QUESTIONS FOR FURTHER STUDY

1. If you had to choose three important ideas from this chapter, which would you choose? How can you apply these ideas to your larger knowledge of teaching English as a new language?

2. Make a simple chart summarizing the important characteristics of function words described in this chapter.

3. If you teach very young children, think about ways you can set up children's literacy for working with morphemes at a later time. What morphemes do you think would be the best starting place?

4. Without using an electronic device, choose a prefix or suffix and see how many words you can write down that use that affix in 1 minute. Remember, the spelling of the affix may change in different surroundings.

5. Using Table 5.1, add *-s/-es* to the following words and classify their pronunciation (for /s/, /z/, or /əz/): *watch, mess, get, kick, sing, hold, help, wash, trust, hum, play, go, sign, stop, hang.*

6. Using Table 5.2, add *-ed/-d* to the following words and classify their pronunciation (/t/, /d/, or /əd/): *waste, live, save, raid, cook, start, play, interest, try, watch, toss, turn, sort.*

7. Choose three roots in one of the content-area morphemes in Appendix 5.2 and see how many words you can think of with that root. Was it difficult? Why or why not?

8. Choose another language you are familiar with and make a list of 6 to 10 affixes in it. Then compare them to similar affixes with the same functions or meanings in English. How could these similarities be displayed in a chart or table used in the classroom?

9. With others, have a contest to see who can find the word that contains the most affixes. Can you find one with four affixes? five? (For this game, we will not count the notorious *antidisestablishmentarianism*!)

10. Make a chart of words that are countable and become uncountable by adding a suffix, such as the example of *friend* (countable) and *friendship* (uncountable) in the chapter.

11. Fill in the columns for the 50 most common American English words in Appendix 5.1 by content words and function words. The first 10 have been provided as a guide. Talk about what you have discovered. Why are two of the top ten classified as both content and function words?

12. Look at the spellings *spilled* and *spilt,* or *burned* and *burnt.* Which spellings give more morphological information? Which give more phonemic information? Why?

13. CHALLENGE QUESTION: Try to create a graphic organizer to show the morphophonemic effects of English on the spelling or pronunciation of words. Why do you think one teacher said, "It should be called the *morphophonemicgraphemic* principle"?

14. CHALLENGE QUESTION: Create a game based on some of the morphemes found in one or more sections of this chapter, and try it out with your classmates or coworkers. What did you learn by writing and piloting it?

The 50 Most Common American English Words

The 50 most common words in American English	Content or function?	Germanic, Old English, or Latin?
1. *the*	F	
2. *be*	C/F	
3. *and*	F	
4. *of*	F	
5. *a*	F	
6. *in*	F	
7. *to*	F	
8. *have*	C/F	
9. *to*	F	
10. *it*	F	
11. *I*		
12. *that*		
13. *for*		
14. *you*		
15. *he*		
16. *with*		
17. *on*		
18. *do*		
19. *say*		
20. *this*		
21. *they*		
22. *at*		
23. *but*		

(continued)

The 50 most common words in American English	Content or function?	Germanic, Old English, or Latin?
24. *we*		
25. *his*		
26. *from*		
27. *that*		
28. *not*		
29. *n't*		
30. *by*		
31. *she*		
32. *or*		
33. *as*		
34. *what*		
35. *go*		
36. *their*		
37. *can*		
38. *who*		
39. *get*		
40. *if*		
41. *would*		
42. *her*		
43. *all*		
44. *my*		
45. *make*		
46. *about*		
47. *know*		
48. *will*		
49. *as*		
50. *up*		

Note. Data from Word Frequency Data (2016).

Common Morphemes from Content-Area Vocabulary

Some Key Science Morphemes					
sol	aero	hydro	paleo	astro	physio
bio	ecto	endo	ortho	chemo	cyto
meta	geo	therm	eco	electr(o)	micro
macro	quant	qual	trans	techn	syn
Some Key Mathematics Morphemes					
grad	graph	deci	centi	milli	circ
meter	plex	numer	equa	tri	quad
angl	hemi	sphere	add	sub	tract
fract	penta	hecto	octo	vert	hor
Some Key Social Studies Morphemes					
multi	proto	poli	agri	metro	ethno
anthro	hist	demo	gyn	homo	andro
poly	mono	bi	mega	hetero	gen
morph	popu	arch	aqua	theo	psych
cult	edu	logy	soph	etic	emic
Some Key Language Arts Morphemes					
biblio	script	auto	comp	improv	infere
solos	meta	orat	studere	spect	littera
rhetoric	genus	narrare	krisis	dict	caput

Note. Some morphemes change spelling when adopted into English.

APPENDIX 5.3

The Compound Noun Game

1. Print the game cards and cut them into pieces. If possible, use card stock or laminate the cards. If the class is larger, create more compound noun pairs. If students are at a very beginning level, pictures can be added to the words.
2. Each student picks out one card with half of the compound word written on it. They will walk around and find a person whose card completes the compound word (e.g., if your word is *water*, you can make a compound noun with the person who has the word *fall—waterfall*).
3. Once the students find their partners, they discuss why it is a compound word and what it means. Explain to the students that sometimes compound words are made up of two random words (e.g., *butterfly*).
4. Now, collect all the words and mix them up. Have two sets of partners pick out four new game cards. Put them together in any order to make a new compound word! Be creative and have fun! Students can use the word in a sentence and draw a picture of the new word. They can also create an advertisement for their new word if it is an object.

ANIMAL COMPOUND NOUN GAME

Try doing this same activity with the set of animal compound words below. When the cards are shuffled, students can create their own animals!

catfish	dragonfly	bulldog	jellyfish	starfish
ladybug	anteater	bluebird	lionfish	grasshopper
sheepdog	seahorse	bullfrog		

When they create the animal, have them draw it and describe what it does.

ANOTHER COMPOUND WORD GAME (COMPOUND WORD LADDER)

1. Give the students a compound word. Take the word and think of another word that has part of the first word. Keep going to make a compound word ladder!

Example: *snowman*
snowball
basketball
football
footprint
fingerprint
fingernail

2. When you can't think of any more words, try a new compound word!

(continued)

CARDS FOR THE COMPOUND NOUN GAME
(ENTERING OR BEGINNING LEVEL)

back	pack
day	dream
sail	boat
water	bed
book	case
flash	light
lunch	box

CHAPTER SIX

Word Formation Processes, Cognates, and Collocations

New Vocabulary in This Chapter: *homonyms, homophones, homographs, polysemous words, semantic field, coinage (neologisms), borrowing, compounding, blending (portmanteau words), clipping, acronyms, abbreviations, backformation, conversion (category shift), scale change, paired-word sound play, multiple processes, cognate, false cognate, cross-linguistic homograph, cross-linguistic homophone, collocation, idiom, listeme, semantic map*

The previous chapter examined the ways in which words can be learned through the powerful tool of morphemes. In this chapter, we will discuss more vocabulary learning techniques at the word and phrase level with a focus on (1) English word formation processes, (2) cognates, and (3) collocations. Although we will look at these techniques as they apply to English, all of these ways of learning new words apply to many languages, and if you know another language, you will quickly find analogies in that language. Learning about these varied forms of word formation will help ELLs create the toolkit they need for successful reading comprehension and dynamic writing. What's more, learning about the surprising ways in which words are created, enter, and evolve in English stimulates motivation and curiosity for learning more.

Vocabulary: The Bottom Line
for Reading in Any Language

It stands to reason that the more word meanings one knows, the easier it is to construct meaning when reading. Educators have looked at the relationship between reading comprehension and vocabulary for many years and found it to be a strong one. Decades ago, Thorndike (1973) researched the relationship between L1 vocabulary and reading comprehension across different languages. He collected data from students in 15 countries who were learning to read in different first languages and found that students' vocabulary and reading comprehension levels correlated at a very significant level across a wide range of grades. This strong relationship has been corroborated in other studies (e.g., August & Shanahan, 2006; Fitzgerald, 1995). The National Reading Panel, after a comprehensive review of reading research in 2000, came to the same conclusion, stating, "growth in reading power relies on continuous growth in word knowledge" (National Reading Panel, 2000, p. 4-15).

For English language learners, vocabulary is just as decisive, if not more so. A 2,000-word threshold is considered by many to be the minimum number of words learners need in order to function when they enter a school setting. By the age of 6, native English speakers already have between 5,000 and 7,000 words in their listening vocabulary (Grabe & Stoller, 2002), and the large discrepancy in vocabulary knowledge between American children from middle class backgrounds and children living in poverty has been shown to have effects on school success (Hart & Risley, 1995). Although many ELLs are not even at the threshold of speaking 2,000 English words, much less 7,000 words, they are expected to make up the difference in English vocabulary size at the same time they are learning academic content. Meanwhile, native speakers alongside them are also busy adding to their vocabulary. For this reason, we can say that ELLs must acquire twice as much English vocabulary, twice as fast as native speakers, often without interacting in English outside of school. That is no small feat—but fortunately, it is entirely achievable!

English, a Richly Generative Language

English has the largest vocabulary of any language in the world, more than 250,000 words by some estimates (How many words are there in the English language?, 2017) and three quarters of a million by others (How many words are there in English?, 2017). The size of the English lexicon is due to at least three factors: the eclectic origins of English, the "accommodating" disposition of English toward new vocabulary, and the digital revolution, which speeds up the rate at which new words are promulgated and shared. English easily absorbs and allows for the creation of new words in myriad ways that captivate linguists—and bedevil countless English learners.

In Chapter 5, we looked at the ways that English words can be formed and modified through derivational morphemes (prefixes and suffixes) and inflectional morphemes (suffixes at the end of words). In addition to all of the new words that can be counted when a word like *stand* takes the forms *stands, standing, stood*, there are many other ways that new words can be formed, and this portion of the chapter highlights some of the most common. The many sources of English words and the wide variety of English word-making options bear upon how easily ELLs acquire English vocabulary. Some aspects of English are relatively straightforward, such as its word order and grammatical categories, the lack of gendered nouns and adjectives, or case endings. It's getting a handle on English vocabulary that can prove challenging. However, when teachers of ELLs bring word formation study into the classroom and make it a topic of inquiry, the enthusiasm for English word learning can become contagious. We hope this chapter will have that effect on you!

Etymology

One of the reasons that English is so rich and widely used around the world is that there are many historical contributions to the English lexicon, or collection of words in the language. Etymology, as we explained in Chapter 5, is the study of the origin of words and how they evolve. It can be fascinating to learn about where words come from as well as the many subtle and dramatic ways their meanings can change.

Ambiguous Vocabulary in English

The opacity of English and its diverse sources combine to create many ambiguities and multiple meanings of words. Words containing differing spellings, pronunciations, or meanings are often lumped together into the catch-all category *homonyms*, but we prefer to separate them into three distinct categories: *homophones, homographs,* and *polysemous words*. Their characteristics are summarized in Table 6.1.

1. *Homophones* are two or more words with the same sound but different spellings and meanings. Because English spelling is so opaque, these words abound. Homophones also account for a great number of spelling errors; even when students know the meaning and sound of a word, they aren't sure which possible spelling pattern represents the meaning they are trying to convey. Spell checking often does not catch homophones

TABLE 6.1. Ambiguous Vocabulary in English

Type	Same sound?	Same spelling?	Same meaning?
Homophones	Yes	No	No
Homographs	No	Yes	No
Polysemous words	Yes	Yes	No

because both of the choices are real words. In addition to homophones with two spellings, such as *slay/sleigh, do/dew, weight/wait,* and *pair/pear,* some of the most high-frequency English words have not just two, but three different spellings and meanings, such as *there/they're/their, right/ write/rite,* and *to/two/too.* Homophones are the cause of many spelling errors.

2. *Homographs* are two words with the same spelling but different pronunciations and meanings. Since the multiple meanings of the words are spelled the same way, they are not likely to be misspelled, like homophones, but they may be mispronounced, misread, and their meanings may be confused. Common homographs that are spelled with the same letters but have different pronunciations and meanings include *bass* ("fish" or "a musical instrument"), *bow* ("weapon for shooting arrows" or "bend from the waist to show respect"), *wound* ("the past tense of *wind*" or "to injure"), and *wind* ("twist a rope" or "a perceptible movement of air"). There are also many words like the word *permit,* which has different word stress and different meanings according to whether it is a noun or verb.

> I bought the *permit* from the city. (noun)
> Do the owners *permit* tenants to own dogs? (verb)

Some homographs cannot be disambiguated without their context, like *read* in the sentence "They read the newspaper," which could be in either present or past tense when the word is in written form. It is only by hearing it read aloud, or seeing in a larger context, that we can know the meaning.

3. *Polysemous* words are pronounced and spelled the same way, but have different meanings that often do not appear to relate to each other. The root morpheme may give us information about an aspect of its meaning, but it also may not. Examples of common polysemous words in English are *bat, bank, fly,* and *bill.* Many very common English words are polysemous, and figuring out their additional meanings can be very tough. For example, ELLs in a class we observed were reading a story from a

basal reader about Native Americans. The students were confident that they knew the meaning of the word *game*. Looking at it in context, however, they realized that the sentence "They hunted *game* with bows and arrows" didn't make sense with the meaning they knew for the word, as "something you play." In linguistics, these new meanings allow a word to belong to different *semantic fields*; for example, the semantic field for *game* as something you play would include the words *chess* and *badminton*, and the semantic field for the second meaning related to hunting would include words like *pheasants, wild boar, deer,* and *elk*.

English content words often take on a variety of specific meanings in different content areas, and students need to know these precise definitions as they advance through the grades. Learners need both general academic vocabulary, which crosses disciplines, as well as content-specific vocabulary for particular subject expertise. Sometimes the same word can have different specific meanings depending on the context. For example:

> A *volume* of a book is one of the books that makes up a set.
>
> Calculating the *volume* of a cylinder requires applying a mathematical formula.
>
> The *volume* of an acoustic signal is its amplitude (loudness).

Students need to learn both the common meanings and the content-specific meanings of words. Ogle, Blachowicz, Fisher, and Lang (2015) caution, "The small words are often the ones that can cause difficulties. For example, *compare, design, look, work, average, equivalent, vary,* and *reasonable* are all words with common meanings that may have explicit meanings in math" (p. 105).

Many times, the content-area teacher or text will introduce the new word without any reference to its meanings in other contexts, and students may carry a different understanding of the word in their minds. This is true not only for native English speakers but also especially for ELLs who have made a mental translation of the word to their L1 that covers one definition, but not another. For example, the French word *la glace* can be translated into three different English words: *ice, ice cream,* or *ice cube*. Over time, ELL students can learn that it's not unusual or problematic to find multiple word meanings; in English, it's natural.

Both English homophones and polysemous words are likely to be found in *puns*, which are jokes based on wordplay. Many puns derive their humor from the clash between the first and second meaning of a word, creating humorous dissonance. For amusing examples of puns on signage, look at the photos in Figure 6.1.

FIGURE 6.1. Examples of English word formation using puns.

A Dozen Word Formation Processes in English

The digital revolution has facilitated the formation of new words at a faster rate than ever before. Dictionary editors and publishers are challenged to constantly introduce—and retire—English words for their latest editions, and this challenge gives the edge to online dictionaries, which do not need to wait for a new printing. Although words seem to enter English randomly, they can be classified into certain linguistically distinct categories. Once students learn about these categories, they will quickly find evidences of English word formation every day and can incorporate the words into their listening, speaking, reading, and writing vocabularies. You may also find that they create a few new words themselves!

Here are 12 of the ways new words can be formed in English. New meanings can also be formed by combining words or by assigning new meanings to existing words. By the way, these word formation methods are not unique to English; they can be found in all languages because they are linguistic in nature.

1. *Coinage (neologisms).* These words are made up from scratch to suit certain purposes. They often do not contain an identifiable morpheme. They are often invented by companies with new products and then are extended to more generalized use. Examples include *xerox, Kleenex, Skype, Etsy,* and *Tylenol.*

2. *Borrowing (loanwords).* These are words taken from other languages and incorporated into English. Sometimes the original meaning is modified, and the pronunciation may change. Since some words were borrowed long ago, it can be hard to recognize their foreign origins. Examples include *cuisine* (French), *pajamas* (Hindi), *banana* (Wolof), *chipmunk* (Algonquin), *alfalfa* (Arabic), and *gung ho* (Chinese).

3. *Compounding.* This common way to form English words consists of combining two free morphemes to create a new word with a new meaning, called a compound. The new word may be hyphenated or combined without hyphenation. Compounds may be composed of two nouns, an adjective plus noun, a verb plus preposition, or other combinations, as seen in the examples below. Sometimes compound nouns, especially with longer words, maintain two separate words with a space between them. In spoken form, the first of the two words receives the strong stress. Examples include *whiteboard, sailboat, makeover, sandbag, frontload, bailout,* and *giveaway.*

4. *Blending (portmanteau words).* This most creative word-making tool of English consists of combining morphemes or phonemic fragments from two different words to create a new "hybrid" word with a

single morpheme and new meaning. They start out with topical short-term uses, and they are often humorous. Eventually they may become standardized in the language or disappear. Some examples are *brunch* (*breakfast* + *lunch*); *smog* (*smoke* + *fog*); *guesstimate* (*guess* + *estimate*); and *webinar* (*web* + *seminar*).

5. *Clipping.* Words are made by shortening a longer word or phrase. It's usually a shortcut for words both parties already know and are familiar with. The word is usually clipped at the end, but it might also be clipped at the beginning, and may even cross morpheme boundaries for ease of pronunciation. Examples include *professional* → *pro, condominium* → *condo, laboratory* → *lab, telephone* → *phone, weblog* → *blog,* and *carbohydrates* → *carbs.*

6. *Acronyms.* The first letter of each word in a group of words is combined into a single word, which is pronounced as a whole. The resulting word may be in all capital letters. When *acronyms* are well established, the words that make them up may be forgotten, as in these examples: *radar* (radio detection and ranging), *scuba* (self-contained underwater breathing apparatus), *pin* (personal identification number), *zip* (zone improvement plan), *AIDS* (acquired immune deficiency syndrome), and the restaurant chain Arby's (America's Roast Beef–Yes Sir!).

7. *Abbreviations.* The first letter of each word in a group of words is combined into a single word, but the letter names are pronounced separately. Examples include *ASPCA* (American Society for the Prevention of Cruelty to Animals), *AKA* (also known as), *RIP* (rest in peace), and *URL* (uniform resource locater). Some words are also an alloy of acronyms and abbreviations, such as *AWOL*, which means a soldier is "absent without leave" and is pronounced as two syllables.

Acronyms and abbreviations can be especially tricky for ELLs if they are spoken aloud without explanation. A Panamanian ESL teacher, who is herself an ELL, describes her frustration.

> *I see a lot of abbreviations, and I am constantly asking people about them. I used to find these abbreviations as new words when going to the doctor, and it was very intimidating and uncomfortable. When I would hear them, I would not even know they were abbreviations, so my brain would be busy trying to figure them out. It was awful when it was medically related. It added unnecessary stress.*—MARIA ISABEL MARQUEZ

8. *Backformation.* This is a multistep process in which, most commonly, a word of one type, usually a noun, is reduced to a word of another

type, usually a verb. It is done by lopping off the end of the noun and changing it to a verb, as in *editor* → *edit, donation* → *donate, magnification* → *magnify, teacher* → *teach*, and *preacher* → *preach*.

9. *Conversion (category shift)*. In conversion, the grammatical category of a word is changed, without changing any morphemes. Some examples are *butter* (noun → verb: pass the *butter* or *butter* the bread), *empty* (adjective → verb: an *empty* bottle or *empty* the bottle), *must see* (modal verb → noun: you *must see* this movie or this movie is a *must-see*), *chair* (noun → verb: sit on a *chair* or to *chair* the meeting).

10. *Scale change*. In scale change, an existing free morpheme adds a free morpheme, bound root, prefix, or suffix in order to indicate a change in its dimension or scale. In English, we have a common suffix to indicate a diminutive, which is the /iy/ sound. It can be spelled several ways, and it can be added to names, foods, and many other things (e.g., *Bobby, Slurpee, puppy*). There are also diminutive morphemes in other languages, such as *-ito/-a* in Spanish (e.g., *burrito, abuelita*) or *-et/-ette* in French (e.g., *livret, coquette*). Scale changes to indicate quantity or size can be shown at the beginning of words, such as in *macroeconomics, microwave*, and *megabucks*, or at the end of words such as in *hoodie, dinette, booklet*, and *nappie*.

11. *Paired-word sound play*. Two kinds of paired words rely on sound play. In the first kind, the second word sounds like the first, except for a change of vowel, such as *hip-hop, mishmash, wishy-washy*, or *singsong*. Interestingly, the second vowel of the pair is usually produced at a lower place in our vocal cavity. The second kind is rhyming paired words, such as *Wi-fi, freebie, hobo*, or *chugalug*. There may be a slight onomatopoetic association (it sounds like the action it is describing), but not always. English has an exceptional number of rhyming phrases due to its opaque orthography. Humans apparently like to hear similar-sounding vowels in consecutive words; in fact, the ability to hear and make rhymes is a milestone in phonological awareness development. English also abounds in rhyming phrases, such as *wine and dine, fair and square*, or *shake and bake*.

12. *Multiple processes*. A combination of the above processes forms a new word, as shown in these examples: *deli* is borrowed from German (*delicatessen*) and then clipped; *snowballed* is compounded from two free morphemes to form a noun, then converted into a verb with the suffix *-ed* added (the event *snowballed*, etc.); *cyberbullying* is a compound of the root *cyber* and the lexical morpheme *bully*, which is then converted to a verb, and then converted to a gerund (noun) by adding the suffix *-ing*.

Figure 6.2 features 12 photos that illustrate English word formation processes. Can you match them with the appropriate kind of word formation?

The English language is constantly in motion, as illustrated in these three interesting examples.

*I didn't know what "to TP a house" meant. My students had to explain it to me. I learned that TP is an abbreviation of toilet paper, which is then converted into a transitive verb. The house is the unfortunate object of the verb, when it is "decorated" with dozens of rolls of toilet paper in the middle of the night.—*TENENA

*My teenage daughter and her friends often use the new word ish. Ish was originally a derivational suffix. As we know, when it is added to a root or stem, it modifies a characteristic, like greenish, starting an event at 12-ish, or newish for "kind of new." Now it has been clipped, and the suffix has become a root, forming a new word. When I ask her if she had a good time at a party, she may shrug her shoulders and answer, "Ish!" in an offhanded way. It means "I had a moderately good time."—*KRISTIN

*I haven't heard the word ish, but I've certainly heard the word meh to mean the same thing as ish. For example, when I asked my neighbor's son if he liked a movie, he shrugged and answered, "Meh."—*LEAH

Using Cognates

Depending on the other languages that ELLs know, cognates may be a rich source of information for word study in English. Therefore, we give this strategy special attention.

A *cognate* is a word with a common or similar meaning in two languages and which comes from the same root. The word may or may not look or sound the same in both languages, depending on the language distance. English derives about 60% of its words from Latin or Greek (Freeman & Freeman, 2004), and the percentage of Latin and Greek words in other languages is also high.

Cognates from Latin and Greek can be found in science, philosophy, mathematics, and the social sciences in most of the Indo-European languages. ELLs can benefit dramatically from studying cognates if their first language is an Indo-European language, but the words they share will vary according to which historical branch of the Indo-European language their language belongs to. The most plentiful cognate words shared with

FIGURE 6.2. Examples of English word formation processes.

FIGURE 6.2. (*continued*)

FIGURE 6.2. (*continued*)

English are from the "Romance language" branch, which includes Spanish, French, Romanian, and Portuguese, owing to the extensive contact between these language groups beginning with the Norman Conquest in 1066. There is an entirely different set of cognate words shared with English from the "Germanic" branch of Indo-European languages, such as Dutch, German, Danish, Swedish, Norwegian, and others. These cognates are often the historically older words of English and may be spelled differently from the English word in those languages. (If you are interested in this topic, you can search "language family trees" on the Internet or in good dictionaries such as the *American Heritage Dictionary*, 4th edition.)

English cognates from Latin and Greek tend to be academic language. Jim Cummins (2007) put it succinctly: "English is a romance language when it comes to academic language, just like Spanish and Romanian." The fact that CALP words in English look like common words in Spanish gives Spanish-speaking ELLs an enormous potential boost in developing their academic language, but only when these words are pointed out and practiced in the classroom (Beeman & Urow, 2012). Here is just a small sample of academic verbs used in English classroom settings and their Spanish cognate equivalents:

examine	*examinar*
describe	*describir*
imagine	*imaginar*
analyze	*analizar*
appear	*aparecer*

Table 6.2 gives a few examples of how English and Spanish words can be generated from their common Latin roots.

ELLs whose L1 is a Romance language may be more familiar with the longer word in English than they are with shorter word from German and Old English because the longer word is a cognate. For example, ELL students may be more familiar with the term *elevation* than the word *height* because *elevation* is a cognate word in many languages but *height* is not. In other words, the same words that are "harder" for native speakers of English may in fact be "easier" words for ELLs if the words are cognates from their languages and they are familiar with the word in their L1. Table 6.3 shows English words with Latinate origins compared to Spanish words next to English words of Old English/Germanic origins. As you can see, Spanish words share cognates with English words from Latinate roots, but they do not share cognates with English words from Old English/German roots.

TABLE 6.2. Generating Words in English and Spanish from a Common Latin Root

Spanish words	Related English words	Root meaning
primero	*primal*	*prim* (Latin, first)
primavera	*primarily*	
primitive	*prime*	
primeramente	*primordial*	
primo	*primitive*	
principal	*primary*	
	principal	
servible	*subservient*	*serv* (Latin, servant)
servidor	*serving*	
servilleta	*self-serving*	
servicio	*servitude*	
	serviceable	
	service	
escritorio	*inscribe*	*scribere* (Latin, to write)
escrito	*describe*	
escribano	*description*	
escribir	*scribble*	
	nondescript	
	scripture	
	script	

Note. Using a common Latin root, it is possible to generate words in English, Spanish, and other Latin-based languages. As an example, here are three Latin roots and related Spanish and English words derived from them.

We use Spanish words as examples, but these similarities occur in the languages with Latin roots. English words such as *photosynthesis, botany, velocity,* and *hydroelectric,* for example, can be found in many Latin- or Greek-influenced languages in the same or similar forms. Even when the full English version of the word is not found in a learner's first language, there may be clues in the morphemes, such as *hydro* being related to water.

False Cognates and Other Misunderstandings

On the other hand, beware of *false cognates, cross-linguistic homographs,* and *cross-linguistic homophones* (oh my!)! False cognates have the same appearance or sound as a word in another language, but have a different meaning. An example is *molestar,* which means "to bother" in Spanish, unlike the much more serious meaning of "molest," or "sexually violate," in English. Another example is *passer un examen* in French, which means "to take an exam," but not necessarily to pass it, unlike the English *pass*

TABLE 6.3. English Words from Latinate Origins Compared to English and Spanish Words

English word from Germanic or Old English origin	English word from Latinate origin	Spanish word from Latinate origin
get	*obtain*	*obtener*
fix	*repair*	*reparar*
keep	*retain*	*retener*
breathe	*respire*	*respirar*
meet	*encounter*	*encontrar*

an exam, which means "to have a passing grade." We have provided a list of some of the most "notorious" false cognates of English and Spanish in Appendix 6.1 at the end of the chapter. We highly recommend that any teacher working with Spanish-speaking ELLs or endeavoring to learn Spanish pay close attention to them! Of course, false cognates cut both ways—our learners will use them in English, just as we might when learning a new language. Teachers will want to focus on false cognates with a completely different meaning or connotation, as seen in the following example.

> *Imagine my surprise when I received a card on the last day of class, signed by all of my Hispanic ELL adults, which read "In Deepest Sympathy." I didn't dare tell them that it was a card we use to comfort someone at the death of a loved one. They meant to tell me that they found me very nice and kind!*—LEAH

False cognates share a root but have different meanings because their morphemes veered off in different directions over time. The second kind of misunderstanding is cross-linguistic homographs, or words that share common letters but not meanings. An example of a cross-linguistic homograph would be *pie*, which means "foot" in Spanish and is pronounced completely differently from the same word in English that means "a sweet dessert." The only thing they have in common is the same string of letters—they don't even share a morpheme. The third misunderstanding is cross-linguistic homophones, which share common sounds but not meanings. An example of a cross-linguistic homophone is the Persian word pronounced as *party*. In Persian it means "clout," which is not at all like the English definition of a party (although people with clout may give or attend a lot of them!). Although the two words sound similar, they do not share spellings or meanings. These two forms can be amusing, but they are not as problematic as false cognates, which can be very common and very misleading.

Collocations: Phrasal Verbs, Idioms, and Listemes

English vocabulary words whose meanings cannot be understood through single words alone are referred to as *collocations*. Collocations can be defined as a string of words commonly used together. Pinker (1999) notes that collocations "are remembered as wholes and often used together" (p. 24). Part of learning to break text into "chunks" while reading is learning to keep collocations together as a single chunk. Although we can find common groupings of words in all reading materials, collocations tend to be overlooked in targeted vocabulary, usually in favor of teaching nouns. However, collocations are pervasive in written and spoken English. Collocations are used not only in social settings, but in the academic language of school.

We consider phrasal verbs, idioms, and listemes to fall into the category of collocations, and will describe them here.

Phrasal Verbs

Phrasal verbs are verbs composed of a verb and a preposition or occasionally a verb and an adverb. These are very common in everyday English. The common action verbs *get up, come in, pick up,* and *put down,* for example, are all phrasal verbs. If you were asked to make a list of common verbs in English, you would quickly find that part of the reason that they are so common is because they combine into many phrasal verbs. You can see that the "integrity" of the verb's meaning is lost if we take away its preposition, because in fact, both words are part of the meaning of the verb. You will also notice that phrasal verbs tend to be a combination of short words that are not cognates with Latin-based words. Once again, it may be easier for ELL students to understand a longer verb with a Latin root than two short Germanic-based words that form a phrasal verb. Therefore, these require explicit teaching and attention. For a sample of Latin-based verbs matched with common English phrasal verbs, see Table 6.4.

Because phrasal verbs are so common in spoken English, many ELLs will acquire them through their social language interactions. However, some of them will not be obvious, and, additionally, many phrasal verbs have multiple meanings. For example, when Isho, a fourth-grade L1 Assyrian ELL, read a story in a basal reader that said, "The workers *picked up* the pace," he asked his teacher what *picked up* meant. Did it mean "lift,"

**TABLE 6.4. Selected Phrasal Verbs
and Their Latin-Based Equivalents**

Phrasal verb	Latin-based synonym
ask about	*inquire*
find out	*discover*
fix up	*repair, rehabilitate*
get over	*recover, surmount*
help out	*assist*
keep on	*continue*
make up	*reconcile, invent*
run into	*encounter*
set up	*plan, organize*
show up	*arrive, appear*
think up	*invent, create*
try out	*experiment, audition*

as in "pick up a sack," or "gather," as in "pick up the pieces of the broken glass," or even "learn informally," as in "She picked up a few words of Japanese while traveling in Japan?" he wondered. In fact, in this text, *picked up* has a fourth meaning, to "increase the speed of an activity." As you can see, two short, common words can carry a lot of freight, depending on their context.

> *Word combinations are always evolving. You might hear one meaning of a phrasal verb, which is then extended into a new area through song lyrics or something on the Internet. Phrasal verbs can acquire new meanings all the time, and that's what makes them so interesting. They also bear careful instruction, however, because so many of them pick up sexual connotations.*—LEAH

In writing and speaking, ELLs often omit a preposition, choose the wrong preposition, or add a preposition when they use English phrasal verbs. This may be due to a word-by-word translation from their first language. Look at the following anecdote from a teacher who emigrated to the United States from Mexico at age 10.

> *I remember exactly what a guest speaker said to me, in the fifth grade. I had recently arrived in the United States and was in the first stage of language development: Entering. The guest speaker was going around*

the class asking everyone what they liked to do. I remember thinking to myself, "Me gusta bailar," and when my turn came, I said very proudly, "I like dance." The guest speaker corrected me and said, "I like to dance." I could not comprehend why she added a "to" if I had translated it correctly: Me gusta = "I like" and bailar = "dance." There were no additional words–where did the "to" come from?—XIOMARA GUERRERO

Idioms

Idioms are metaphorical expressions whose meanings cannot be discerned by looking at the individual words alone (Pinker, 1999). Often colorful and humorous, idioms give us insights into the cultural underpinnings of societies. For example, the English idiom *straight from the horse's mouth* stems from a historical context in which the stable boy in daily contact with a racehorse is most aware of its overall condition. Now, it has come to mean "coming from the highest possible authority." Figure 6.3 is an illustration by a sixth-grade student of another idiom about horses. Can you guess what it is?

Colorful idioms enhance the communicative power of a writer or speaker tremendously. Also, they can teach us fascinating history that might otherwise be lost. Linguist Ben Zimmer (2011) notes:

> Idioms are like barnacles on the ship of language. Oftentimes they long outlive their original intent, confounding generation after generation seeking clarity in the linguistic shreds that they've inherited.

There are thousands of idioms in English, just as in any language, and learning them is part of the fun of learning a new language. Often the story behind the idiom adds a bit of spice to reading, writing, and speaking. For example, when we say "Don't put the cart before the horse," we imagine what it looks like when a cart is in front of a horse—the cart can't move, because the horse is behind it and can't pull it! From that story, we can extend its meaning to the situation in which the idiom is being used. It helps us understand that we need to do things in the correct sequence in order to move a project forward.

Zwiers (2007) identified a number of academic idioms that teachers often use, "phrases such as *all boils down to, the gory details, that answer doesn't hold water, a thin argument, a keen insight, crux of the matter, on the right track,* and *dissect the article.* Many of these academic idioms serve to describe cognitive processes and school tasks" (p. 108). Sometimes teachers say the first part of an idiom as a way of making a humorous commentary in class (see Table 6.5 for examples).

Saying half of an idiom represents a complex task for an ELL student:

FIGURE 6.3. Idiom drawing: What is the idiom?

He or she must be able to mentally complete the idiom fragment first, recognize its meaning, and then apply it to the situation, rapidly enough to chuckle with the rest of the class. This is no small feat! Teachers of ELLs need to carefully monitor not only the speed and clarity of their speech, but also limit their use of casual witticisms, or "asides," to make sure all of their students are able to get the joke.

> *One of my students mentioned that her fourth-grade ELL students had learned the word* capiche *from a previous teacher. They figured out that it meant "understand," but no one had ever told them it was an Italian word, not necessarily understood in English. She had to explain that it was Italian, used idiomatically in English.*—KRISTIN

> *I have used the word* capiche *in my graduate classes. I picked it up because of my contact with Italian friends who always said it. Everyone seems to understand it, or at least no one has ever asked me what it means!*—TENENA

The word "up" combines with hundreds of verbs to form a vast number of subtle meanings. You might want to check the interesting list of expressions that use the word *up*, which is considered the "most confusing two-letter word in English" at the website *www.proofreadnow.com* (Most confusing two-letter word, 2016). You start to realize that prepositions by

TABLE 6.5. Examples of Partial Use of Idioms

"Let the chips fall . . . " in the food section of a daily newspaper

The headline is above a picture of different kinds of potato and vegetable chips in midair. English readers know that the full idiom is "Let the chips fall where they may," meaning "Accept the minor consequences and keep going." The idiom comes from advice given to lumberjacks whose axes created chips on the ground while they were chopping down a tree. In the context of the article, it gives the idea that other chips are just as acceptable as potato chips.

"It's six of one . . . " in a group of people discussing two options

The phrase is the beginning of the idiom "It's six of one, half a dozen of the other," which means "they're equal" or "they're the same." To understand the idiom, we need to know that a dozen consists of 12 items, so a half dozen is 6, and they are the same size.

"In one ear . . . " in a teacher's lounge

The phrase is half of "In one ear, out the other" which means, "It was heard but not remembered or learned." To understand this idiom, we have to picture an empty head that ideas flow right through. The idea is that there is no brain in the middle to process the information!

themselves do not have directionality or relationships, but in combination with verbs.

Listemes

Listemes are words that commonly appear together. In addition to phrasal verbs and idioms, there are English expressions with words in a fixed order that are memorized as a whole. Some linguists refer to them by the general term *collocations*, but a more precise term is *listemes*. Listemes are created when millions of members of a language community use a word combination so often that it is understood as a whole unit and used in that way. Some examples of these fixed expressions are "up and down," but not "down and up"; "they lived happily ever after," which is how European fairy tales routinely conclude; or newer phrases from the digital era, such as "copy and paste," "the World Wide Web," or "in case you missed it (ICYMI)." Other listemes, like the paired words *mumbo-jumbo, higgledy-piggledy,* and *wishy-washy,* are bound together by their ease of pronunciation and the enjoyable reaction we feel hearing their similar sounds (Pinker, 2000). Some linguists consider individual words that have irregular forms, such as irregular past tenses or plurals, to be listemes too (e.g., *goose/geese* or *take/took/taken*), but our focus is on listemes that are composed of more than one word.

　　Collocations can be confusing for ELLs because very simple words may be combined in ways that are not at all simple, as can be seen in the cartoon in Figure 6.4.

Learning to recognize and use the collocations of English is an integral part of learning to read and write. The more collocations we know, the better we are able to comprehend spoken and written English. In turn, the more collocations we can use and explain in our own speaking and writing, the better we can help ELLs develop their unique language styles and self-expression.

HOW DOES THIS LOOK IN THE CLASSROOM?

Playing with Words Is the Fun Stuff of Language Learning

Wordplay builds vocabulary through uproarious fun. Between morphemes, cognates, and diverse word formation processes, there are many ways to get students excited about words, and these are but a few.

Taking Cameras into the Community

Using cameras and phones to hunt for examples of word formation is a wonderful project. The images can be turned into photo stories, either by

FIGURE 6.4. An English idiom. Reprinted with permission from Martha Rosenberg.

individuals or the whole class, and posted in class or uploaded to a website. In addition to analyzing the environmental print surrounding us, the project also gives students an opportunity to talk about their neighborhoods. In multilingual neighborhoods, it can also be fun to look at signs in other languages posted in ethnic neighborhoods, where the same word formation processes can be seen. Examples of some signage with Spanish word formation processes can be seen in Figure 6.5.

Idiom Calendars

To practice idioms, high school ELL reading teacher Barb Willson uses what she calls idiom calendars. This is a class calendar displayed in the room featuring a different student-illustrated idiom every week. When the idiom appears on the calendar, students practice the idioms through illustrations, dialogues, and skits. When ELLs share idioms from their L1, it is also a great way to enjoy linguistic comparisons while teaching metalinguistic concepts.

Collocations in Song Lyrics

Pop songs and country songs are chock full of phrasal verbs, idioms, and listemes that reflect common speech. Listening to, analyzing, and singing along with song lyrics are natural, effortless ways to practice using these expressions. Songs also help ELLs express their feelings and develop shared cultural experiences while lowering their affective filter. Furthermore, using songs and music in the classroom helps to foster classroom community (Lems, 2001b, 2002, 2016).

Pulling out Phrasal Verbs

One way to highlight phrasal verbs is to pull them out from different kinds of texts, including song lyrics, fiction, poetry, and Readers' Theatre scripts. Sometimes phrasal verbs may be overlooked as the "easy words" in a text, but they carry rich associations and warrant explicit teaching. For example, when an ELL high school student at the Developing level chose to do a presentation about the mysterious song "Hotel California" by the Eagles, he did not recognize the irony of the line "living it up at the Hotel California," because he didn't know the idiom *to live it up*. The placement of that idiom, in a song about being mentally trapped, heightens the song's power. Collocations should be introduced and practiced as they appear in groups, not word by word. They can be put up on the wall or included in vocabulary notebooks, just like individual words.

Polysemous words, including phrasal verbs, can be represented on a graphic organizer that allows each meaning of the word to be shown in its own section. The word *will*, for example, can be put in the middle of

FIGURE 6.5. Examples of Spanish word formation processes.

a *semantic map*, a graphic organizer showing relationships among words and concepts. One branch of the map can show the definition of *will* as a verb signaling future tense, while another branch can show the definition of *will* as a document people create to distribute their possessions after their death. Yet a third branch defines *will* as determination. To differentiate for less-proficient learners, the definitions on the map can be provided by the teacher, and students instead identify the word and write it in the center of the map.

Creating New Product Names

Advertising copywriters create new words all the time as they try to come up with new products and company names to entice the buying public. For example, "Bubblicious" is a blend that is the brand name of a successful product. When we see its name on the gum package, we know that it is *bubble gum*, and we also get an association with the word *delicious*. Advertisers hope that this winning word blend will make us want to buy the product.

First, have students find several products at a store or elsewhere and break their product names into morphemes, analyzing how the morphemes are combined to create an effect. Evaluate how well the created names sell the product. Then have students create a new product name for a common product, such as toothpaste, soap, a pair of gym shoes, a robot, a drone, or a car. Next, have them write an ad for the product. Discuss what word formation processes students used to create their product name. If appropriate, have students vote on the best product name created in the class.

Idiom Matching Game

Write idioms on heavy stock paper, then cut the pieces of paper with longer idioms into two halves and scramble them (see Figure 6.6). Have students work in small groups to put the idioms together, and ask them to define the idioms in their own words and use them in an original skit. Here is a sample of idioms that can be divided into two parts to get you started.

Too many cooks	*and into the fire.*
One swallow	*lie.*
Let sleeping dogs	*spoil the broth.*
Out of the frying pan	*doesn't fall far from the tree.*
The apple	*does not a summer make.*

Note: Idiom matching games only work with idioms that have divisible phrases or clauses—and many do not! For example, the idiom *living it up* mentioned previously cannot be divided in a way that retains the seman-

FIGURE 6.6. Teachers trying out the idiom matching game.

tic association, but *out of the frying pan and into the fire* can be divided into *out of the frying pan* and *and into the fire* at its natural phrase break.

Dictionary Resources

The Internet has changed the way people find and learn words, and it is a wonderful supplement to bound dictionaries. More people now access the *Merriam-Webster Dictionary* through smartphones than laptops, according to its editors (Sokolowski, 2016). A wonderful source for ELLs is the Learner's Dictionary site hosted by Merriam-Webster (Learner's Dictionary, 2017). The completely free site includes visual support for vocabulary, guides to pronunciation, and examples of usage, using a base of 3,000 words. The open source etymology reference called *Etymology Online*, mentioned in Chapter 5, is also rich and is constantly updated. Traditional bound dictionaries allow students to master many important academic skills, such as using alphabetical order, reading abbreviations, understanding typographic symbols within a definition, exploring multiple meanings of words, and noticing words related to the one they were looking up. For traditional bound dictionaries, *The American Heritage Dictionary of the English Language* and *The Oxford English Dictionary* include word etymology. No classroom should be without at least one dictionary that includes etymology, and every student should be expected to use it. In addition, books tell amazing stories about English words. Teachers will enjoy adult-level books by Bill Bryson, such as *Mother Tongue* (1990) and *Made in America* (1994); *The Story of English, Third Revised Edition* (McCrum, MacNeil, & Cran, 2002); *The Stuff of Thought* (Pinker, 2008), and *Word by Word: The Secret Life of Dictionaries* (Stamper, 2017).

Online Resources for Word Study

YouTube videos, blogs, and websites trace the origins of English words. Videos from publishers, language schools, and individual entrepreneurs are sprinkled throughout the Internet, and now it is a question of finding the best materials rather than feeling lucky to find any! We like and use etymology videos on YouTube from Gina Cooke, Kori Stamper, Peter Sokolowski, John McWorter on TED-Ed, and Tom Scott.

There are also excellent websites for learning idioms. One of the best is a free, downloadable American idiom reference guide called *In the Loop*, written for the Office of English Language at the U.S. Department of State; it can be found at the American English website of the State Department (*https://americanenglish.state.gov/resources/loop*).

QUESTIONS FOR FURTHER STUDY

1. If you had to choose three important ideas from this chapter, which would you choose? How can you apply these ideas to your larger knowledge of teaching English as a new language?

2. Think of a word that has multiple meanings and create a semantic map with each definition on a different branch of the map and a blank in the center, and try it out on classmates or on your students. Share the experience.

3. Words and phrases are always entering the English language. Can you think of some new ones you might have read in the newspaper or online or heard on TV or the radio? If you teach, what do you hear your students saying lately? After jotting down the words, write a short definition of each one, and share it with others. Could you ask your students to write definitions of these words?

4. In your work or in your life, have you found acronyms or abbreviations to be troublesome? If so, which ones in particular have given you a hard time? What ideas do you have to make acronyms and abbreviations more accessible to students as readers or listeners?

5. Table 6.2 gives examples of words in English and Spanish that are generated from a common root. Try to do the same with the Latin roots in Appendix 6.2. If you don't know Spanish, but know another language with common Latin roots, try to think of words from that language instead. If English is your only language or the only language with Latin roots that you know, see how many words you can generate on the English side alone. Share with a partner or with the class, and discuss ways the words reflect the meaning of the root.

6. With a partner or alone, classify these words by the word formation processes listed in the chapter. If the word is in the multiple processes category, describe the processes that go into the mix. (See p. 168 for the answers to this question.)

whiteboard	*spam*	*FYI*
translate	*waste*	*Skype*
gadget	*Humpty Dumpty*	*dashcam*
sci-fi	*SCOTUS*	*ecocide*
	ciao	

7. If you have studied another language, make a list of some cognates with English that you are aware of. How do you use these cognates to remember new words? Have you ever used any false cognates? If you have any stories about this experience, share them with others. If not, ask around to find stories from others.

8. Classify the following puns based on either homophones or polysemous words.
   - Q: What is the best fruit for studying history? A: Dates.
   - Q: What two animals go everywhere you go? A: Your calves.
   - Q: What is the strongest day? A: Sunday, because all the rest are "week"days.
   - Q: What letter is never in the alphabet? A: The one that you mail.
   - Q: What should be looked into? A: A mirror.
   - Q: Why did the Palmers name their cattle ranch "Horizon"?
     A: Because that's where the sons raise meat (sun's rays meet).

   Find some other jokes that are based on polysemous meanings or homophones of words. Better yet, do this with your students!

9. Idioms have rich cultural resonance. With a partner or alone, and without consulting the Internet, see how many idioms you can think of about one of the following topics: baseball, cooking, travel, weather, or birds. Then look at what kind of prior knowledge one needs to understand the idiom. How could you explain these idioms to your students?

10. Literal meanings of idioms cannot always be shown, but often they can. Choose two idioms and think about their literal meanings. How could you best teach the figurative meaning of some of these idioms? Can you draw them?

11. Choose one of the following verbs and see how many phrasal verbs you can create with it. Then create a lesson to practice the various meanings and try it out on colleagues or students. Do some, or all, of the phrasal verbs that you can make with the same base verb have similar underlying actions?

_____ *run into*	*a. initiate*
_____ *talk about*	*b. tolerate*
_____ *think over*	*c. sacrifice, quit*
_____ *make up*	*d. contemplate*

    _____ *put up with*   e. *encounter*
    _____ *give up*   f. *depart*
    _____ *get out*   g. *reconcile, invent*
    _____ *start up*   h. *discuss*

12. Without consulting the Internet, think of some additional phrasal verbs and their Latin-based equivalents. If you're stuck, look at Table 6.4 again for ideas.

13. The three photographs in Figure 6.1 (p. 145) contain puns, but require both linguistic knowledge and cultural background knowledge to understand the joke. Explain each one and cite the linguistic and cultural background knowledge needed to understand it.

14. CHALLENGE QUESTION: Make a list of 10 listemes and share them with others. (A test of a listeme is that another person can easily finish the expression for you when you start it.) Create a lesson for students in which they match them.

15. CHALLENGE QUESTION: Pick one of the following homographic words and explore its multiple meanings, including its occurrence in idioms and in phrasal verbs: *bass, tip, wind, mass, right, lead, game, bill*. Create a lesson to teach its multiple meanings.

Answers to Question 6

whiteboard	compounding
spam	multiple (clipping and blending of *spiced* + *ham*)
FYI	abbreviation
translate	backformation (translation changed to a verb by removing syllable)
waste	conversion (from N to V)
Skype	coinage (neologism)
gadget	scale change (-*et* indicates it is small)
Humpty Dumpty	paired-word sound play
dashcam	multiple (clipping and blending of *dashboard* + *camera*)
sci-fi	multiple (paired-word sound play, clipping, blending)
SCOTUS	acronym (Supreme Court of the United States)
ciao	borrowing (Italian)
ecocide	multiple (clipping and blending *ecology* + -*cide* morpheme for "death")

APPENDIX 6.1

Selected False Cognates between English and Spanish

Spanish translation for English word	English word	Spanish word that looks/sounds similar to English word	True meaning in Spanish
avergonzado	embarrassed	embarazada	being pregnant
estreñido	constipated	constipado	having a head cold or congestion
engaño	deception	decepción	disappointment
emocionado	excited	excitado	being sexually aroused
abarrotes	groceries	groseriás	spoken vulgarities
eficaz	effective	efectivo	cash
requisitos	qualifications	calificaciones	grades
éxito	success	suceso	event, happening
realmente	actually	actualmente	at this time
apoyar	support	soportar	put up with, tolerate
ayudar	assist	asistir	attend
alfombra	carpet	carpeta	folder
darse cuenta de	realize	realizar	achieve
tela	fabric	fábrica	factory
salida	exit	éxito	success
asistir	attend	atender	take care of

More English and Spanish Words from Latin Roots

Related Spanish words	Related English words	Root meaning
		solo (Latin, alone)
		cent (Latin, one hundred)
		circulus (Latin, ring)
		vacare (v) (Latin, to empty) vacuus (n)

CHAPTER SEVEN

"The Same, but Different"

Reading Fluency in English as a New Language

New Vocabulary in This Chapter: *fluency, automaticity theory of reading, processing efficiency, oral reading fluency (ORF), miscues, prosody, rate, accuracy, chunking (parsing), washback, phonological decoding, phonological loop, cognitive load*

Reading fluency has been considered a core literacy skill since the National Reading Panel (NRP) called attention to it in 2000, and it continues to be part of balanced literacy programs throughout the United States and beyond. Once considered a neglected area of reading research and practice, reading fluency is now well represented in both research and in the curriculum.

This chapter briefly reviews research on reading fluency assessment and instruction for both native English speakers and ELLs, discusses the instruments and the measures used to assess fluency, and shares best practices. We also adopt a critical stance with regard to fluency assessments and ELLs.

A Working Definition of Fluency

According to the NRP (2000), "The fluent reader is one who can perform multiple tasks—such as word recognition and comprehension—at the same time" (p. 3.8). Samuels (2007) defines it even more simply: "In order to comprehend a text, one must identify the words on the page and one must construct their meaning" (p. 564). Achieving reading fluency is the stage of the reading development process in which readers are able to advance from identifying individual words to being able to construct meaning from connected text. Because of this connection, fluency is often considered the "bridge" between decoding and comprehension, and fluency-building activities are seen as the way to cross that bridge. Figure 7.1 gives a visualization of the fluency bridge.

In the field of ESL and foreign language learning, *fluency* has a completely different meaning from the definition used in the reading field, and the difference has created some confusion. In language learning, when we say a person is fluent, we mean that he or she has native-like proficiency in speaking a new language. We want to distinguish this definition of fluency from the definition of reading fluency, which is also called simply *fluency,* or the ability to simultaneously decode and construct meaning from print. *Fluency* has the Latin root *fluentem,* meaning lax, relaxed, or flowing, and other words with this root include *fluid, flow, flowing,* and *fluidity.* Although the first definition is about oral proficiency in a new language and the second definition is about reading, both have the root idea that the activity is effortless, smooth, and trouble free. A fluent speaker of a foreign language has no trouble communicating orally on any subject, and a fluent reader can easily handle reading material with ease and confidence. In this chapter and throughout the book, however, we use *fluency* only to refer to a reader's ability to simultaneously decode and comprehend a written text.

Automaticity Theory

Why is fluency important to reading? A theoretical explanation can be found in LaBerge and Samuels's *automaticity theory of reading* (1974). Their theory is based on the idea that people have a finite supply of cognitive resources available while reading. Skillful readers engage in rapid, unconscious, and automatic decoding of texts. When readers achieve automaticity, they can devote their cognitive attention to constructing meaning while reading. In effect, readers who cannot process text fluently don't have enough mental energy to construct meaning while reading. Fluency might also be described as *processing efficiency* (Koda, 2005). When decoding is inefficient and cumbersome, with many stops and starts, it's hard to devote mental resources to the active process of reading comprehension because so much energy must be taken up in identifying the individual words. We can apply this concept not only to reading, but also to any activity that takes a lot of concentration before we get good at it. For example, a beginning piano student cannot learn to play pieces of music until he or she learns basic keyboard techniques and basic sight reading.

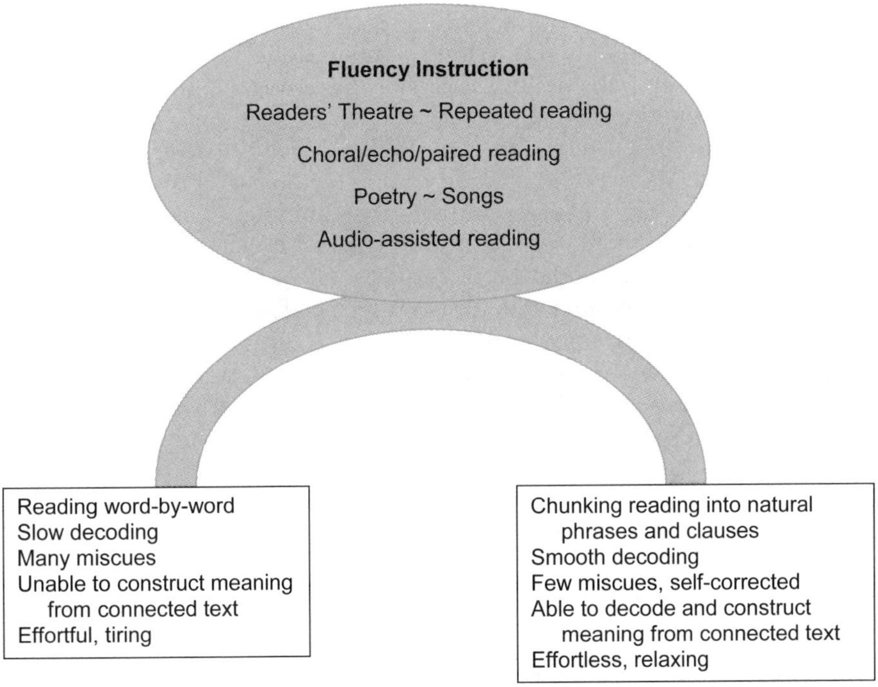

FIGURE 7.1. Fluency: The "bridge."

If we apply automaticity theory to ELLs and reading, it's easy to see why it would take ELLs longer to become fluent in reading. ELL readers need to recognize the English words and access their meanings as they appear in a text, even though their knowledge of English words and their understanding of English sentence structures is still developing.

The idea of processing efficiency meshes well with Birch's (2015) hypothetical model of the reading process discussed in Chapter 2. It stresses the importance of efficiency in the use of low-level or "bottom-up" language knowledge as an indispensable component of reading comprehension.

Measuring Reading Comprehension

Oral Reading Fluency as a Proxy for Reading Comprehension

In planning language arts instruction, teachers need to be able to evaluate the reading levels of their students. Historically, reading comprehension has been assessed mainly by (1) answering questions about a reading through a written test, (2) writing responses or reflections based on a prompt, or (3) through retelling, especially for younger children. To make judgments about the reading level of a child based on these kinds of assessments requires much time and care. In 1985, Deno discovered another, quicker way to identify the reading comprehension level of students: by asking them to read a passage out loud for 1 minute. Their oral reading fluency, or "ORF," score was highly correlated with their reading comprehension level from a standardized reading test. *Oral reading fluency (ORF)* measures were sensitive enough to show even small improvements in reading—when reading comprehension went up, so did oral reading fluency scores (Deno, 1985). These informal ORF assessments were usually 1 minute long and used a method of counting words correct per minute—the number of words read minus the number of errors or *miscues*. Correlations between curriculum-based oral reading and silent reading comprehension were confirmed in many studies (e.g., Fuchs, Fuchs, & Maxwell, 1988; Shinn, Knutson, Good, Tilly, & Collins, 1992), and based on the robust research, oral reading fluency assessments gradually began to be used in the classroom.

Prosody as an Additional Measure

When oral reading fluency began to be measured in many classrooms, some researchers noticed that the profile of "expressive reading" by students also seemed to provide information about their silent reading comprehension, sometimes correlating even better with silent reading comprehension than words correct per minute (Dowhower, 1991). *Prosody* refers to features of "expressiveness" in oral reading, such as pausing, vocal intonations, the loudness and softness of words, and vowel lengthening. Differences in prosody reflect an understanding of the syntactic structure of sentences, which goes above and beyond mere word reading. Prosody is part of the listening comprehension "endowment" that children receive when adults read to them; expressive reading gives listeners information about the characters in the story, especially in their direct speech. For example, an expressive reader makes sure that the Wolf in the fairy tale has a low, growly voice to reinforce its scary role in the story. The auditory information available in prosodic reading is a tool children use to comprehend text before they are ever exposed to written text. Studies of prosody supported the finding that children who read with more "adult-like" intonation in second grade became stronger readers (Miller & Schwanenflugel, 2006). Once prosody entered the conversation, ORF assessments began to include expressive reading as one of the measures of oral reading, and rubrics that included prosody were implemented.

However, evaluating prosody is bafflingly difficult to objectify, and words correct per minute continues to be the preferred measure.

ORF measures, or "fluency snapshots" can provide teachers with a handy way to do flexible grouping, match children with books at an appropriate level, keep track of student progress, and flag students who need early intervention because their reading is not progressing to grade level.

ELLs and Fluency Research

How does this method of assessing reading apply to ELLs? Despite the enthusiasm for reading fluency, there is limited research to validate ORF assessments as measures of reading comprehension for ELL students. Much fluency research in the reading field intentionally omits ELLs from the control and experimental groups, and large research studies and white papers tend not to disaggregate results for ELLs (Lems, 2012, p. 244).

There is some research focused on ELLs, however. Baker and Good (1995) found that an ORF measure predicts reading comprehension for second-grade Spanish ELLs as well as for their L1 English peers. Ramirez (2001) found higher correlations between fifth-grade Spanish ELLs' oral reading fluency and their silent reading comprehension than she found in correlations for their reading comprehension and other reading scores. Mild correlations were found for 1-minute oral reading fluency scores and state reading tests for third-grade Spanish-speaking ELLs (Vanderwood, Linklater, & Healy, 2008), and third- through eighth-grade Spanish-speaking ELLs (McTague, Lems, Butler, & Carmona, 2012). Quirk and Beem (2012) found that correlations for ELLs in grades 2, 3, and 5 generally matched those of native English speakers; however, a substantial number of the ELL students had significant comprehension gaps. In the absence of large studies that focus on ELLs, it is impossible to conclude that ORF assessment is a valid and reliable measure of ELL reading comprehension (Crosson & Lesaux, 2010).

Fluency Instruction

We shift our focus from a discussion of the promises and perils of ORF as a representation of silent reading comprehension to the other side of the coin: What activities can actually improve silent reading comprehension? And is it possible that some kinds of oral reading practice have a positive impact on silent reading?

Components of Fluency Instruction

Fluency instruction is characterized by one or more of the following:

1. Some kind of reading repetition or practice.
2. Modeling by an expert or more proficient other.
3. Some kind of progress monitoring (Rasinski, 2003).

As you can see, none of these components specifically requires oral reading; however, fluency instruction usually does involve it.

Many kinds of activities fall under the umbrella of fluency instruction. They include such diverse techniques as Readers' Theatre, poetry performance, audio-assisted reading, echo reading, lyric singing, paired reading, timed repeated reading, simulated TV broadcasts, podcasts, choral reading, and more (Rasinski, Blachowicz, & Lems, 2012).

In some fluency programs, the reading levels of striving readers have been boosted by several grade levels in only a few months. There is also widespread anecdotal evidence that students enjoy these activities, too, and that they increase students' motivation to read. In addition to assisting in more automatic retrieval of words, fluency instruction ensures that striving readers are reading more words than they otherwise would. For ELLs, this is even more important: "It is clear that if fluent reading is to be developed by English language learners," warned Hiebert and Fisher (2006), "the amount of exposure to texts that students have in classrooms needs to increase" (p. 291).

Benefits of Fluency Instruction with ELLs

There are six distinct benefits to using fluency instruction with ELLs, and they go above and beyond benefits that accrue to native speakers.

Chunking and Prosody

In addition to increasing the *rate* and *accuracy* of word recognition, fluency instruction gives ELL readers practice in developing two important reading competencies: *chunking* and *prosody*. *Chunking* (which is sometimes called *parsing*) is the ability to separate or combine written text into meaningful phrase or clause units. It requires knowledge of syntax, and it develops unconsciously for native speakers as they learn the patterns of a language through listening to it and speaking it. When they start to learn to read, they apply their auditory memory of how words cluster together in spoken form and apply that to the words they see across a line of text.

For Kiennesha, a native speaker of English, developing the chunking skill is closely related to her auditory memory of the sounds of the words. For example, when Kiennesha pauses at periods or changes her intonation pattern for a yes/no question, she is showing that she can chunk the phrases or clauses of a sentence correctly as she "reads the punctuation."

However, prosody goes well beyond the ability to chunk the words in a sentence. It includes interpretive features such as "getting into character" for reading certain texts by speaking more loudly, using variations in voice tone, or pausing for emphasis. When working with ELLs, we reckon that these additional oral reading skills might come considerably later than chunking skills or may not come at all. Because of their developing oracy in English, ELLs may have limited knowledge of how a written text might sound in terms of its expressive features. Therefore, for ELLs, we may expect their knowledge of chunking to precede—or even exceed—their expressive reading. In fact, it may be premature or unrealistic to expect ELLs to read expressively. Nonetheless, practicing both chunking and prosody are important ways to boost reading comprehension, and they can be practiced together.

Expressive Reading

Expressive reading can assist in comprehension. It is usually thought to include pausing, intonation patterns, and word lengthening. Interestingly, Johnson and Moore (1997) found a moderate but significant relationship between the reading comprehension scores of ELLs and how "native-like" their pausing behaviors were when reading English aloud. Seeing how prosody looks and hearing how it sounds are very useful for ELLs, and fluency practice gives them a chance to do both at the same time. In spoken English, the most important words in a text are longer, louder, and higher pitched, which underscores their importance. Reading along silently or quietly with a text that is being read aloud helps students create these associations. Oral reading practice probably has positive effects on teaching and learning, or positive *washback,* on ELLs' pronunciation and speaking fluency, too, but this has not been validated.

A Spanish teacher at Addison Trail High School in Addison, Illinois, says the following about oral reading.

> *Whenever I have to read aloud in front of an "audience" I never comprehend what I am reading. The weird thing is, though, when I don't understand something that I have read silently, I read it aloud. As I am reading it aloud, I accentuate the words of importance and then I understand. This seems odd to me since I would classify myself as a visual learner. Even when I write, I usually speak aloud as I write. It really helps me to hear and see what I am trying to understand.*
> —KATHLEEN MCCOLAUGH

Phonological Decoding and the Phonological Loop

Phonological decoding, or pronouncing written words, is a vital skill for beginning readers. The ability to decode and pronounce words is one of the most powerful predictors of reading success, even as early as first grade (Bowers, Golden, Kennedy, & Young, 1994; Share & Stanovich, 1995; Torgeson & Burgess, 1998; Wagner, Torgeson, & Rashotte, 1994). This ability has been found in many languages, including those with other kinds of orthographies. Koda (2005) ranks it as "number one": "Phonological decoding is perhaps the most indispensable competence for reading acquisition in all languages" (p. 34). The reason is that, even for mature readers, having a good phonological representation of a word helps retrieve it from working memory. It is a core literacy skill (p. 185).

When we see or hear a written word that we know, we retrieve it from our long-term memory and move it into our short-term memory for use. How does the word get into our memory to begin with? It is stored through a process called the *phonological loop* (Baddeley, Gathercole, & Papagno, 1998, p. 1158; Birch, 2015). When we encounter a new word for the first time, the phonological loop converts the visual or audio stimulus of the word into a sound-based "phonological image." The brain, in turn, creates a short-term "slot" to hold the word, which can be filled with semantic associations at that time or later, at which time we have learned it. The phonological loop is like a messenger, taking the information and moving it into auditory memory. The loop moves data from the eyes or ears into short-term and then long-term storage. Rehearsal solidifies the word in long-term memory through visual and auditory repetition.

What ELLs do not have available in their long-term memory is that reservoir of remembered words, the listening vocabulary, that native speakers accumulate through the natural, automatic process of acquiring our first language. As a result, it's really important that ELLs have enough exposure to a word to secure it in memory through the phonological loop, and fluency practice provides that exposure. In fact, ELLs in a repeated reading study cited repetition as one of the factors contributing to their reading comprehension progress (Taguchi, Takayasu-Maass, & Gorsuch, 2004).

Stamina for Reading Connected Text

In addition to vocabulary growth, fluency practice helps build stamina in the key skill of reading connected text. Hiebert and Fisher (2006) note that there are reports of sharp discrepancies in the ability of first-grade Spanish ELLs to read individual words from a list compared with reading connected text (p. 291). Reading comprehension requires moving swiftly and accurately through connected texts in many genres, and fluency helps students build the endurance to keep moving and bring text processing up to speed.

Confidence and Motivation

Children who have the opportunity to listen to or practice passages multiple times develop more self-confidence and independence as readers (Koskinen et al., 1995), provided they are in a setting in which their affective filter is low. These techniques might include a performance, a home–school program with audiotapes, or partner reading.

Reading Rate

The rate at which people read in a second language is slower than that of their first language, and below a certain rate, it is impossible for readers to keep up with an academic curriculum (Birch, 2015; Rasinski, 2000). ELLs benefit from opportunities to learn techniques to increase their reading rate so that they can become successful readers of academic texts. Rate-building activities include timed repeated readings (oral or silent), charting progress on a graph, or repeating reading until a certain target rate is reached (Anderson, 1999).

Success in Fluency Instruction for ELLs

Research has shown impressive results for ELLs in fluency programs. We feature three here: repeated reading, audio-assisted reading (Taguchi, Gorsuch, Lems, & Rozzwell, 2016), and Readers' Theatre.

Repeated Reading

Repeated reading gives students practice in learning syntax patterns as well as unknown vocabulary. In a key work, "The Method of Repeated Readings," Samuels (1979) found that when students silently read the same passage up to four times, their comprehension of not only that passage but other passages improved dramatically. Hiebert and Fisher (2006) found that first-grade ELLs benefited from daily fluency interventions that included repeated reading and modeling by the teacher, whether they were reading highly decodable books or those with more high-frequency, high-imagery vocabulary. The benefit of repeated reading has been verified through eye-tracking technology, which tracks the time a reader's eyes stop, or "fixate," on words, how many words they fixate upon, and how many times the eyes return to a word. When L1 readers engaged in repeated reading, eye-tracking technology found that they "spent less time fixating on words, made fewer fixations per word, and revisited the previously fixated parts of the text progressively fewer times as they became more familiar with them" (Taguchi et al., 2016, p. 109).

Audio-Assisted Reading

Audio-assisted reading, sometimes called reading while listening, or "assisted RR" when combined with repeated reading, consists of looking at the words of a text while also listening to an oral performance of the text, whether prerecorded or live. When Pluck (2006) implemented an audio-assisted reading fluency intervention for L1 Maori ELLs and native English speakers in New Zealand, she found almost double the level of progress in word recognition, accuracy, comprehension, and spelling for the ELLs compared with the native English speakers. Koskinen et al. (1995) used audio-assisted book reading as part of a home–school literacy program with first-grade ELLs, and both the teacher and parents noticed a marked increase by the children in daily conversations about books as well as an increased motivation to read. In addition, children became able to read more difficult books. At the university level, Woodall (2010) found that low-proficiency ELLs made more gains in reading comprehension when they were able to listen to an audio version of the text while reading than those made by their "reading only" counterparts.

Many reading programs now have audio-assisted versions that ELLs and others can use to practice reading aloud. Listening to audiobooks available through digital devices, an audio track in a classroom or computer lab, or singing along with a musical recording are all excellent techniques for modeling language for ELLs and providing access to the sounds, appearance, and meanings of English. One caution should be kept in mind, however: Passages read by a voice synthesizer, and some Internet audio samples, do not have natural prosody, and therefore may not assist students in acquiring natural language.

In Pluck's intervention, ELLs gained an average of 2 years in their reading comprehension level from a 15-week audio-assisted reading program for 1 hour a day (Pluck, 2006). The students read short, high-interest stories along with listening to a tape, repeating their practice until they could perform the reading on their own. The program from which the study came, Rainbow Reading, is now widely used in New Zealand and other English-speaking countries.

Readers' Theatre

Kozub (2000) discovered that Readers' Theatre was very effective in developing the fluency of her ELLs. Initially, the language instructor can model the text with exaggerated stress and intonation to highlight its prosodic contours. Practicing the prosody of a poem or dramatic performance allows students to develop the expressive features so important to the development of L2 oral fluency and adds a positive social dimension to the practice. Also, the performance itself can be motivating, and students may practice intensively before the date of the Readers' Theatre "debut" performance.

Besides these techniques, research supports the success of several other techniques for developing ELL reading fluency. Lems (2001a) and other teachers have used poetry performances in adult ESL classrooms. Li and Nes (2001) studied Chinese ELLs who received weekly English language paired reading activities at grade level, led by a skilled adult. The children made impressive gains in accuracy and fluency, even during the maintenance period, when the sessions became less frequent and then ceased. In another case, McCauley and McCauley (1992) successfully used teacher-led choral reading to promote language learning by ELLs and confirmed its success.

Recorded Books as a Resource

Whether they are found in a listening center in the classroom or in the school or public library, or sent home in book bags, books with CD or audio files help ELLs practice listening comprehension and build vocabulary. Many teachers already know this, but they may not realize that the listening element is not only a bridge to reading growth, but also is a listening comprehension practice in its own right. When students listen as they read or read as they listen, they get a double dose of comprehensible input.

Breaking Text into Smaller Units

Because the sheer volume of listening required for ELLs is exhausting, teachers should keep the amount of their instruction manageable. Lectures should be avoided in instructional settings with ELLs—and that includes lengthy teacher explanations about what is planned for the day! It is particularly important for content teachers, especially at the high school level, to find interactive ways to explain course content without lecturing and reading from the textbook. Some of the ways teachers can guide ELLs in building their listening vocabulary in the content areas include:

1. Clearly displaying key words and concepts on the board or screen.
2. Previewing and reviewing concepts to serve as "fence posts" for the core curricular content.
3. Using pictures and video clips.
4. Creating small-group activities in which peers can help each other.

Building the Comprehension Habit

Professor Yvonne Gonzalez, a specialist in bilingual special education at Texas Women's University, checks comprehension as her ELLs read aloud by asking them to read a sentence for her, then stopping them halfway through and asking them to look up and finish the sentence. "If they are really constructing meaning while they read," she says, "they will be able to finish the sentence with a logical sentence ending" (Gonzalez, personal communication, January, 2008). Another way of checking comprehension is to ask students to retell the gist of each paragraph to a partner.

Problems with Fluency Assessments

As the habit of taking regular ORF snapshots has become standard in thousands of schools, two concerning changes have occurred: an overemphasis on oral reading to the detriment of practicing silent reading comprehension strategies and the questionable validity of the assessment. We will briefly sketch out the problems in these two areas.

When ORF assessment became widely adopted in classrooms, oral reading practice was also introduced, and with it, a shift away from a focus on comprehension. In 2009, Applegate, Applegate, and Modla, in a study of students in grades 2–10, found that fully one third of children considered strong readers by fluency assessment measures were weak in their ability to demonstrate thoughtful comprehension of text. It led the researchers to wonder whether "the freed up resources that result from automaticity and fluency do not necessarily or automatically flow toward comprehension" (p. 519). The researchers reported that reading teachers noticed "an overemphasis in their schools on the development of oral reading indicators such as rate and accuracy without an accompanying emphasis on comprehension" (p. 512).

There are also inherent weaknesses in the testing setting and the assessment process itself. Children are often asked to do "cold readings" in noisy hallways, sometimes by paraprofessionals or even parent volunteers, because the teacher does not have time to evaluate each student. The passages themselves are not usually curriculum based, but are downloaded, or purchased from publishers who specialize in such assessments, and the passages may or may not be vetted for cultural sensitivity, background knowledge, or word frequencies. The readings are completely out of context of the curriculum. Most important, in a mixed school building, modifications to ORF testing are not made for ELLs. ELLs are expected to do a timed, cold reading of passages in English that they have never seen before, often in front of an unknown rater with a stopwatch. This is a perfect recipe for a sky-high "affective filter" that may cause blowback into the classroom.

Look at the effect that an overemphasis on oral reading had on this Polish ELL, who is now a teacher.

My science teacher had us read entire chapters aloud in class. She would move up and down the rows and have each student read one paragraph at a time. Because I was an ELL and I was very self-conscious about reading aloud in front of my peers, I would count out which paragraph I would have to read so that I could rehearse it ahead of time before my time came to read. As a result, I would not be paying attention to the previous paragraphs that were being read aloud and, when my turn came, I would focus on my pronunciation, rate, and prosody, instead of the meaning of the text. My own oral reading experience in Science class made me dread science. I did not understand anything that was read by others or by me aloud in class, not only because I was busy rehearsing my assigned paragraph, but also because the language was just words that oftentimes were unfamiliar to me. As a result, I not only hated Science class, but also science. This, in turn, limited my own professional opportunities as I never wanted to enter the medical field because I just never considered myself good in science and I never found myself enjoying learning about it.–Sylwia Bania

As a result of widespread "pullout" 1-minute fluency testing, many students have gotten the message, either directly or indirectly, that the goal of reading is to read as fast as possible. Even if the instructions invite them to "read with expression," students do not take the time to slow down and may have no idea what that instruction means. In fact, they may realize that expressiveness is really not counted in the score, only words correct per minute, so they will think only about speed. Students are interested in their numerical scores, and this syndrome has been described and commented upon by teachers we teach, in numerous settings, for a number of years. As consultants, we have also witnessed and inadvertently taken part in this system.

The idea that reading fluency equals fast reading is problematic, but there is a second mutation of fluency assessment that is even more serious. It has now become a widespread practice to give students random passages to read, and to expect students to read these passages cold, while being timed, and then ask them to immediately answer comprehension questions about the passage.

There are serious problems with using the same passage for oral reading and for answering comprehension questions. Teachers know from their classroom experience that when students read out loud in class, their ability to construct meaning at the same time is reduced. They are too busy performing the text to be able to comprehend it deeply. The same is true for educated adults! To make an analogy, it would be like taking Karima, a new driver, out on the road for a driving test and then at the same time judging her posture at the wheel!

The original research and the confirmatory research on fluency did not combine oral reading with an assessment of reading comprehension using the same text; in fact, the correlations between oral reading fluency and silent reading comprehension were all established using different texts, at different times.

Problems Specific to ELLs

Using oral reading as an assessment of ELLs' reading comprehension is problematic for three key reasons beyond those facing native speakers of English (Birch, 2015; Helman, 2005; Lems, 2005; Riedel, 2007): the foreign-accent factor, differences in processing time, and word calling.

The Foreign-Accent Factor

The first is the "foreign-accent factor": ELLs may mispronounce a word because some of the sounds do not exist in their first language and they have not learned to say them in English, or because the letters they are trying to pronounce map to different sounds in their L1. As a result, raters listening to the oral reading may mark mispronunciations as miscues (mistakes) in the reading performance even though the ELL reader knows the meaning of a word. For example, native speakers of Persian, the language of Iran, may pronounce the letter *w* as a /v/ in English because the closest equivalent to the *w* in English is pronounced as a /v/ in Persian. Therefore, Mina, a Persian ELL, might read the word *went* as/vent/, and a rater might deduct it as a miscue even though Mina correctly identified and understood the word. Teachers may say, "Oh, we accounted for the foreign accent and didn't deduct the word," but this decision is often anecdotal and creates an unreliable assessment. The foreign accent issue becomes even greater when ELLs start their study of English in adolescence, when their foreign accent is more likely to be set permanently in place.

Differences in Processing Time

The second difference is that ELLs may take a longer time to retrieve and pronounce words because of their limited English vocabulary, limited pronunciation skills in English, and interference from their L1 orthography. These factors may result in a score that places them in a lower proficiency reading group than they are capable of, based on rate alone, or provide reading materials that are less challenging than they should be.

ELLs may have difficultly with preparing to pronounce a word correctly, even if they know the word, or if it is not an obstacle to their comprehension. In particular, proper nouns, such as place names and family names, are especially opaque in English. As a result, ELLs may spend a long time trying to sound them out, as can be seen in the story below.

> *When I analyzed the oral reading of adult ELLs for my doctoral dissertation, I found that they made a large number of miscues on proper nouns in the reading passage. For example, most of the Chinese ELLs in the study were stopped cold by the name* Indianapolis *in the passage. They struggled mightily to pronounce it, mostly coming to an unsuccessful conclusion after several tries. That one word added several seconds to their reading rate, and the miscue was deducted anyway.*—KRISTIN

> *When ELLs are reading words of foreign origin aloud, they often don't know whether to pronounce the word with Anglicized pronunciation or the pronunciation from the original language, and they freeze. I've noticed this problem with the words* Des Plaines, Illinois *and* Des Moines, Iowa.—LEAH

ELLs and Word Calling

The third issue of concern is *word calling*, or decoding a text without comprehending it. If ELLs are able to decode and pronounce English words accurately, they may still not have the English words in their listening vocabulary, and thus may not comprehend the text. Word calling, famously dubbed "barking at print" by researcher Jeanne Chall (1983), can occur with L1 English speakers, but research tends to support the notion that it is not commonplace (Meisinger, Bradley, Schwanenflugel, Kuhn, & Morris, 2009). Students who are slow and inaccurate oral readers are also weak in answering grade-level comprehension questions (Markell & Deno, 1997). Also, researchers found that teachers who consider their students to be word callers may be using subjective criteria (Hamilton & Shinn, 2003).

However, word calling may be a real phenomenon for some ELLs. Helman (2005) notes that Spanish ELLs she studied in Arizona struggled with comprehension questions in an oral reading assessment and warned, "A classroom teacher may make the assumption from hearing students reading out loud that comprehension is occurring. This assumption is less likely to be true for ELLs, who may have adequate accuracy and fluency on lower-level passages, but may not understand the vocabulary and content" (p. 221). A longitudinal investigation of 261 Spanish ELLs from first through sixth grade revealed that although their word decoding was on pace for the norm, their reading comprehension scores began to fall behind, starting in the third grade (Nakamoto, Lindsey, & Manis, 2007).

Samuels (2007) echoes this concern: "As Riedel reports in his research, about 15% of the students who take the Oral Reading Fluency test [of the DIBELS] get misidentified as good readers, when, in fact, they have poor comprehension. These misidentified students are often English-language learners who have vocabulary problems that interfere with comprehension" (p. 564). Kim (2012) found that Spanish-speaking ELL first graders had similar oral reading scores for word reading rate and accuracy in English, but lower reading comprehension scores than their L1 English counterparts, leading to the conclusion that fluency and comprehension may map differently for children whose first language is not English.

Because of the complicated nature of cross-linguistic influence and the diverse backgrounds and experiences ELLs bring to the classroom, oral reading for ELLs appears to be a less valid measure of reading comprehension than it is for L1 English speakers, at least when learners are at the Beginning or Developing levels of English proficiency (Lems, 2005). Thomas and Collier (2002) note that it takes 5–7 years for ELLs to achieve a level of English proficiency on a par with native English speakers of their age, and this lag can be reflected in fluency scores for some time. A score below the mean for a certain time of year at a certain grade level may not warrant the concern that would be raised for a native speaker of English because the ELL student is learning an additional language. In addition, if an intervention is prescribed, it may not be appropriate. In short, any important decisions about the reading program for ELLs should not rely solely on oral reading scores and should take into account student language growth, teacher observations, and forms of informal assessment, such as retellings and discussions.

Even when ELLs decode well and know the words they are reading, the *cognitive load*, or mental engagement, required is considerably heavier because the words are not in their first language. For all of these reasons, ELLs should not be evaluated according to the same benchmarks as those used for native speakers (Birch, 2015; McTague et al., 2012). All of that being said, monitoring the progress of an individual student over time can still be useful because increases in oral reading scores reflect increases in reading level for both L1 English learners and ELLs (Fuchs, Fuchs, Hosp, & Jenkins, 2001; Lems, 2005).

Many researchers have come to the conclusion suggested by Quirk and Beem (2012): "Practitioners should be cautious when making identification and instructional decisions for ELL students based solely on oral reading fluency data" (p. 539). Oral reading fluency can be thought of as an additional source of data, in a one-on-one setting, for an informal snapshot of classroom progress.

Many teachers have never had the opportunity to try repeated oral reading of a passage and process the experience through adult eyes. To provide an opportunity to have this experience, we have included a passage for repeated reading (Appendix 7.1), as well as a demonstration of three ways that text can be marked for oral reading (Appendix 7.2). We have also provided a chart on which you can score your own performance and a chart that can be used to track student scores across several passages (Appendix 7.3).

HOW DOES THIS LOOK IN THE CLASSROOM?

Increasing Reading Rate

Timed repeated reading and other fluency rate practices can help students increase their reading rate and serve as motivators. When doing repeated reading to increase reading rate, passages should be at the students' already attained reading level so that the focus can be on processing text more rapidly rather than on guessing the meanings of unknown words.

Some digital software and apps can also help increase reading rate. However, rate building shouldn't be the main point of fluency practice, or even of repeated reading practice (Zutell, Donelson, Bevans, & Todt, 2006, p. 270). When students practice in order to increase their reading rate, they are not building the habit of reading for comprehension. Although an increase in reading rate may transfer to other reading passages, the reading done in timed settings is not likely to yield high levels of comprehension. Of course, this is exactly what so much high-stakes testing asks students to do; it forces them to rush through random passages and answer comprehension questions with little time for reflection or rereading. If we know this practice is not good in the classroom, why is it used for so many standardized tests?

Segmenting Text

Segmenting text into lines that break at natural phrase endings, or by marking with slashes, is a great technique for ELLs. In one study, segmented text produced better comprehension in young readers than conventional text (O'Shea & Sindelar, 1983). This technique was validated in research comparing it to other techniques that used only repeated reading (Hoffman, 1987). Of course, poetry naturally segments phrases into different lines, and lines from a skit or Readers' Theatre show the breaks of different partners in a conversation. All of these methods are good places to start to look for authentic text that is naturally segmented. Rasinski (1990) proposed an alternate method of tracking chunking knowledge, not by having students read aloud, but by having them check the text at phrasal breaks themselves, using a pencil. To be sure there was high reliability, Rasinski first had skilled readers mark the texts. A correct score for the students consisted of a check made by at least 50% of the skilled readers. Example of these three ways to segment text is shown in Appendix 7.2 at the end of the chapter.

Choral Reading, Echo Reading, Popcorn Reading

There are many different ways to arrange oral reading in class, and educators unhappy about the stressfulness of round robin reading have found ways that are less stressful but still motivating. Do you remember the stress of waiting for your turn in round robin reading? This bilingual art teacher certainly does.

> *My earliest memory in a school setting, reading aloud, is from second grade. I was a slower reader than my peers at the time and was insecure in my academic abilities. I can remember the aluminum can of popsicle sticks from my teacher's desk and the stress I felt each time she vigorously shook the container. I feared my name being selected because I knew that she would make known each of my mistakes as I made them.*
> –BEATRIZ LAPPAY

Whole-group instruction can give students the opportunity to hear the teacher modeling expressive reading. Here is what a third-grade teacher does to ensure that students do not experience anxiety about oral reading.

I very rarely do read-alouds as a whole group, and none of those read-alouds are done without the students choosing to participate. I never call on students to read aloud without their consent. I also find that a whole-group lesson is a great time for me to model fluent reading and listening comprehension, and I use guided reading and partner reading as opportunities for the students to practice their own fluency.
–MARY HELMSTETTER

Choral reading, with the instructor in the lead, works very well for beginning ELLs and very young readers who do not know the sounds of words and do not want to be singled out. Echo reading, in which students chime in right after the instructor, allows for a little more individual performance but still allows the student to safely shadow the main speaker.

In popcorn reading, students take turns reading a short passage, then stop when they feel like it and pass the reading on to the next person. Here is how one math specialist handles it.

We do have a popcorn reading activity where students who start reading aloud can call on a classmate to read aloud. As a class we've decided a reader needs to read a complete sentence as a minimum, but they are welcome to read as much past that complete sentence as they would like. Some of my students that struggle with oral reading fluency have expressed they enjoy popcorn reading because they aren't forced to read a lot, but they can read something to the class. Each student also has a pass at least once during the session. I tend to have students read aloud only for a second reading of text and after we have discussed many of the content vocabulary words that students may encounter when reading. I'm much more concerned that students feel safe to participate as that is not what I experienced for others in my classes as a child.—MISTY J. RICHMOND

Cross-Grade Reading, Buddy Reading

Older students, whether ELLs or native English speakers, can benefit from the opportunity to read to younger students. Here is how a sixth-grade teacher of ELLs set up a cross-grade fluency project.

In my own classroom in order to start practicing fluency, I started having them read Green Eggs and Ham. *It was challenging, but students enjoyed it. I also talked to the kindergarten teacher, and we had my sixth graders go read to her kindergarteners. My sixth graders would practice their book so that when they read it to the kindergarteners they would sound "like a teacher."*–MALITZINA SALAZAR

Even when students are the same age, having them take turns reading passages to each other in pairs can be useful. When it is a regular activity, they get used to the routine and get right to work. Buddy reading, also called partner reading or paired reading, is one of the five core activities in the popular "Daily Five™" curriculum—in the category called "Read to Someone" (Boushey & Mozer, 2014). Kids settle in nooks around the classroom and take turns reading paragraphs, each holding his or her own copy of the text. They can also time each other with a stopwatch for fluency-rate practice, or they can paraphrase their partner's reading, to focus on listening comprehension. Buddy reading engages ELLs in actively using language as listeners, speakers, readers, and communicators, and keeps the affective filter low.

Rhythm Walks

In this kinesthetically focused fluency activity, after reading a poem or short story together as a class, the students and the teacher divide the reading into phrases or clauses, write them on construction or flipchart paper, and lay them out in sequence on the floor around the room (Peebles, 2007). Students walk around the room and read out each phrase as they come to its page. They can repeat the path several times, practicing the reading each time.

Classroom Fluency Norms and Diverse Assessments

Establishing classroom fluency norms makes sense because native speaker fluency rates do not always reflect rates of ELLs. If you work in a setting with many ELLs, we suggest creating local norms by collecting students' reading fluency scores over time and building the database as more students are assessed. If school fluency measures are already taken, disaggregate the scores for ELLs as a group and individually, and be prepared to expect somewhat lower scores from students whose native languages are orthographically distant from English. When using fluency assessments with a comprehension component (not recommended), allow ELLs to read a text silently more than once, do not impose an arbitrary speed limit, and be sure that students clearly understand that there is a comprehension component before they begin the activity.

Digital Resources for Fluency Practice

The digital revolution has made available a multitude of free resources for audio-assisted reading. Children can read a book and listen to it at the same time at the Starfall website (*www.starfall.com*), which has many folk and fairy tales. We especially like this site because the text is clean and readable, the stories are well written, and the readers are children with delightfully clear and expressive voices. Another resource is the set of picture book stories read aloud by the actors at Storyline Online (*www.storyline.net*), a website run as a community service from the Actors Guild.

It is also easy to find stories read aloud by authors at their author websites or their publisher websites. Teachers will also find wonderful short interviews and book trailers by authors and illustrators at publisher and author websites and fan sites. A few of our favorite author and illustrator interviews and sites at the time this book was published include early childhood author/illustrator Eric Carle (2017; e.g., *The Very Hungry Caterpillar*), graphic novelist Gene Yuan (2017; e.g., *American Born Chinese*), J. K. Rowling (1997–2016; the *Harry Potter* series), and Mem Fox (2016; e.g., *Possum Magic*).

QUESTIONS FOR FURTHER STUDY

1. If you had to choose three important ideas from this chapter, which would you choose? How can you apply these ideas to your larger knowledge of teaching English as a new language?

2. With a partner, practice reading the passage provided in Appendix 7.1 aloud for 1 minute. Using the scoring charts in Appendix 7.3, repeat the timed reading four times, and plot your scores. Note the changes in words read. In addition to any change of number of words read, what other differences did you notice about doing the passage reading four times?

3. If you are able to listen to the oral reading of ELLs, jot down notes about their reading performances. Did anything surprise you?

4. Did you read aloud in school as a child? How did you feel about it? Share with a partner. How might that experience influence how you would plan oral reading activities?

5. Have you ever read a text aloud without understanding a word of it? Talk about it.

6. Do you know people who read well, but cannot read aloud expressively? Do you think reading aloud expressively is an important skill for teachers, or is it optional? Do certain kinds of teachers need to read expressively more than others?

7. Looking at the statement from Kathleen McColaugh (p. 177), do you feel that hearing your own voice as you read helps you, or hinders you? Why? Relate your discussion of this answer to the main ideas of this chapter.

8. Have you had any experience with a fluency instructional technique? If so, how did it go? What did you learn from it?

9. CHALLENGE QUESTION: Find a folktale from a culture you are less familiar with, and create a short Readers' Theatre piece at the reading level of the students you teach or will be teaching. After piloting it with

colleagues, bring it to a class and have students use the piece. If time allows, have them perform it. What did you learn from this experience?

10. CHALLENGE QUESTION: Find a new text and prepare it for use in oral reading fluency assessment, based on a topic you are teaching or plan to teach. There should be two copies of the text: a "clean" copy, in large font size, for the students, and an instructor copy with numbered lines, enough space between lines to note miscues, and a place to write the scores for repeated oral reading. Administer the reading to several students and report on what you learned from the process.

11. CHALLENGE QUESTION: Look at the three ways the sample text is presented in Appendix 7.2. Find three different people and ask each one to read the text in one of the three ways: unmarked, marked, or separated by lines, covering up the two that are not being used. Compare the performances. Which way of presenting the text do you think would be most appropriate for English readers at the Entering or Beginning level? At the Developing, Expanding, or Bridging levels? At the Reaching level? Did you notice differences in rate, accuracy, phrasing, or expression with the different presentations of text? Talk about it.

Sample Text for Oral Reading

	Our increasing reliance on the Internet and the ease of access to the vast resource available
17	online is affecting our thought processes for problem solving, recall and learning. In a new
32	article published in the journal *Memory*, researchers at the University of California, Santa
45	Cruz and University of Illinois, Urbana–Champaign have found that "cognitive offloading," or
58	the tendency to rely on things like the Internet as an aide-mémoire, increases after each use.
74	We might think that memory is something that happens in the head but increasingly it is
90	becoming something that happens with the help of agents outside the head. Benjamin Storm,
104	Sean Stone, and Aaron Benjamin conducted experiments to determine our likelihood to reach for
118	a computer or smartphone to answer questions. Participants were first divided into two groups
132	to answer some challenging trivia questions—one group used just their memory, the other
147	used Google. Participants were then given the option of answering subsequent easier questions
160	by the method of their choice.
166	The results revealed that participants who previously used the Internet to gain information
179	were significantly more likely to revert to Google for subsequent questions than those who
193	relied on memory. Participants also spent less time consulting their own memory before
206	reaching for the Internet; they were not only more likely to do it again, they were likely to do
225	it much more quickly. Remarkably 30% of participants who previously consulted the Internet
238	failed to even attempt to answer a single simple question from memory.
250	Lead author Dr. Benjamin Storm commented, "Memory is changing. Our research shows that
263	as we use the Internet to support and extend our memory we become more reliant on it.
280	Whereas before we might have tried to recall something on our own, now we don't bother.
296	As more information becomes available via smartphones and other devices, we become
308	progressively more reliant on it in our daily lives."
317	This research suggests that using a certain method for fact finding has a marked influence on
333	the probability of future repeat behaviour. Time will tell if this pattern will have any further
349	reaching impacts on human memory than has our reliance on other information sources.

(continued)

362	Certainly the Internet is more comprehensive, dependable, and on the whole faster than the
376	imperfections of human memory, borne out by the more accurate answers from participants in
390	the Internet condition during this research. With a world of information a Google search away
405	on a smartphone, the need to remember trivial facts, figures, and numbers is inevitably
419	becoming less necessary to function in everyday life.

TOTAL: 426 words

Note. Text is from "Cognitive Offloading: How the Internet Is Increasingly Taking Over Human Memory."
Taylor & Francis Newsroom, August 16, 2016. Retrieved from *http://newsroom.taylorandfrancisgroup.com/S=ca
b1064056a90282853372f7a8f295c7173ed04f/news/press-release/cognitive-offloading-how-the-internet-is-increasingly-
taking-over-human-mem#.V7aMIfkrLIX.* Journal reference: Benjamin C. Storm, Sean M. Stone, Aaron S.
Benjamin. Using the Internet to access information inflates future use of the Internet to access other
information. *Memory,* July 18, 2016.

Three Ways to Mark Text for Oral Reading

A. Original text (first paragraph only)

1	Our increasing reliance on the Internet and the ease of access to the vast resource available online is
19	affecting our thought processes for problem solving, recall and learning. In a new article published
34	in the journal *Memory*, researchers at the University of California, Santa Cruz and University of
49	Illinois, Urbana–Champaign have found that "cognitive offloading," or the tendency to rely on things
64	like the Internet as an aide-mémoire, increases after each use. We might think that memory is
80	something that happens in the head but increasingly it is becoming something that happens with the
96	help of agents outside the head. Benjamin Storm, Sean Stone and Aaron Benjamin conducted
110	experiments to determine our likelihood to reach for a computer or smartphone to answer questions.

Procedure: Place text in table with one row for each line of text; use "word count" function for each line, calculate word count for first word at beginning of each line (there may be faster ways, but we use this one).

B. Text divided into phrases, retaining punctuation marks (first two sentences of passage only)

General guideline: start a new line for comma, between the end of a subject and beginning of a predicate (verb phrase), after a period, or before a prepositional phrase or a relative clause inside a long clause

Our increasing reliance on the Internet
and the ease of access to the vast resource available online
is affecting our thought processes
for problem solving,
recall
and learning.
In a new article published in the journal *Memory*,
researchers at the University of California, Santa Cruz
and University of Illinois, Urbana–Champaign
have found that "cognitive offloading,"
or the tendency to rely on things like the Internet
as an aide-mémoire,
increases after each use.

(continued)

C. Dividing text by slashes (first two sentences only)

one slash / = "half stop" (pause, for a comma, or between the end of a subject and beginning of a predicate/verb phrase)

two slashes // = "full stop" (longer pause, at the end of a sentence or long phrase)

Our increasing reliance on the Internet / and the ease of access to the vast resource available online / is affecting our thought processes / for problem solving, / recall / and learning. // In a new article published in the journal *Memory*, / researchers at the University of California, / Santa Cruz / and University of Illinois, / Urbana–Champaign / have found that "cognitive offloading," / or the tendency to rely on things like the Internet / as an aide-mémoire, / increases after each use. //

Note. Complete text is in Appendix 7.1.

Scoring Charts for Repeated Reading

Chart for a Single Reading

340				
330				
320				
310				
300				
290				
280				
270				
260				
250				
240				
230				
220				
210				
200				
190				
180				
170				
160				
150				
140				
130				
120				
110				
100				
90				
80				
Title of passage:	First reading	Second reading	Third reading	Fourth reading
Slowest score	Fastest score	Difference:		

(continued)

Chart for a Set of Readings

340						
330						
320						
310						
300						
290						
280						
270						
260						
250						
240						
230						
220						
210						
200						
190						
180						
170						
160						
150						
140						
130						
120						
110						
100						
90						
80						
Best score from each passage	Name of passage:	Name of passage:	Name of passage:	Name of passage:	Name of passage:	Name of passage:

CHAPTER EIGHT

Achieving Comprehension in L2 English Reading

New Vocabulary in This Chapter: *reading comprehension, reading comprehension strategy, strategies, preteaching, frontloading, lemma, lexeme, keyword method, punctuation, inferencing, signal words, transitions, and connectors, graphic organizers, T-chart, Venn diagram/H-chart, content frame (semantic feature analysis grid), text structure, visualization, audio imaging, metacognition, think-alouds, literacy advantage, wait time, extensive reading, drop everything and read (DEAR), sustained silent reading (SSR), free voluntary reading (FVR)*

In previous chapters, we reviewed some of the components that are needed to create a "syndrome of success" for an ELL reader—proficient oracy; effortless decoding; an understanding of morphemes, word formation processes, cognates, and collocations; and the attainment of reading fluency. This chapter focuses on how these work together to bring about *reading comprehension*, the ability to construct meaning from a given written text. Reading comprehension is not a static competency; it varies according to the purposes for reading and the specific text that is involved. When the prerequisite skills are in place, reading becomes an evolving interaction between the text and the background knowledge of the reader. This is accomplished through the use of both cognitive and metacognitive strategies.

Comprehending Connected Text
in a New Language Is Hard!

Even if an ELL is an able decoder in English, the level of effort required to read for meaning in academic contexts can be a monumental task. Look at how author Richard Rodriguez (1982) describes his own reading in English as a new language.

> Most books, of course, I barely understood. While reading Plato's *Republic*, I needed to keep looking at the book jacket to remind myself what the text was about. (p. 64)

One might ask how Rodriguez could be reading a book at such an advanced level in English but still not be reading with comprehension. How could he read and yet not read? And what is it that makes reading in a new language so overwhelming? Perhaps part of the answer can be found in the fact that ELLs have less extensive listening vocabulary from which to draw when reading written words they have never seen before. When we read words that we haven't seen or heard, we don't have the advantages of the phonological loop, the cycle that helps us retrieve words from long-term memory by means of phonological information. Perhaps it is partly due to the opacity of English orthography, which makes it harder to "hear" the way unknown words look on the page. Or it may result from incomplete knowledge of the syntax and grammar patterns of the sentences of English. But surely it is also due to the limits of working memory. When we struggle with sentences in a new language, reading takes a great deal of cognitive energy. As a result, retaining the gist of the previous sentences or previous paragraphs in working memory is harder to do as we move through a text.

Even when decoding is no longer very effortful, it is still much harder to read through a text and construct meaning from it as we read in a new language. We might describe this as a real-time cognitive "delay." When the rate of constructing meaning from text can't "catch up" with the rate of our decoding, the result may be the strange phenomenon of decoding but not comprehending, as lamented by Richard Rodriguez above. Native speakers of English experience this phenomenon, too, and reading teachers have developed many strategies, such as highlighting text, or reading and retelling to a partner, to help them develop the comprehension habit as they read.

These techniques work for ELLs, too, and *reading comprehension strategies* are even more necessary—if such a thing is possible! One rule of thumb is to practice strategies using texts that are at a student's independent reading level. For example, Sara, a 10-year-old ELL from Peru, developed several comprehension strategies by reading informational text that was easy for her. By doing so, she will find it less overwhelming to read for comprehension when content-area texts become denser and longer. For ELLs and native English speakers alike, if texts become too overwhelming too soon, the struggle associated with reading makes the whole enterprise unpleasant, and a vicious cycle develops. In this syndrome of failure, the student avoids reading, and this avoidance causes the student to fall further and further behind in both reading proficiency and academic content. Stanovich (1986) calls it "the Mathew effect," comparing the phenomenon to the Bible story of the parable of the talents, which can be paraphrased as "the rich get richer, and the poor get poorer."

Making the transition from general vocabulary, both oral and written, to the content-specific language of the classroom is hard even for native speakers, but it is especially challenging for ELLs. Often ELLs are mainstreamed from bilingual and sheltered English programs just at the exact moment that content reading and writing are becoming much more complex, and they are not prepared to perform the needed academic activities in English. For this reason, developing strategies to cope with academic language is a must.

Good ELL readers are able to orchestrate a repertoire of strategies that serve them as they read different kinds of texts for a variety of purposes. It is important to remember that these strategies are performed together while reading. For example, when we analyzed our reading comprehension experience with an editorial in our local newspaper last week, we found that we did the following things.

1. Identified that it was an editorial from its layout and placement in the newspaper.
2. Recognized the name of a politician in the text and activated background knowledge about her.
3. Read a direct quotation from that politician and applied it to the discussion of a current issue.
4. Visualized a humorous scenario proposed by the editors within the next paragraph.
5. Engaged in wordplay in order to chuckle at the pun in the "punchline" in the last sentence.

Proficient readers employ all of these strategies and many more as they move through different kinds of texts at a comfortable clip.

When we were writing this chapter, Tenena asked the meaning of the word clip *in our phrase "at a comfortable clip." Leah and Kristin mentioned that it was a certain pace in horseback riding, and Tenena asked if it was like a "trot." Leah answered that it was faster than a trot. We realized that Tenena, himself an ELL, had the cognate* trot *from his knowledge of French, but not the Old English word* clip. *When we looked the word up, we realized that our background knowledge of* clip *was also limited because the word referred to the speed of clipper ships.*–KRISTIN, LEAH, AND TENENA

Strategy Use by L1 Learners

Reading comprehension requires the use of strategies before, during, and after reading. In the context of reading comprehension, *strategies* can be defined as deliberate actions that readers take to establish and enhance their comprehension (Jimenez, Garcia, & Pearson, 1996; Pritchard & O'Hara, 2008). As we learn to read in our first language, we acquire a collection of working strategies that we employ for different purposes for reading. Once we know how to activate and effectively use a set of strategies, we can apply them to new texts and new tasks.

Better readers in any language use more strategies and use them more effectively. A study of resilient and nonresilient ELLs found that resilient ELLs employed more successful strategies while reading (Padrón et al., 2002). Schoonen, Hulstijn, and Bossers (1998), in a study of middle school and secondary Dutch ELLs, found that knowledge of vocabulary and use of reading strategies were decisive factors in their successful reading comprehension in English.

Pritchard and O'Hara (2008) noticed that the strategies L1 Spanish ELLs used in reading texts in their first language were not the same as those they used in reading English, even though they were proficient readers in both languages. They were able to use analytical and critical strategies in Spanish, their native language, but used more sentence-by-sentence analysis in reading English. Fitzgerald (1995) did a meta-review of research on L2 academic reading and came to the conclusion that in academic tasks, the more proficient an ELL reader becomes in English, the more his or her processing strategies resemble those of a proficient L1 English reader, both in the number and appropriateness of strategies used. Other studies lend credence to this view (see Fender, 2001; Jimenez et al., 1996). These studies support the threshold theory (Chapter 2), which asserts that second-language proficiency is needed to activate first-language literacy. Evaluating the use of strategies in a comprehensive research review, August and Shanahan (2006) noted, "Strategies of various types are unlikely to help students who do not have the requisite language proficiency to comprehend the text" (p. 355).

Students need to understand how strategies work through modeling and support, and they need many chances to practice them. We should not expect students to figure out all the various reading strategies in a new language by themselves. It would be like putting someone in a kitchen for the first time and expecting a banquet! We need to introduce the tools one by one, systematically, and demonstrate how they work with a text through careful guidance. Only then can we truly "cook!"

In the following section, we introduce some key strategies that fit with best practices for ELLs. Many vocabulary strategies were introduced in the previous chapters. Here, we work our way across single-word strategies to longer discourse-level strategies, using the following organizational format: word-learning strategies, phrase- and sentence-level strategies, paragraph- and discourse-level strategies, and metacognitive strategies. We fold these strategies directly into the body of the chapter in lieu of describing classroom practices at the end of the chapter.

Word-Learning Strategies

Native speakers and ELLs need to learn such a colossal amount of vocabulary during their academic lives that it is impossible to teach them all of the words that they need to know. Lesaux, Kieffer, Faller, and Kelley (2010) have established three principles for vocabulary study with ELLs, based on research: (1) words should be studied deeply so that the words chosen for study are encountered multiple times and used in all domains, rather than using sets of word lists that are quickly studied and replaced; (2) words should be carefully chosen academic words of high value across disciplines, rather than obscure or colorful words that will not be applicable to many classes; and (3) direct teaching should alternate with teaching strategies for word learning to help learners increase their proficiency on their own (p. 198).

Vocabulary learning is a cumulative process in which the initial and subsequent meanings of words are built upon over time. For ELLs, it is especially important to receive ample exposure to new words in order to activate the phonological loop. The best way to ensure that ELLs will be active vocabulary learners over the long haul is to help them master strategies and skills that can be used independently, throughout and beyond their years of schooling, rather than high-maintenance strategies that can only be done under the tutelage of an instructor.

All of the following vocabulary-learning strategies can be effective in sheltered, bilingual, or dual-language instructional settings.

Using First-Language Resources

Since ELL students start school already speaking and understanding another language, their L1 vocabulary can be a tremendous resource for learning English vocabulary. In this respect, ELL children have a potential advantage over monolingual English-speaking children because they have an additional reservoir to draw upon. However, when using first-language resources to build vocabulary, teachers need to take two important considerations into account in order to be most effective.

The first is that teachers cannot assume that children know the vocabulary item in their first language or that their understanding of the word is complete. Children in the stages of early language acquisition are often learning words in both languages for the first time, and this is easy for a teacher to support. For concrete words, young children can create picture cards with a picture and the word in both languages. For example, on one side, a Spanish-speaking ELL can write *martillo* and draw a hammer, and on the other, write the word *hammer*. However, for children in the elementary grades and above, we can't be so sure when it comes to understanding words that represent processes, concepts, or ideas in English as a new language. It's more difficult to know if, or how thoroughly, they understand these more abstract words in their first language. For example, the first-language meaning of "parade" might have completely different associations for a child whose family is used to Mardi Gras in Brazil, or military parades in China. This demonstrates one of the big advantages of bilingual and dual-language education. When ELL students are in rigorous programs that teach content material and strong literacy in their first language, teachers can be more confident that students have the needed academic vocabulary in place, and PCI can occur. However, such programs are not always available, and are sometimes not rigorous, so teachers need to carefully unpack word meanings and check comprehension often as words become more difficult.

The second consideration is that many languages share cognates with English, which can be a very helpful tool for students from such languages, but students do not notice them until they are pointed out. As we have discussed previously, cognates derive from a common root and look or sound similar and have similar meanings in two or more languages. To be useful, cognates need to be explicitly pointed out so that students get into the habit of looking for and recognizing them. Some cognates share the same root and have language-specific derivational morphemes, and these can be very useful for "cognate hunting." For example, the adjective suffix *-ous* in English often translates to the Spanish suffix *-oso/-osa* in a consistent way. When students learn this fact, they can easily make connections between these words.

precious	*precioso*
famous	*famoso*
mysterious	*misterioso*

Having conversations about cognates is helpful in raising children's metalinguistic awareness even if a cognate does not exist for many English words. That being said, it's important to remember that cognates do not exist between English and some other languages, so not all students will have the benefit of this powerful technique. With these two considerations taken into account, teachers can draw upon students' first-language vocabulary resources, both informally and systematically.

Preteaching Vocabulary

Preteaching vocabulary (Bamford & Day, 1997) is a proven method of enhancing knowledge before reading a new text, as well as introducing the cultural aspects of a text. In the literacy field, preteaching vocabulary before reading a text is sometimes called *frontloading*. Preteaching or frontloading clears up some unknown vocabulary through oral activities so that by the time the new words are found in the reading, they are already familiar (Hoyt, 2002). Freeman and Freeman (2004) consider learning new vocabulary as part of a continuum, which "involves learning about something, talking about it, wondering about it, and then reading and writing about it" (p. 198).

In order for this strategy to work smoothly, teachers have to figure out which words need to be pretaught, how many of them to choose, and how to best preteach them. High-frequency words with key importance in a text should always get top priority.

Lemmas, Lexemes, and Word Families

A *lemma* is a single form of a word, or an entry in a dictionary, and these words are often the focus of vocabulary instruction. However, a lemma belongs to a larger group of words that have the same morpheme and meaning but appear in different forms. In language arts classrooms, these groups of words may be called word families, and in linguistics, they are called lexemes. In linguistics, *lexemes* are the set of variations of a lemma that are created from adding different derivational and inflectional morphemes to a root or stem (Kempen & Huijbers, 1983). For example, the lemma *write* is connected to the lexemes *writing, writer, wrote, written,* and *writes.* It makes sense to teach the lexeme, not just the lemma. ELLs may not be aware of all the forms of the word or realize that the forms of the word have the same root. To a native speaker of English, it's intuitively obvious that *write* and *wrote* have the same root, but it may not be obvious at all to an ELL student who is still learning the irregular past tense forms of English verbs. Also, the more teachers introduce and provide practice for the variations of a lexeme, the more opportunities it gives ELL students to use lexemes in writing and speaking. One good way to account for the forms of a lexeme is to use a "spider" graphic organizer. The lemma is written in the center, and its lexemes are written in the branches surrounding it, resembling the spokes of a wheel. An example can be seen in Figure 8.1.

Saying It with Pictures

When new words are introduced with pictures, understanding improves enormously. Printed picture dictionaries featuring many specialized words on different topics that ELLs once used have been replaced by Internet-based image and video banks that make it easy to provide visual support for new vocabulary. When students are also given the opportunity to draw the new word, say it, write it down, or even physically demonstrate it somehow, the odds go up that students will understand, retain, and use the word.

Word Cards/Word Rings

Using a simple set of index cards can generate hours of effective practice. It is easy for young ELLs to create picture cards, described earlier, and older children can also add a simple definition to the card. The cards can be kept in a box and sorted according to different criteria. They can also be hole-punched and slid onto a big key ring—something students enjoy. The kinesthetic aspect makes it more likely that an ELL will recognize and

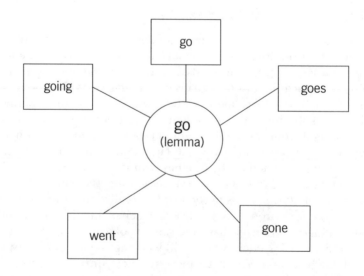

FIGURE 8.1. Lemma and lexemes.

understand the word. It's also possible to generate card sets at Quizlet (*quizlet.com*) and other online vocabulary practice sites. Nation (2001) says, "There is thus plenty of evidence that, for the simple word form–word meaning aspect of vocabulary learning, direct learning from word cards is an efficient and highly effective practice" (p. 299). In fact, there is some evidence that L2 vocabulary is retained best by using a simple L1 or L2 synonym (Fraser, 1999). Variations of the word card technique abound, and teachers can choose the ones that work best in their teaching setting. Some variations can include asking students to use the word in a sentence, finding its opposite, writing synonyms, or writing a definition "in my own words" below a dictionary definition. (One caution: beware of including "antonyms" in the template because many words don't have them). The word cards can be grouped using many systems, including color coding by part of speech, thematic unit, or by structural characteristics of the word, such as its morphemes. When students are just learning to read, they can use word cards to practice sight words or to sort words by sounds, spelling, or syllables. When children sort cards according to whether or not they confidently know a word, they are getting great metacognitive practice. As students move the cards from the pile of words they are learning to the pile of words they know, they feel rightfully very empowered.

Word Walls and Labeling

Teachers who have their own classrooms can create word walls. There are many varieties of word walls. They are most often arranged alphabetically, but can just as easily be arranged by concept or topic, bilingually, or by characteristics of words. These might include words with initial consonant blends starting with *gl-* or *scr-*, for example, or by endings, such as words ending with *-tion* or *-ious*. Pictures can also be included next to the words. Sight words, or the words that are hard to decode, are often placed on word walls as an aid to memory for emergent readers. Teachers can put labels for common classroom objects around the room, which is a natural way for Entering- and Beginning-level learners to access the print environment. Bilingual word walls may be color coded by language. A science word wall based on morphemes can be found in Chapter 5 (Figure 5.2, p. 131); Figure 8.2 shows examples of two more kinds of word walls. The first is color coded by content area, and the second shows words accompanied by pictures.

The Keyword Method

The keyword method has been shown to be superior to several other methods of word learning (Ellis & Beaton, 1993) although its main value

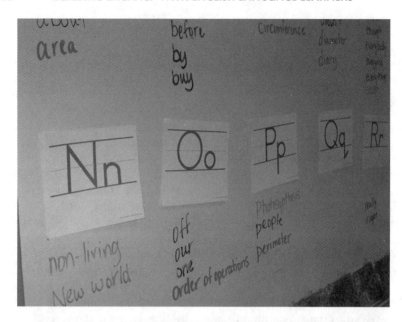

FIGURE 8.2. Two kinds of word walls. *Top:* This color-coded word wall uses red for math words, light blue for science words, and black for language arts. *Bottom:* This third-grade word wall includes a picture with each word.

is in recognition, not production, of the new word. In the *keyword method,* the teacher encourages students to form a mental image connected to the meaning of a new word, often through its sound (Baumann & Kame'enui, 1991). This combined auditory and visual memory aid is often effective for hard-to-learn words.

When I was learning the word pool *for swimming pool, I made a mental image of a hen, which is* poule *in French, the language that I studied in school in Ivory Coast, flapping around in a swimming pool. Picturing that hen in the water allowed me to remember the word* pool.—TENENA

Providing Enough Repetitions

Hiebert et al. (2004) found that words are repeated much less frequently in beginning reading series than they once were. This is a problem for ELLs at the Entering or Beginning levels who are using beginning reading books because they often do not encounter the words frequently enough to learn to easily retrieve and comprehend them. The authors propose that new words be introduced with "an emphasis on a handful of familiar yet compelling categories across a set of texts [as opposed to] different categories of items in every text" (Hiebert et al., 2004). In other words, new words can be "bundled" into high-interest categories or topics, just as they can be bundled into lexemes when their root is similar. Having these high-interest categories, along with an opportunity to interact with the activity these words represent, will help ELLs construct background knowledge as they learn new words. For example, bundling together the vocabulary involved with maintaining a fish tank in the classroom will allow for many conversations that are generated around repeated use of related vocabulary.

Making Daily Use of Dictionaries

Dictionaries are an indispensable resource for ELLs, but must be introduced and used properly for full effect. As mentioned in previous chapters, although there are excellent online dictionaries available now, it's still important to have good dictionaries within easy reach around the classroom. Many activities can be included to scaffold dictionary use, including alphabetizing, looking for synonyms, finding word etymologies, or even playing the game Balderdash, which is a board game for adults that can be played at the high school level. In Balderdash, a small group of players hears a word, and all but one of the group members creates an imaginary definition for the word, while one person holds the correct definition. Each player reads his or her definition, and then all vote for the definition they think is the real one. The winners are the ones who identify the correct definition, as well as the one who had the most convincing "fake definition."

In some classrooms, part of the routine is to ask students to find a word in a large, open dictionary in the room and call out its meaning to the whole class.

Phrase- and Sentence-Level Reading Strategies

Punctuation

What's the use of those little specks all over the text? Do they convey any meaning? *Punctuation* is an incomplete attempt to codify the ways words are spoken aloud. We can call them the "traffic signals" of language—they tell us "to slow down, notice this, take a detour, and stop" (Truss, 2003, p. 7). Punctuation separates sentences into thought groups, which are phrases, clauses, and sentences. English punctuation, like all the other aspects of English we have covered in the book, is language specific. However, it also shares commonalities with much punctuation in many other languages. For example, English shares PCI with Chinese with regard to the period, or full stop, at the end of a sentence. This mark will transfer effortlessly when learning to read English as a new language. However, for Chinese readers and writers, the dot is floating above the line, rather than sitting on it, and it's "hollow." Therefore, even this symbol, although similar, is slightly different.

Other features similar to punctuation, which are usually called part of "mechanics," may also cause interference when they are not the same in the two languages. For example, in French, the first letters of months, days of the week, and nationalities are not capitalized, unlike in English, and French-literate ELLs will need to learn that. In German, on the other hand, many nouns whose first letters are capitalized are not capitalized in their English equivalents.

Punctuation can make a tremendous difference in the meaning of sentences. Take these sentence pairs, for example.

A woman without her man is nothing.
(=Women need men to have value.)

A woman: without her, man is nothing.
(=Men need women to have value.)

Of course, when we read these two sentences aloud, there is no problem distinguishing their meanings. Our voices provide the clue to meaning through our intonation and our pauses, which represent the punctuation. However, in written form, the punctuation is all important! To help ELLs understand the meaning functions of punctuation, it is important that they hear text read aloud as they look at it. In this way, when they see and hear the punctuation at the same time, they will develop a sense of how punctuation contributes to the meaning of words. Learning to "read punctuation" through expressive reading is also an oral reading skill that ELLs can develop with fluency practice.

Truss has written several entertaining books for elementary students about the importance of correct punctuation, including *Eats, Shoots and Leaves: Why Commas Really Do Make a Difference!* (2006) and others.

Inferencing

When we speak of someone who is not very perceptive, we often say that they "take things too literally." We value a person's ability to "read between the lines" and see the hidden dimensions of situations. In reading, knowing how to make inferences is indispensable. *Inferencing* is a large set of skills and strategies that requires actively interacting with the words in a sentence and among sentences. As you recall from the hypothetical model of the reading process in Chapter 2 (Figure 2.2, p. 34), inferencing is represented as the highest of the cognitive-processing strategies. Some inferencing strategies are text based, as can be seen in the model, and others are dependent on both world knowledge and general language knowledge. Inferencing includes the following subskills, which are representative but not exhaustive.

- Making pronoun references (knowing what a pronoun in a sentence refers back to).
- Forming hypotheses about what is coming next in the text.
- Guessing the meanings of unknown words or phrases.
- Forming impressions about character motives and behaviors across multiple locations in a text.
- Knowing not only the denotations, but also the subtle connotations of words as they are used in particular contexts.
- Understanding cause–effect relationships of events mentioned at different times in a text.
- Drawing upon background knowledge in order to fill in gaps within a text.
- Using a detail provided in the text to help make meaning.

ELLs can begin to be inferential in their thinking even before they are reading. Inferencing can be developed through interactive read-alouds and conversations about texts. A question as simple as "What do you think the author might be trying to say here?" can help an ELL begin the process of learning to infer. Listening to mystery stories is one way to make inferencing exciting.

> One of the ways I try to foster inferencing with advanced learners of English is to read them daily mysteries aloud from the book series "Two-Minute Mysteries" (Sobol, 1967). I read the mystery three times slowly, without interruption. Next, they get in small groups and try to solve it through discussing clues in the story. Their listening and inferencing abilities get better and better as they get accustomed to the format. It's a great way to boost reading between the lines, and interest is always high.—KRISTIN

Signal Words, Transitions, and Connectors

Has anyone ever responded "Yes, but . . . " to your great idea? That sentence is a kind of "shorthand" telling you that the person really doesn't agree and is planning to object. Both words are powerful, and their meanings clash. The connector *but* tells us that the "yes" part of the sentence is about to take a turn toward the negative.

Just like traffic signals, *signal words, transition words, and connectors* tell the reader what's coming up and where to go. English has many sets of signal words, transitions, and connectors, which range from the general to content specific. Different teachers and textbook series name and group these sets in different ways, and it benefits your students when you have clear groupings too. For example, it is useful to group signal words for multiplication problems, such as *multiply by, tripled, times as much,* and *factor of,* which can be found in many word problems. ELLs need to understand what mathematical operations these words represent in order to do the problems—it's not enough to understand the math. Connectors can be tremendously useful in providing "traffic signs" and in keeping readers moving along in a text even if they are missing some vocabulary words. For example, when students are reading history, they need to recognize connector words such as *prior to that, after that, at the same time,* and *shortly after* in order to place events in a timeline. If we know the function of a connector, we can stay on track even when we're not quite sure what's around the bend.

Signal words, transitions, and connectors use a variety of syntax patterns and punctuation, and these features can prove challenging to ELLs. In addition, they affect the form of the words that follow them. For example, in an introductory phrase before the subject of a sentence, the word *after* is followed by the gerund (-*ing*) form, such as "After *looking* around, I found a good place to study." Good grammar books and websites can help you, the teacher, learn more about connectors if you have not fully analyzed them. Many teachers have created wonderful charts on Pinterest and Teachers Pay Teachers. Our own favorite English grammar books, consulted extensively as we have learned and taught English, include those by Azar (2003), Raimes (1998), and Quirk and Greenbaum (1973) and can be found in the reference section.

Learning to use connectors in writing can take a long time; however, their semantic purposes can be understood at an earlier stage by means of reading. For example, the words *but, although, nevertheless, regardless,* and *despite the fact that* all signal a contrast even though they are punctuated differently, and the words that follow them are in different forms. We can group these relationships for students by means of charts, word walls, or laminated sheets that can be placed inside student folders.

One more simple and charming way of representing signal words, connectors, and transitions is the "retell rope." The retell rope is a real piece of rope with knots, which can be used as a memory aid as children engage in retelling a story. The knots on the rope can be labeled with these cues: *character, setting, problem, in the beginning, next, then, finally,* and *the problem was solved by.* The knots can also be left unlabeled and simply used as something to grab on to while speaking. Kinesthetic aids can provide comfort and reassurance to ELLs as they collect their thoughts and form their English words, lowering the affective filter.

Paragraph- and Discourse-Level Reading Strategies
Four Graphic Organizers

Graphic organizers are, in a sense, the visualization of the way we store the knowledge we keep in our brains and the methods by which we organize new information. They are useful organizing tools for all students, including ELLs, because they can help manage a great deal of information in a concise way. When teachers carefully choose the appropriate graphic organizer for a reading assignment, the reading task becomes more manageable. Teachers can also provide graphic organizers to help ELLs gather and sort information and to give them a framework to prepare for writing full-fledged compositions.

Many books in the literacy field contain reproducible graphic organizers and guidance in using them to help learners read and write (e.g., Buehl, 1995; Essley, 2008; Zwiers, 2008), and we encourage you to make use of them. We highlight only four graphic organizers we have found to be particularly effective with ELLs for both reading comprehension and writing: semantic maps, T-charts, Venn diagrams/H-charts, and content frames. A small model of each of the four organizers can be found in Appendix 8.1 at the end of the chapter.

Semantic Maps

Semantic maps are graphic organizers used to connect a word with many associations. On an unlined piece of paper, learners create a "map" with the word or concept in the center and associations with the word branching out from it in various directions. Another name for the semantic map is a spider map because it often looks like a spider web. Semantic mapping especially helps activate a student's prior knowledge for reading and for brainstorming before beginning to write. Semantic maps can also be used for showing the lexemes of a lemma, as shown in Figure 8.1.

T-Charts

T-charts can provide an entrée into listing the characteristics of two separate items in columns before discussing how they are related. This helps ELLs initially organize information they find in content reading before they analyze it further. An example of our own T-chart can be found in Chapter 2 (Figure 2.3).

Venn Diagrams or H-Charts

The overlapping circles of *Venn diagrams* are widely used to help students learn how to compare and contrast two ideas or items. However, teachers note that the "overlapping" part doesn't give students enough room to write in the commonalities. A slight variation of the Venn diagram is the *H-chart,* with two long rectangles and a larger center section. It provides students with much more room to write the common features, while still preserving the visual display of comparison and contrast. Venn diagrams and H-charts are great ways to support developing the ability to read and write about contrasts. First graders can learn about the Venn diagram by putting hula hoops on the floor and placing like and unlike objects in different parts of the hula hoops.

Content Frames (Semantic Feature Analysis Grid)

The *content frames* chart is a matrix that allows students to list and compare attributes of several items with respect to a number of different characteristics. For example, different animal names can be placed in the rows in the left column of the organizer, and the qualities animals possess, such as hair, warm-bloodedness, kinds of appendages, and so forth, can be listed in the top row of the chart across the columns. Students evaluate each animal according to its characteristics by checking, writing *yes* or *no*, or adding detailed information in each box. To scaffold less proficient learners, some of the boxes can be filled in beforehand. When students report back on their completed charts, either in small groups or to the whole class, they engage in rich instructional conversation. A content frame is also a good scaffold for writing up a simple report, which is useful for developing expository writing.

The content frames matrix can also be used as a knowledge rating tool for vocabulary learning. Across the top are categories of familiarity with a word: 0—don't know the word; 1—have seen it or heard it; 2—think I know it; and 3—know it well. Vocabulary is listed in the left column. Students assess their vocabulary knowledge of keywords before reading. They return to the same words after reading and reassess their level of understanding (Cobb & Blachowicz, 2007).

Classic and New Text Structures

Text structures define the ways different kinds of information can be organized in written form. The kinds of text structures in use have greatly expanded since the digital revolution, and even traditional textbooks show the effects. Text structures describe such aspects of a text as the following:

1. The length of a text.
2. The number and length of sections in a text.
3. How the text is subdivided by headings and subheadings.
4. How material is accessed through indexes, glosses, and glossaries.
5. How images are used with the text.
6. How charts and tables are integrated within a text.
7. What kinds of learning support or related activities are available, such as questions or projects at the end of the text.

Text structures are related to genres but focus more on the organization than on the content. The text structure of an informal letter, for example, looks very different from the text structure used for a letter of recommendation, an email, a science article in a journal, or a blog entry. Each has its own conventions, and they are culturally specific. ELLs need to be exposed to many text structures and be able to both decode and understand them. Later, they need to learn to write in several different text structures with a range of formal elements.

ELLs grow both as readers and as writers by becoming aware of the ways different kinds of written texts are structured. Research indicates that readers use knowledge of text structure to store, retrieve, and summarize information they read (Meyer, Brandt, & Bluth, 1980). As learners become more familiar with these forms, they create mental templates that make it easier for them to access future texts that contain the same structures.

Students can apply their awareness of text structures in three specific ways that involve both reading and writing.

1. They can quickly preview a text by looking at its text structure.
2. They can use the text structure to organize their note taking as they read.
3. They can practice writing in different text structures.

When students are preparing to read an informational text, it is very helpful to preview the text by previewing the headings and subheadings to get an idea of what will be involved. This is very helpful to ELLs, who work best with "no surprises." Students can also make use of their awareness of text structure when they learn to take notes that follow the structure of a text as they read. Doing so not only creates an active involvement with the text, but also serves as a memory aid and study guide for later use. Similarly, when students learn to write compositions using different kinds of text structures, such as comparison–contrast, problem–solution, or process compositions, they are practicing the organizing skills that will help them recognize those structures when they read. In other words, learning text structure organization "has a profound effect on comprehension and memory" (Peregoy & Boyle, 2005, p. 321).

Teaching text structure has value for both L1 learners and ELLs alike, but the value is even greater for ELLs because text structures provide a scaffold as vocabulary knowledge and sentence-level reading skills are still developing.

Visualization and Audio Imaging

Visualization is a strategy that consists of forming a visual image in the mind in order to remember or evoke a word, event, or idea. Visualizing in reading allows us to "see" in our heads the events that are occurring in a story or account. Although visualization is most strongly applied in language arts classrooms, the strategy can also help learners "see" chemical processes, mathematical shapes, or dramatic moments in history. Strategies that use visualization are excellent for ELLs because they build L2 oracy when they involve oral reading or performing, and they serve as aids to memory as well. Asking students to create a visual representation of something they have seen or read is both an authentic way to check comprehension and a bridge to writing.

Graphic novels are one way that visualizing is made explicit, through their pictorial display of the text. They are a natural fit with ELLs or any language learners, and they are very popular at the middle school and high school level. Comic-like books in the new and evolving genres of *anime* and *manga,* which originated in Japan, now are widely available in English and other languages. Our favorite multicultural graphic novels include Gene Yuan's (2008) *American Born Chinese,* the trilogy *March* (Lewis, Aydin, & Powell, 2013–2016) about the life and times of American civil rights hero Rep. John Lewis, and Marjane Satrapi's (2003–2004) paired comic books, *Persepolis* and *Persepolis 2.*

Audio imaging can also enhance comprehension. Classic television shows and famous movies have musical motifs that have become associated with certain moods or situations. The creepy opening theme of *Twilight Zone,* for example, denotes "something mysterious is going on." Another example is the ticking clock and melody from the television game show *Jeopardy,* which tells us a competition is taking place. Because today's young people are drenched in media and the audio inherent in it, soundtracks can be a real source of information and an additional cueing system. Kids can enthusiastically take the lead in choosing or obtaining these sounds for their own projects, which may include creating photostory and video projects.

It's also possible to add sound effects while stories are being read aloud.

*When one of our teachers did a read-aloud to students with the story of Balto, the heroic Alaskan dog that saved a town in Alaska during a blizzard (Kimmel, 1999), she put on a sound effects tape with the sounds of a violent snowstorm. Some of the children began shivering just from the sound!—*KRISTIN

Metacognitive Strategies

Metacognition is conscious awareness of our own thinking and learning process. It is part of our human heritage and can be found in people with no formal schooling. However, it becomes much more highly developed as we obtain more education, and it has a demonstrable influence on reading and academic success. Metacognition is usually divided into three categories: planning, monitoring, and evaluating one's own comprehension (before, during, and after performing a task). In the beginning, using our metacognitive skills may be a very conscious process, but as the skills become more ingrained, they tend to become less conscious and more automatic. When we read, metacognitive strategies help us prepare for a reading task, monitor the task as we go along, and then evaluate it when we have completed it (Grabe & Stoller, 2002).

Some metacognitive reading strategies are internal to the text and are cultivated as students learn the techniques of close reading. These strategies might include rereading, using graphic organizers, looking for pronoun references and transition words that connect thoughts within and between sentences, or looking up unknown vocabulary. Other metacognitive strategies make conscious use of knowledge outside the text to figure out unknown elements and might include tapping into one's background knowledge, using probabilistic reasoning, or figuring out something by analogy. For example, we might recognize a text structure, such as a mathematics story problem, because we have seen it before, and that memory helps us prepare to tackle a new story problem. Writers use metacognitive strategies when they make careful word choices, read aloud to see if the language "flows," or try to put themselves in the shoes of their readers.

Some metacognitive strategies rely on language-specific characteristics, and others are more universal. Learners can only perform metacognitive tasks in a new language if they know the words that describe the processes. For example, even if Hussein realizes that he needs to find a way to keep notes about a text as he reads it so that he can go back and review it later, he still has to know exactly what to do when the teacher says to "highlight" or "annotate" in class.

When good readers realize that their comprehension has broken down, they use several strategies to get it back on track. Rereading is the one that is most obvious and universally used. We also employ such strategies as these:

- retelling
- paraphrasing
- looking for alternative explanations
- looking for a connection to our own experiences
- checking the illustrations
- looking forward or backward in a text
- stopping and asking ourselves questions

We can also search our prior knowledge to see whether there might be a hint to meaning in a text hidden in something we already know. For example, when a text, or the introduction to a text, mentions the "Jim Crow" era of U.S. racial segregation, students need to be able to activate the associations they have from their prior learning about that period, which may be more extensive than they realize. A teacher can make the time to help them "unpack" what they know before they begin to read.

A *think-aloud* is a metacognitive technique in which teachers orally express how they figure out something they read as they are doing it. Think-alouds, or verbal reports (Anderson, 1999), are a great way for teachers to help students become more metacognitive. These verbal reports are a key technique of early childhood educators. They might involve asking oneself questions or ruminating on what to do, using a conversational and informal tone. Think-alouds are often performed during interactive read-alouds. When teachers model think-alouds often enough, students begin to take part in the conversation, and eventually can try using think-alouds in small groups or pairs. Think-alouds are useful in three important ways.

1. They build metacognitive awareness.
2. They give the teacher a window into the thinking processes of the learner.
3. They give ELLs opportunities to practice using instructional conversation.

Strategies Kick In at Different Times in L1 and L2

Some learners may be able to use both cognitive and metacognitive strategies while reading in their L1, and yet not be able to use them in English because they don't have the requisite language to perform them. This is an instance of the threshold theory described in Chapter 2 (Alderson, 1984, 2000) as applied to strategies. The *literacy advantage* from ELLs' first-language literacy is enormously important in the syndrome of success for reading in a new language. As you recall, in Bernhardt's research-based compensatory model of second-language reading (see Chapter 2, Figure 2.1), L1 literacy accounts for fully 20% of L2 reading comprehension, whereas 30% comes from proficiency in the new language. That proficiency depends on mastering the "bottom-up" skills before the "top-down" cognitive and strategic processing skills can be fully activated. For using connectors, for example, once an ELL has knowledge of connector words in English, such as *therefore, in addition*, or *nevertheless*, for example, it is then possible to apply the PCI they have from reading in their first language to figuring out the meaning of the English text that uses those connectors. Even for using metacognitive strategies, Schoonen et al. (1998), for example, found that metacognitive knowledge contributed to reading in English by L1 Dutch secondary ELLs only when they reached a certain threshold of proficiency.

To make an analogy, let's imagine that Costas, a high school ELL who plans to enter culinary school, is trying to use an English-language cookbook to make banana bread in cooking class, as part of a larger menu. Even with Costas's good background knowledge, he will still have to be able to read the names of the ingredients, the abbreviations for the measuring units in English, and the meaning of the descriptive verbs, such as *whisk, fold,* and *spoon.* His background knowledge and metacognitive strategies—such as preheating the oven or sniffing the kitchen to detect whether something is nearly done—will come into play once he is able to execute the recipe, which he can do when he knows the English words needed to read the recipe. Of course, these days language is less of an obstacle for cooking due to all the cooking shows on TV or cable—another new horizon created by the Internet.

Questioning Strategies

Question–answer relationship (QAR) is a useful question-asking and answering strategy developed by reading experts trying to find ways to help students perform better on standardized tests (Rafael & Au, 2005). They discovered that the kinds of questions on reading tests could usually be classified into four types, in two categories.

In the Text	*In My Mind*
Right There	Author and Me
Think and Search	On My Own

Answers to the first kind of question, Right There, can be found in the text directly, without needing to infer. The second, Think and Search, requires combining information found in several parts of a text in order to get an answer. This is a skill ELLs need to work hard to attain. The third kind of question, Author and Me, requires activating background knowledge to make sense of the words in the text, and the fourth, On My Own, activates non-text-based background knowledge. Rafael and Au found that students felt more empowered to answer questions when they could classify them, and even more so when they practiced writing the questions themselves. QAR charts can be put up in the classroom as a reminder of the four kinds of questions.

Another system is the "DOK," or depth-of-knowledge, classification system. Webb (2002) analyzed texts from different content areas for their linguistic features and classified them into four levels of text complexity: (1) recall and reproduction, (2) skills and concepts, (3) strategic thinking and reasoning, and (4) extended thinking. Webb developed a set of possible questions for each level of text complexity. Many content standards have made use of the DOK classification system, as well as incorporating questions to accompany texts at each of the four levels. For example, a "level-2" question frame might begin, "How or why would you use . . . ?" or "How would you organize _____ to show . . . ?" (Hess, 2013). Interestingly, the WIDA standards have also described the academic activities needed for different levels of text difficulty, but WIDA has further sorted them by content area, grade level, and English proficiency level (Gottlieb, Cranley, & Oliver, 2007).

Wait Time

Educational researcher Mary Budd Rowe studied *wait time* over a 20-year period, in classrooms from kindergarten through college, and she came to some remarkable conclusions (Rowe, 1986). She separated wait time into two categories: Wait Time 1 (pausing after asking a question) and Wait Time 2 (pausing after a student response). She measured and analyzed thousands of interactions, using tape recordings. She discovered that most teachers tend to rush in to fill the silence after their question, waiting an average of less than 1 second for students to respond, and less than 1 second to resume speaking after students do respond. Analyzing the quantity and quality of student responses, she found that a 3-second pause after Wait Time 1 had a strong positive effect on increasing student participation, and a 3-second pause after Wait Time 2 had a dramatic positive effect on the quality and depth of student responses. With ELL learners, wait time is even more critical since they need first to consolidate their understanding of an English question, and then to construct a response in English. Imagine yourself answering questions in a new language about something you have just read in a new language—would you want to be rushed?

Extensive Reading Develops All of the Strategies

There is no doubt that extensive reading is the best universal method to help all learners consolidate their reading comprehension. *Extensive reading*, which can be defined as reading a large amount of text for general comprehension (Anderson, 1999; Krashen, 2004), helps with vocabulary acquisition, content knowledge, familiarity with syntactic structure, knowledge of genres, and reading rate. Strategies that are taught and practiced in the classroom must then be followed up by extensive reading.

It's similar to learning to drive a car in a driving class followed by a great deal of time "behind the wheel." However, out of class reading cannot do the trick unless there is enough silent reading time in the classroom. Hiebert and Fisher (2006) say, "If students are not reading voraciously in their classrooms, it is hard to expect that they would read voraciously at home, especially when language and cultural patterns differ in the two contexts. If English language learners are to read voraciously at home, they also need to read voraciously at school" (p. 291). ELLs need to read "voraciously" during the school day and as part of their homework and summer reading as well.

A good reading "fitness program" involves both intensive and extensive reading. Like any other disciplined activity, it helps "build muscles," but one activity alone will not build overall strength and fitness. A good workout for ELLs affords opportunities to practice many kinds of reading on a regular basis, including close reading, reading for fluency, and reading for pleasure in a variety of genres. There are many reading genres and modes available for young readers to sample. Teachers and schools that are committed to producing strong readers find many ways to support their students' reading habit. Some examples follow.

Daily Silent Reading

Whether it's *DEAR (drop everything and read)*, *SSR (sustained silent reading)*, *FVR (free voluntary reading)*, or a summer reading program sponsored by the library, every student needs and deserves the opportunity to take part in daily silent reading of books of their choosing (Krashen, 2004). During silent reading, teachers also engage in engrossed silent reading. When a teacher reads and values reading, it becomes contagious. After silent reading, ELLs can also benefit by sharing what they have just read with a buddy. Interactive dialogue about books can also get kids interested in books their buddies feel enthusiastic about.

Reading Buddies

Many schools bring together older and younger children to read on a regular basis. There are several formats for these visits. In the most common two, the older children may bring picture books to read with the younger children, or the younger children can practice reading as their older counterparts listen to them. ELLs benefit from reading buddy programs, whether they are older children or younger children. It gives older children a chance to feel a sense of mastery of the book they prepare to read to the younger children, and they enjoy the admiration younger children naturally feel toward their older peers. Younger ELLs enjoy the attention and mentorship of an older student. We have a couple of tips for cross-age groupings with ELLs.

1. Any assignment involving a reading performance should be given well in advance, so that students can practice their parts as much as needed.
2. The reading activity should involve a text that is within the ELL reader's instructional reading level as well as the listening comprehension level of the younger child.

Book Bags

When teachers have good classroom libraries, they can set up a book bag system that allows students to bring books home. Teachers obtain durable, waterproof book bags, enough for each member of the class, and set up a system for students to check out books and bring them home. A book bag is like a tiny, portable bookmobile bringing books into the home! A log sheet in the book bag gives students or their families a place to report on their home reading. The parents or caregivers of younger students can read with the child. Not all parents can read in English, and some cannot read in their first language, and part of the job of a teacher of ELLs is to gently discover what kinds of supports or resources are good for each family. A good way to start is by having a number of titles in the native languages of each student included in the classroom library. It is also helpful to have a set of wordless picture books to circulate so that families can share stories without needing to read at all. Home reading can make a big difference in the vocabulary development of young children. Frequent parental reading to young children has a measurable effect on L2 vocabulary acquisition (Collins, 2005). Of course, different homes are structured in many different ways, and families and caregivers need to establish a routine for reading that works for them. The important element is to have books around and to read them. Trelease (2016) offers numerous, helpful downloadable brochures and posters, some of which are in Spanish, to support families reading aloud. They can be downloaded free and shared with families.

Summer Reading Programs

Especially in the summer, public libraries have many reading incentive programs. Offering entertainment, prizes, friendly competition, and a comfortable place to read, public libraries are a core resource for families with ELL children. Whether it's field trips to the library or writing letters home to parents about library visits, teachers of ELLs should build in visits to public libraries right from the start. Children who visit the school library on a weekly basis are more likely to visit their neighborhood public library, especially during the summer months. Many large chain stores have reading incentive programs as well.

Here is another great idea from one teacher, which she named the "Postcard Challenge":

This summer I am hoping to see what my students return to me. I created a postcard challenge in which students were provided with four postcards, my address, and instructions. I asked that they write me about the books they were reading in the summer and draw me a picture about something in their storybook. I would then give them a prize at the start of the year for completing the task, but the student who read the most books and sent me the most postcards would receive and extra special gift. I hope to be inundated with postcards this summer!
–Patricia Luna

With all of these options, any teacher who is committed to the idea of an extensive reading workout will find that it is easy to do.

Additional Ideas for Developing Classroom and School Resources

Seeking Out Bilingual Titles

Selecting a book that ELLs can already read in their L1 and providing an English version of the book, if it is available, along with it is a great way to boost ELLs' vocabulary. Bilingual texts can be either two separate books or a book with bilingual text on the same page or on opposing pages. When ELLs have already read a book in their native language, for example, they will know the story line, the concepts, words, and characters when they go back to read it in English. There are excellent bilingual publishers and distributers. Lectorum has a large catalogue of K–8 children's literature in Spanish, as do smaller publishers such as Cinco Puntos, and Scholastic has added many Spanish titles to its weekly book club offerings. Searching for books in other languages might take a little more time, but the Internet makes what used to be a chore extremely navigable. One free resource is the International Children's Digital Library, which has free downloadable full-color copies of children's books in many languages, including some low-incidence languages (International Children's Digital Library, 2016). If your school library does not have titles in the languages of some children in your classes, the International Children's Digital Library is a good starting place.

The Need for Books

Building your classroom library and resources can be a challenge. One middle school teacher noticed the following problem in her ESL classes.

When introducing a lesson, one of my strategies is to use tradebooks to teach background knowledge with which my ESL students can connect. Unfortunately, my junior high is lacking in this area and I must rely on the elementary schools or public libraries to loan me picture books to facilitate more meaningful learning.—VIRGINIA RUNGE

If you're teaching at the upper elementary level or above, try to provide picture books that build background knowledge for ELLs whose reading levels are still in development.

Finding sources for books in low-resourced schools can be a challenge, but they are available. One of our favorites is First Book (see *www.firstbook.org/first-book-story*), a nonprofit group that matches classrooms that need books with donors. Donors Choose (see *www.donorschoose.org*) also matches classrooms and donors, not only with books, but with iPads and other classroom materials. Garage sales, church rummage sales, and library sales are also places to find inexpensive, albeit used, books. Used booksellers also offer many titles, sometimes at rock-bottom rates, online. Many community members want to support their schools, and there are many ways for schools to connect with them. One small proviso: keeping your books in good working order is just as important as having good books. Messy or disheveled book shelves give the message that books are just for show, not for use.

Using Many Kinds of Print Sources

Comic books (Krashen, 2004), graphic novels, newspaper and magazine articles, letters, recipes, advertisements, blogs, and websites are all potential sources of reading experiences for ELLs. "Environmental print" such as fast food signs, theatre marquees, road signs, and billboards can be an early print source for very young learners, and this is part of the way they make the transition to print. Reading in many genres also predisposes learners to try writing in a variety of genres.

We hope that you have gotten some good ideas for your classroom as you read about the many reading comprehension strategies in this chapter.

QUESTIONS FOR FURTHER STUDY

1. What are some ways teachers can make vocabulary learning "multisensory"? What are some ways vocabulary could be tied in with speaking practice, the arts, graphic art, or other methods of self-expression?

2. In your experience, what graphic organizers have been useful or not useful for certain kinds of strategic tasks? Explain why some graphic organizers work better for certain kinds of content.

3. Look at the list of metacognitive strategies on pp. 217–219 and apply them to yourself as a reader. Which of them are you aware of using on a regular basis? Are there other metacognitive strategies that you find useful? Describe them.

4. How do you think text structures have changed because of the growing influence of the Internet? How do you introduce these changes to your students?

5. How would you describe the text structure of this book? Look at the different elements of the book. In what ways do you consider this to be a classic textbook format, and in what ways not?

6. What experiences have you had, whether as a student or as a teacher, with extensive reading programs? Have you known anyone in a book club? What effect do you think it has had on the person who took part in it?

7. How can the multimedia available to today's students work in favor of their greater involvement in extensive reading? In what ways does it work against it?

8. Think of some "messages" given by society about reading. Do you think reading for pleasure as described in the reading "fitness program" is a harder sell for children than it once was? How can reading among ELLs be encouraged in school settings?

9. What soundtracks, if any, from TV shows, movies, or commercials have you been able to use with students to set a mood or preview an activity?

10. CHALLENGE QUESTION: If you are in a classroom, try changing the length of your wait time, record your anecdotal results, and share the results with your colleagues.

11. CHALLENGE QUESTION: Choose the kind of reading strategy from this chapter with which you are least familiar, and create a lesson plan that uses it. If possible, try it out with students. Evaluate and modify based on feedback from others and your own reflections. Why is that strategy less familiar to you? Do you think other teachers have gaps in understanding and using that strategy, and if so, why?

Four Useful Graphic Organizers for ELLs

Content frame

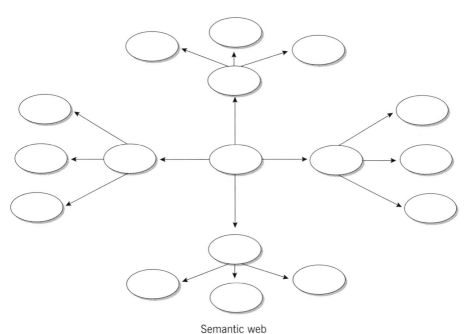

Semantic web

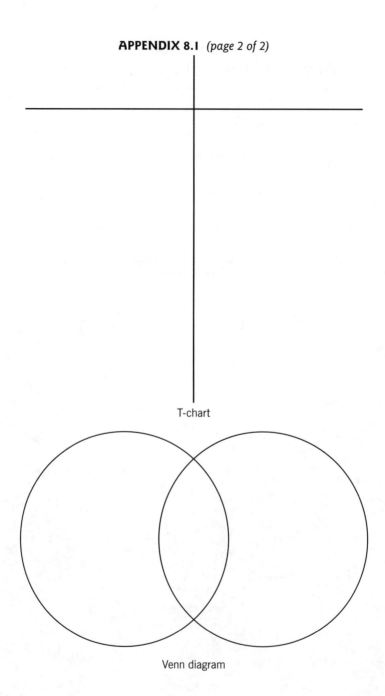

T-chart

Venn diagram

CHAPTER NINE

Writing to Learn in English across the Curriculum

New Vocabulary in This Chapter: *redundancies, learning logs, reading logs, process writing, writing workshop, prewriting, prompts, independent writing, revising and editing, publishing, telling versus composing, expressive writing, responsive writing, expository writing, focus on form (FoF), recasts, uptake, linguistic complexity, vocabulary usage, language control, dictocomp, language experience approach (LEA)*

The development of writing, unlike oral language, is not inevitable, and not all societies have a written language. Writing is an invention, and it is a way to compress, organize, store, and transmit vast amounts of information in a symbolic form. The act of writing can also be a path to understanding ourselves and others. When we write in a new language, it is a real accomplishment and something to feel very proud about. It is also true that it is difficult for teachers to teach writing. At the same time that we recognize the technical complexity of learning writing, we take the view that it can make a huge difference to have a window into the inner life of a child or young adult, and we hope to convey a sense of respect for that privilege.

If there weren't any writers, there would be nothing to read! Writers create the material that makes all reading possible. When other factors, such as topic, difficulty, and interest levels are accounted for, a skilled writer makes reading pleasurable; bad writers make reading unpleasant. Both readers and writing teachers know this.

Writing is challenging, and for ELLs, it is the last of the language domains that will reach native-like proficiency, if ever. Pinker (2007) explains that writers must write without the ability to converse with the reader, without knowing the background knowledge of the reader, and must remove themselves from the center of focus in order to move the text along. "This makes writing a difficult craft that must be mastered through practice, instruction, feedback, and probably most important, intensive exposure to good examples" (p. 416).

Interactions between Reading and Writing

There is a close and complex relationship between writing and reading, the two big domains of literacy. Table 9.1 lists some of those similarities. Both the reading and writing enterprises can be thought of as "drawing from a common pool of cognitive and linguistic operations" (Kucer, 1985, p. 331).

TABLE 9.1. Similarities between the English Reading and Writing Processes

- Both activities are centered around written language and do not exist in languages that are unwritten.
- Both reading and writing consist of a wide variety of genres with which students need to be familiar in order to succeed in school settings. These genres vary in formality, complexity, and breadth of vocabulary, as well as discourse structures.
- Both require an understanding of the relationship of phonemes and graphemes that make up words.
- Both are complex activities with many component processes enfolded in them.
- Both reading and writing are a way of creating, selecting, and organizing information that can be stored for later use.
- Academic vocabulary expectations for both reading and writing become more challenging as students move up through the grade levels.
- Both are context reduced. Meanings are able to be communicated through words alone.
- Both reading and writing may use English structures that are more complex and lengthy than oral speech and lack the redundancies and clarifications of spoken English. Written sentences can be longer than sentences in oral English.
- Reading and writing vary according to different purposes, audiences, and contexts.
- Reading and writing are the cornerstones of academic success.

Research confirms the close interactions between reading and writing development (Grabe, 2003; Kucer, 2001; Tierney & Pearson, 1983, 1985; Van Dijk & Kintsch, 1983). Tierney and Shanahan (1990) did an exhaustive review of the reading–writing connection and concluded, "Writing and reading together engage learners in a greater variety of reasoning operations than when writing and reading are apart or when students are given a variety of tasks to go along with their reading" (p. 272).

The interrelationships between them are so close, in fact, that the reading field has renamed itself to include reading, writing, and oral language in a more unitary concept, "literacy." Teaching reading and writing together, as a tool for learning, allows students to process their academic knowledge more thoroughly, remember it better, and enhance their overall literacy (Oded & Walters, 2002). Although reading and writing skills do not necessarily develop in parallel, even for L1 speakers of a language, we can make a good case for combining them in the ESL classroom.

Of the five domains of language learning (listening, speaking, reading, writing, and communicative competence), writing requires the conscious orchestration of the largest number of skills. Regardless of the content area, students need to use formal and discipline-specific registers of language to report on their understandings of the material they're studying, and to share in print their reasoning processes, supporting evidence, experiences, feelings, and beliefs. As children advance through the school system, writing becomes more and more closely connected to overall academic success. Because of its importance and the long time frame needed for good writing to develop, writing practice with ELLs needs to start as soon as possible.

Written Language: Not Just Frozen Speech!

In Chapter 3 we talked about the grammar of oral language and the ways oral grammar can be understood through context clues and *redundancies*, or repetitions of the same material in slightly different ways. The grammar of written language, on the other hand, relies more on the organization of the words themselves, and it has fewer redundancies. Also, writing lacks the gestures or expressive qualities of human speech, and the listener/reader is usually not there to give immediate feedback. Therefore, "writing requires a double abstraction: abstraction from the sound of speech and abstraction from the interlocutor" (Vygotsky, 1986, p. 181). When children make the transition from speaking to writing, they proceed through a number of specific stages, which have been classified by Sulzby (1991). These stages track the child's recognition that spoken language has a representational form, and it requires abstract understanding. Because of its inherently abstract nature, writing is the hardest domain for native speakers and ELLs alike to master.

Written language, and especially academic language, is distinct from oral language in several important ways that take on added meaning in the context of teaching writing to ELLs. Some of these differences are similar to the differences between BICS and CALP discussed in Chapter 2.

- *Written sentences are longer* and use such structures as passive voice, embedded clauses, conditionals, ellipsis, and other features that aren't normally found in spoken English. Because of the limits of our working memory, we cannot keep track of long, complex sentences when they are spoken aloud. Written English, on the other hand, does not have this restriction because we can always go back and reread the text. The reverse is also true. Long introductory phrases and clauses are likely to be found in written English, but are rare in spoken English because it's too hard for the listener to keep the introductory information in working memory.

As an example, let's look at this sentence from a magazine advertisement for a watch.

From the sweeping second hand to the illuminated numerals on the unique ivory-colored face, every detail has been carefully reproduced.

In spoken form, we would say something like "They copied every detail from the second hand to the numbers. . . . " We make (at least) six distinct changes when we convert the written sentence into oral text.

1. We move the introductory phrase ("From the . . . second hand") to the middle of the oral sentence.
2. We change the verb *reproduced* to the more common word *copied.*
3. We drop the adjectives *sweeping* and *illuminated.*
4. We change the verb from passive to active voice.
5. We change the verb tense from present perfect ("has been carefully reproduced . . . ") to simple past ("copied").
6. We change several other words to conversational BICS language.

The written form has a more dramatic effect through well-chosen descriptive words and elegant word order. In oral speech, our vocal expression, not the words and syntax, conveys the dramatic effect instead.

Students become familiar with a variety of written genres by encountering them through listening or reading. They then can practice them in speaking or writing. As they also become familiar with more written patterns over time, students are more likely to use them in writing.

- *Written texts use a much wider range of vocabulary words*, both in content words and function words such as connectors. Written text includes more low-frequency or even rare words, more concept words in noun form (Fang, 2008), and connectors not found in contemporary spoken English. For example, the connector "hence" is found in written language, but it is seldom spoken. In spoken English, we would be more likely to say the words *therefore* or *so* to express the same meaning as *hence*.

- *Punctuation takes on critical additional meanings* in written English. Fluency instruction can help students learn to "read" punctuation with vocal expression and understand the functions of periods, some commas, question marks, quotation marks, and exclamation points. However, other punctuation marks cannot be rendered by reading aloud because they show subtle relationships among words in the text that can only be understood in written form. The more "academic" punctuation marks include semicolons, apostrophes, colons, parentheses, and hyphens, and they abound in academic writing. The semicolon, for example, can be used in many of the same places that a period is placed, but writers choose it to indicate a close relationship between the words before and after the semicolon. Look at this sentence: "The raft was ready for release; they lowered it into the water." The semicolon in this context tells us that these actions came in close succession. The semicolon allows us to dispense with a connector like *then*. Academic writing is full of these "shortcuts," and good writers use them a lot.

A Change in the Philosophy of LI Writing

In the early 1960s, researchers as well as teachers began to consider new approaches to writing instruction. Graves (1973), in researching the classroom environment, concluded that the writing curriculum, with its focus on correctness and its lack of authentic purposes, did not encourage students to become actual writers. Educators such as Atwell (1987, 2002), Clay (1968), Calkins (1984), and Fletcher and Portalupi (1998, 2001) examined writing as a thinking process. In so doing, they helped bring about a major overhaul in the way writing was taught in schools. These understandings are still core concepts in a balanced literacy curriculum.

This paradigm shift supports the belief that helping students develop the love of writing is as important as helping them develop their skills and confidence in it. This integrated view of writing sees no reason to wait for a certain level of readiness; writing activities can be set in motion very early in a student's education and can continue through all the school years, right into adult life.

In this model of writing, teachers are encouraged to view themselves as writers too, through professional development programs like the National Writing Project. The idea is that when teachers like to write, their students are more likely to as well, so the first place to address improving student writing is to get teachers writing. When students see teachers working on their own writing, it reinforces the idea that learning to write is a lifelong process. Here is what one eighth-grade teacher does.

> *I think it is important for teachers to view themselves as writers and discuss the process of writing with students as they move through it as well. For example, in my class, I write the same papers that I ask my students to write and we go through the process together. I edit my paper, rewrite things, and peer edit with my colleagues so that students can see how I am a writer and I work through the process as well. I think that is really important.*–PATRICIA GRIVAS

The notion that has emerged is that writing is a tool not just for finished products, but also is a part of a process of self-discovery and metacognition. It is now widely understood that writing, in combination with reading and oracy, needs to be part of the cognitive activity of every kind of class, from language arts to physical education.

Math teachers, for example, expect students to be able to jot down the steps they used to arrive at an answer, and sometimes the written description of the process receives as much credit as the answer itself. In some language arts classes, teachers ask students to keep *learning logs*, summarizing what they have learned or have questions about; *reading logs*, used during or after reading to help students apply comprehension strategies; or notes that they share periodically with the teacher. All of these journaling activities help students develop metacognitive skills and use writing as a learning strategy.

Writing often and for many purposes helps students overcome anxiety about writing and makes it easier to pick up the pen or pencil, tap away at the keyboard, text message a friend, or create on a smartphone, all in the service of developing the writing habit.

Process Writing and Writing Workshop

In the *process writing* model, the writing curriculum is segmented into steps. The most widely used model of process writing is *writing workshop* (Calkins, 2006; Fletcher & Portalupi, 2001).

Writing workshop consists of four main stages: prewriting, independent writing, editing and revising, and publishing. Students may be engaged in any one of these four processes on a given day and cycle through them as they undertake new writing. Writing occurs 3 to 5 days a week, on a reliable basis. Writing workshop usually starts off with short mini-lessons the teacher presents to the whole class (Calkins, 2006). Mini-lessons teach writing skills explicitly, beginning with making a connection to the students' experiences, followed by modeling or making a teaching point, often by means of a think-aloud or a demonstration.

During *prewriting*, students brainstorm ideas through many different kinds of stimuli, including scribbling, pictures, memories, dialogues, semantic maps, or even a set of *prompts*, or suggested writing topics, from which they can choose. Prewriting helps students find personally meaningful topics and details. During *independent writing*, students are shown strategies for developing their ideas in conferences with the teacher and produce a rough draft, analyze their own text, and comment on the writing of others. In the *revising and editing* stage, peers, the teacher, tutors, or others help guide writers as they refine their ideas. In this stage students develop the discipline and stamina to create multiple drafts. The process differs in length for each student and should not be rigidly timed. Finally, in the *publishing* phase, students publish their work by sharing it with an audience either through creating a book, for example, or by reading for their classmates in the "author's chair" (Graves & Hansen, 1983). Students have the satisfaction of sharing a finished product with their peers and experiencing their appreciation.

Changes in Writing Due to the Digital Revolution

It would be impossible to overstate the importance of the digital revolution in the writing process. What was once possible only with writing "utensils" can now be performed with software that can transcribe speech into text and transfer large swaths of text from one place to another and with apps that can translate text from one language to another. The digital revolution has given rise to many new genres of writing, from tweets to blogs to discussion threads—and more. The graphic novel has allowed writers to express themselves through cartoons and comics, not only for kids' fun, but for serious mature themes. Seasoned educators may shake their heads in wonder at the changes, and feel that the end of writing is at hand! It is true that the education field has been struggling to keep up with the breakneck pace of new technology, and there are gaps in new protocols; however, researchers have already come to understand how good writing can occur and how it looks, regardless of its medium.

Writing Workshop and ELLs' Writing Needs

Several aspects of the process writing model coincide with research findings about how ELLs learn best.

- There is extensive classroom time given to develop writing skills; students are not expected to learn them at home or on their own.
- The writing atmosphere is relaxed, lowering the affective filter.
- Students choose their topics, which gives ELLs a chance to validate their prior experiences and write to their strengths.
- Each student has the opportunity to write at his or her own level. Even labeling of drawings can be considered part of writing workshop when ELLs are at the Entering or Beginning level (see Appendix 2.1). Calkins also points out that writing in one's L1 may be appropriate in some contexts and at some stages (2006, p. 89).
- Working closely with peers in collaborative settings is of particular value for L2 acquisition (Waxman & Téllez, 2002).
- The predictable routine of writing workshop can be comforting for an ELL getting adjusted to many new classroom routines.
- There is an opportunity to share finished writing with peers, encouraging relationships and mutual respect.

On the other hand, writing workshop is not a perfect fit for ELLs for the following reasons.

ELLs Need Closer Guidance from Teachers

In order to perform the cognitively demanding task of "generating meaningful text in a second language" (Myles, 2002, p. 4), ELLs need considerable teacher guidance. In a process writing model, ELLs may be left in a small group without guidance from an expert peer or adult. Teachers need to guide ELL writers in topic selection, vocabulary selection, sentence structure, paragraphing, editing, spelling, and punctuation, all areas in which ELLs need explicit teaching. Even for college-level ELLs, Silva (1993) found that when they revised their own work, the editing tended to be at a superficial level and required guidance from the teacher.

Peer Editing Requires a Language Proficiency Threshold

Before ELLs can benefit from peer discussion and peer editing, they need two things: a sufficient level of reading comprehension to be able to read, appreciate, and provide relevant comments on each other's writing, and enough language proficiency to be able to understand and benefit from feedback given by other students, who may not be very articulate or clear. These are high-level, nuanced skills, and involving ELLs in peer editing when they are not at a proficiency level to benefit from it is not a good use of time for either member of the pair. Several studies of peer editing by ELLs failed to show improvement in their writing quality (Shanahan & Beck, 2006, pp. 434–435).

Academic Writing Encompasses Both Telling and Composing

Myles (2002) points out that writing in academic contexts does not just involve *telling*, or narrative writing, but the more difficult skills of *composing*. Composing requires taking information about a subject, gathered from a variety of courses, and "transforming or reworking" that information. Writing workshop works best in helping learners create narrative pieces, and it is usually done during language arts time. These experiences are very important for creating a welcoming environment and developing a child's identity, but ELLs also require a great many opportunities to learn to create, or compose, the expository prose needed to perform academic tasks in the content areas, and this area may not receive enough attention. Composing can take years to learn and needs careful scaffolding, especially since it requires utilizing ever-increasing content knowledge vocabulary.

Coherence

Writing rubrics usually consider "coherence"—consistency across paragraphs or sections—a valued attribute, but ELLs may not be writing to manipulate information across paragraphs. If they are not very familiar with the writing structures they are expected to produce, their text may not appear to be coherent above the sentence or paragraph level. Coherence requires mastering many discourse connectors in English (e.g., signal words, connectors, and transition words), and these connectors take a long time to learn. Extensive practice is necessary. Very often, these connectors are not taught very "coherently," making it even harder to write coherently. Learning signal words, connectors, and transition words may require more explicit, direct instruction than allowed for by the mini-lessons in the process writing model.

One bilingual teacher, herself an ELL, remembers this process as a writer:

I believe that the most challenging task for me as a writer in English was coherence. It was difficult to manipulate information across my paragraphs as I didn't know enough about the discourse patterns of English. Not only did it take more time and extra metacognition effort, but depending on the teacher I had, there were times when I felt discouraged and wanting to give up, and other times when I felt proud and wanting to write more.—ADRIANA IUHAS

Zwiers (2007, 2008) has unpacked the language requirements that comprise academic tasks faced by ELLs. He characterizes academic language as a "dialect that describes cognitive processes, complex relationships, and abstract concepts" (2007, p. 96). This academic "dialect" is part of the cultural capital possessed by teachers and students from middle-class, educated backgrounds, who understand these processes, relationships, and concepts from long-term exposure to them. However, the language of school and academic dialect needs to be clearly explained and taught to those from other socioeconomic and cultural backgrounds, including ELLs (Bourdieu, 1991; Delpit, 1995). This task might require some self-examination on the part of teachers, who are not in the habit of examining their own academic assumptions. For example, Zwiers (2007) points out that in the process of ensuring that ELLs are receiving comprehensible input, teachers may simplify complex content temporarily in order to clarify it, but then neglect to figure out how to bring the students back up to the level of complexity that the content requires. If that second step doesn't occur, providing comprehensible input may just end up in enabling failure. Teachers need to analyze what writing skills are needed, how to introduce them to ELLs, and how to ensure that they are practiced enough to become second nature.

Instructional Settings

Even for native speakers of English, the writing instruction provided by teachers across grade levels can be contradictory and confusing. For ELLs, the inconsistencies in what they are asked to do in writing can be bewildering. For example, McCarthey, Garcia, Lopez-Velasquez, and Shumin (2004) took a look at writing assignments for ELLs at the fourth- and fifth-grade levels in several programmatic settings and found the writing tasks and requirements to be both complicated and "fragmented." They also discovered that interactive dialogue about the writing was infrequent.

An 8-year longitudinal study in 13 California secondary schools showed encouraging results for ELL students whose teachers implemented a *cognitive strategies approach* (Olson & Land, 2007). In the cognitive strategies approach, students were exposed to a rigorous language arts curriculum; explicit teaching, modeling, and guided practice in a variety of writing strategies; and participation in a community of learners. Their academic writing showed significant improvement for 7 consecutive years. In addition, their grade-point average exceeded that of a control group, and they performed better on standardized tests and in high-stakes writing assessments. The findings reinforce the importance of teaching critical thinking strategies, having high expectations, and exposing ELLs to a rigorous language arts curriculum.

A Framework for Analyzing School Writing Tasks

We have developed a framework that helps analyze the varying writing demands on ELLs and others in school settings and suggests ways to meet them. We have categorized them into three broad levels: expressive writing, responsive writing, and expository writing. Table 9.2 provides a description of each level, common writing assignments likely to occur at each level, and activities teachers can use to develop and bridge the levels.

Expressive Writing

This first level is typically performed by learners at the Entering, Beginning, or Developing stages of English proficiency. *Expressive writing* is writing based on a learner's own experiences. It uses a minimum of formal language, and it is not usually about classroom content. It may be used at all stages of language proficiency, but it is the only kind of writing low-language-proficiency students will be able to do in class. When ELLs have only limited oral English, their writing will probably look like their oral English. It will use the same words, and the words may look like a transcription of their speech. Here is an example of expressive writing, written by a ninth-grade Spanish ELL at the Beginning level as a caption to a drawing:

> *What I like to improve was my Inglish because I don't speke to much.*

We note that she is writing what she would say in English. She is unsure of the verb tenses and spelling: she is using her BICS language in writing. Expressive writing is a starting point for writing narrative essays and short paragraphs. As the student develops her English vocabulary and reading base, she will learn to make sentences that use more CALP language and more formal conventions.

TABLE 9.2. Three Levels of Formality and Complexity in English Writing

Level of writing	Description of writing demands	Examples of common writing assignments in this type of writing	Scaffolding to help ELLs at level and to prepare to advance to the next level
Level I: Expressive writing TESOL Proficiency Level: Entering, Beginning, Developing	• Drawing representational drawings • Labeling • Drawing and labeling • Describing lived experiences • Describing familiar people, places, and things • Writing simple and compound sentences • Writing a short paragraph • Filling out a simple form	• Labeling • Drawing people, objects, and events • Drawing cartoons; depicting events • Stories • Poetry • Diaries • Journals • Personal narratives • Songs • Fantasy • Friendly letters • Captions for a photo essay or cartoon	• Teacher modeling of sentences and stories • Language experience approach • Shared writing—each student contributes a sentence, all transcribed by teacher, and coherence, connectors are talked about • Paired writing with more capable peer, tutor, teacher, adult • Sentence walls • Retelling fieldtrips, holidays, etc., and creating a class book with illustrations • Performing written compositions for parents, the class, others • Providing kid-friendly rubrics to remind ELLs of what good writing looks and sounds like • When doing interactive read-alouds, pausing to discuss author techniques and discussing ways to apply them to one's own writing • Having lots of writing and drawing materials on hand to encourage creative expression • Allowing and encouraging native language writing resources • De-emphasizing "correctness" in favor of developing writing comfort

Level II: Responsive writing TESOL Proficiency Level: Developing, Expanding		
• Using connectors to create complex sentences • Using transitions to connect paragraphs • Creating topic sentences • Giving examples • Describing less-familiar topics • Making judgments • Giving opinions • Using academic vocabulary • Explaining steps in a process • Indicating topic through a title • Making comparisons • Making recommendations • Giving reasons for preferences • Rereading and revising three-paragraph compositions, five-paragraph themes • Developing a sense of voice and point of view in differing writing tasks	• Filling in simple forms • Writing responses to readings • Learning logs • Dialogue journals • Interviews • Recipes • Book reports • Movie reviews • Reports on an event, person, or place • PowerPoints showing main points • Short compositions based on information in a graphic organizer • Peer editing and peer review • Filling in graphic organizers • Writing about the same event from multiple perspectives • Note taking • Blogs	• Modeling specific skills involved in the writing process to the whole class, in small groups, and one on one • Teaching academic language to describe the processes writers use, using ample examples • Including writing workshop in the literacy program • Doing interactive read-alouds of informational texts and discussing author technique • Providing exposure to and practice in a wide variety of text genres • Working with ELLs in centers during guided reading • Setting up process writing procedures • Training students to do regular peer editing, using a written rubric • Modeling editing and revising with sample papers • Modeling reflective skills through think-alouds • Encouraging writers to enhance reader comprehension of compositions using supportive illustrations such as graphic organizers • Having rubrics for writing on the classroom walls and alluding to features of good writing throughout the curriculum • Allowing and encouraging use of native language vocabulary as appropriate

(continued)

TABLE 9.2. (continued)

Level of writing	Description of writing demands	Examples of common writing assignments in this type of writing	Scaffolding to help ELLs at level and to prepare to advance to the next level
Level III: Expository writing TESOL Proficiency Level: Expanding, Bridging, Reaching	• Creating a thesis statement and support over a longer composition • Reporting on research obtained from several sources • Creating a formal essay • Showing formal voice through word choices • Showing conventions of formal writing in paragraphing, citing, or quoting • Creating a summary based on reading • Creating a summary of an experiment • Explaining cause–effect relationships • Providing written interpretation of information on graphs	• Creating graphic organizers • Research reports • Writing for school publications • Timed writing on high-stakes standardized tests • Essays submitted for college admissions • Final reports for content classes • Science lab reports • Comparing key points of several documents on the same topic • Writing an in-depth analysis of a work of fiction • Preparing note cards, summary sheets, or graphic organizers for writing or speaking tasks	• Involving library staff and aides in teaching research writing and referencing skills • Modeling how to integrate information into a common composition, using very easy texts as a model • Modeling how to integrate information into a common composition, using small excerpts of challenging texts • Breaking writing into smaller sections and discussing ways to recombine • Focusing on using larger range of connectors and transition words • Developing editing skills and metacognitive skills for self-editing and peer editing • Planning timetable for completion of challenging writing assignments

Responsive Writing

We call the second level *responsive writing* because it is usually created in response to something occurring in the curriculum. It might be responding to a reading, movie, or class lecture; it might be part of a project or report, using some of the "composing" skills described earlier. At this stage, writers increasingly learn to use academic language and formal features of writing; now, writing no longer simply resembles speech. Writing genres begin to be introduced, and the connectors and language needed for formal presentation of ideas become more important. Students at the Developing and Expanding proficiency levels need a substantial amount of modeling and guidance in this kind of writing. During this stage, students are introduced to many different kinds of writing genres, including writing tasks in each content area, and they develop the skills needed to use writing as a learning tool. Learning logs and note taking are some of the many ways to develop responsive writing. Here is an example of responsive writing from a ninth-grade ELL in an ESL pullout program.

Divergent

There are many things that the Book Divergent reminds me of. For example, when i was in eighth grade i was the tallest boy in school. Everyone else was shorter than me by a lot. Except one boy who was the same height as me. I felt divergent because i was different from everyone else. I wasn't sad about it but i knew that i was just a little different. Being different is not bad but it is awkward sometimes.

This paragraph, written to a prompt about the book *Divergent*, shows that the student is activating his own experiences to respond to something he read and understood and using appropriate words and phrases, but he is still in the process of developing many skills, such as avoiding sentence fragments, capitalizing the word *I*, and widening his use of vocabulary.

Expository Writing

The third level, *expository writing*, uses the language of the content areas to demonstrate academic knowledge and skills. It is strictly CALP language. Vocabulary is specific to the writing genre and the content area, and formal elements need to be in place. This is the area in which ELLs struggle the most. Even when they are deemed capable of exiting an ESL instructional program, ELLs tend to lag behind in expository writing. The demands of expository writing increase dramatically throughout the grade levels, and by high school, students are asked to perform many complex and challenging writing tasks. If they aren't fully prepared for the transition to expository writing, it can come as a great shock and capsize their academic aspirations. Informational writing falls under the category of expository writing.

All too often, the writing activities taught in expressive and responsive writing do not provide a bridge to expository writing. Learners may believe they are strong writers, only to discover that the qualities they developed in narrative and essay writing did not prepare them for the new demands of expository writing. Teachers must ensure that this doesn't happen by strengthening ELLs' expository writing every step of the way.

Current instructional writing programs often do not adequately prepare students to produce expository writing. That is unfortunate because weakness in this one key area can lead to discouragement or poor grades that may result in nothing less dramatic than failure to graduate from high school. Therefore, a good program for ELLs must incorporate a strong expository writing component, with strong emphasis on practicing specific skills, good modeling, and an assumption of multiple rewrites.

Mistakes and Errors in ELL Writing

There are many reasons that ELLs might make mistakes and errors in writing: they may overgeneralize language rules, be unsure of rhetorical or text structures, be unclear about what they want to say or lack the vocabulary to say it, or experience L1 interference. All of these issues may be manifested as mistakes. Writing mistakes dog many a dedicated ELL writer, and the stubborn persistence of errors even after a mistake has been explained, demonstrated, or practiced in class can be exasperating both for the student and the teacher.

Research on contrastive analysis (CA) found that often the errors made by ELL writers were developmental and not related to their L1 (Lightbown & Spada, 2011). Errors may be based on an incomplete understanding of a rule in the new language, including overgeneralization or simplification, rather than applying the rules of the first language directly. Learners may also refrain from trying to write certain structures in order to avoid errors, so we do not always know what the learner knows or does not know. Lightbown and Spada (2011) summarize: "It is often difficult to determine the source of errors" for ELL writing (p. 82).

Producing good writing is a skill that is above and beyond any one language. Of course, too many grammar errors can impede meaning. All of us who have studied or taught another language are probably aware of the differences between the structures of various languages. In particular, syntax differs from one language to another, and it is very easy to use our L1 syntax when writing in a new language. The problem is that in using our L1 syntax, we do not notice that it is wrong until we have internalized an understanding of the new syntax.

The *focus on form (FoF)* approach (Doughty & Long, 2003; Doughty & Williams, 1998) to error correction is one that was developed for ESL students in higher education settings but has been used with some school-age learners. In FoF, teachers guide ELLs in the direction of noticing and correcting errors by means of *recasts*. Recasts consist of restating or rewriting the incorrect form generated by the student into a grammatically correct form. *Uptake* occurs when students accept and use the recast. This attention to form, or grammar accuracy, "often consists of an occasional shift of attention to linguistic code features—by the teachers and/or one or more students—triggered by perceived problems with comprehension or production" (Long & Robinson, 1998, p. 23). The important goal of FoF is to instill self-monitoring strategies in learners so that they can use them outside of their classrooms. The goal should remain effective writing, as opposed to error-free writing.

Cultural Aspects of Writing in English

Expressive writing involves self-revelation and self-discovery through journaling, peer editing, and the like. Revealing oneself in print may be alienating or even threatening to ELLs or their families if they are from cultures in which writing is not used in that way. For one thing, issues of privacy differ among cultures, and being asked to write down one's challenges or personal experiences may seem like prying to some families. To avoid self-disclosure, students may feel compelled to produce "formulaic" compositions, with many platitudes. They may also fabricate stories.

Also, peer editing is sometimes questioned by ELL families, who may feel uncomfortable with the idea that their children are judged by peers rather than by the teacher. ELL families are eager for their children to have expert models, and they may be wary of group work. In classrooms that contain native speakers and ELLs, there is also a valid concern that peer editing of an L1 writer by an ELL with less language knowledge can create a stressful situation for both.

Cultural considerations also influence vocabulary choices in writing. For fear of writing a wrong word, language learners often choose to "play it safe" by writing only the words they are absolutely sure of, making for a very dull read. Engaging in language play in the classroom will help ELLs develop the courage to go out on a limb and try to use unique words and phrases—even if they don't pan out the first few times. By the way, praise by teachers helps a lot! Teachers can also add points to a rubric for trying to use new words, idioms, or figurative language.

Understanding Plagiarism

Cultural norms defining copying and plagiarism differ dramatically among cultures, and concepts of plagiarism in the U.S. school system are often confusing or obscure. Some ELLs may not clearly understand what plagiarism really is; many teachers rush through a discussion of the topic at the beginning of the year, and others do not cover it at all. Few teachers explain plagiarism and review it during the year. Also, insecure ELLs looking for a model from which to write may think that wholesale imitation of a valued writer is the best way to be a good student. They may have no idea what the teacher is looking for, so they provide the writing they think is most likely to please him or her. Problems with plagiarism have multiplied a thousandfold in this era of digital technology and the Internet. Therefore, it needs to be folded into the curriculum in a clear and consistent way.

Spelling and Handwriting

Spelling

ELLs are likely to have more spelling errors than L1 writers because of their less-developed probabilistic reasoning (see Chapter 4) about the graphophonemic system of English or because of interference from their L1 sound and writing systems. However, learning to spell in English gives teachers an indication of the students' reading development. Spelling helps assess reading because "what they can spell, we know they can read" (Bear et al., 2003, p. 76). We can think of spelling as the skill of "recoding," which is part of the writing skill. All too many writers, however, both native speakers and ELLs, believe they cannot write well simply because they make spelling errors. Spelling can be checked while writing multiple drafts, and again in the final stages of editing, during proofreading. Let's face it—opaque English will always be a "spelling-problem" language, so we need to keep spelling in perspective, and make sure it isn't a reason to abandon writing.

Handwriting

The role of handwriting in the overall development of literacy is explored in Chapters 4 and 10, and research on its changing role continues to unfold. A national conversation is occurring about the decline of handwriting instruction in the elementary curriculum and its possible implications for learning (Bounds, 2010; Konnikova, 2014). In one study, copying text using handwriting correlates with developing several reading and writing skills in the elementary grades (Jones, Abbott, & Berninger,

2014). In a longitudinal study, Berninger et al. (2006) found that children in grades two, four and six wrote more words, wrote words faster, and expressed more ideas when they composed by hand than when they used a keyboard (Bounds, 2010). In fact, the same study found that "the ones with better handwriting exhibited greater neural activation in areas associated with working memory—and increased overall activation in the reading and writing networks" (Konnikova, 2014, para. 12). Clearly, handwriting is more than just a motor activity.

Spelling and Handwriting in the Digital Era

The skills of spelling and handwriting have assumed ancillary roles in literacy curricula because of handy tools that can correct spelling and encode speech from a keyboard or a voice-activated device. Students once had to meticulously learn handwriting and typing, and schools bought curricula to teach these skills efficiently. Now, moreover, the writing utensil and even the keyboard are not the only routes to writing. However, before we relegate them to the antique shop, we should note the continuing role for both skills as markers of and contributors to English language literacy.

Guidance from the English
Language Proficiency Standards

The TESOL/WIDA English language proficiency (ELP) standards for writing can be found in Appendix 9.1 at the end of this chapter. They summarize the writing skills needed throughout all the grades of school according to three categories: linguistic complexity, vocabulary usage, and language control. *Linguistic complexity* refers to the ability of a writer to create complex sentences and paragraphs that are well-organized, coherent, and varied. *Vocabulary usage* refers to knowing and choosing words and phrases that best express a wide variety of ideas and purposes while keeping the reader's interest. *Language control*, an issue of special concern in teaching ELLs, refers to having enough grammatical accuracy in writing that errors do not impede comprehensibility of the written text. These three areas can be used as a yardstick for checking on the growth of ELLs' writing skills, whether they are involved in expressive, responsive, or expository writing.

HOW DOES THIS LOOK IN THE CLASSROOM?

Like the listening comprehension activities described in Chapter 3, we can divide writing practice into intensive and extensive activities. Intensive writing activities are skill based and structured, whereas extensive writing activities are more open ended and designed to address the affective rewards of writing. In addition, an important part of writing is writing for learning, which is useful as a support for academic learning. Good writers do all three kinds of writing, which are both overlapping and complementary.

Whichever mode of writing is used, ELLs need to write every single day in class, for homework assignments, and ideally, for summer projects as well. In addition to its other benefits, the time spent on content writing can ultimately save class time needed for review, because writing about content tends to help students remember it better (Tierney & Shanahan, 1990).

Intensive Writing Activities

Intensive writing activities are targeted to specific writing needs faced by ELLs and others; they encompass the skill-building activities used in an L1 writing classroom along with a number of additional skills related to second-language acquisition. Intensive writing includes the mini-lessons that are part of writing workshop; they also include the components of responsive and expository writing that guide students to learn to summarize, to find supporting examples, citations, and quotations, to prioritize the importance of details, to employ formal language, and so forth.

Sentence Frames

Sentence frames provide partially completed sentences students can use to complete a whole sentence or a composition and are a very important technique for improving ELL writing. Sentence frames sometimes consist of "sentence starters" to help organize sentences or paragraphs for different writing genres. For example, a persuasive essay sentence frame may include the frame, "The reason for _____ is because _____" for a persuasive essay. They can also scaffold the use of connectors. Students also get practice in using grammar and syntax patterns effortlessly. The DOK system described in Chapter 8 refers to sentence frames as "question stems," and has different question starters for different text levels. Even when ELLs are at an advanced level, sentence frames are a great way to lock in sentence patterns.

> *A sentence frame I've always enjoyed using with ELL students is "He/ she/it is as _____ as _____." I demonstrate several colorful phrases in English like "The wrestler is as strong as a lion," or "That joke is as old as the hills" and then ask students to think of their own. Often students have amusing phrases from their own cultures. My favorite, provided by Polish students, is "He's as dumb as a door-knob." It's also a chance to talk about the roles animals play in different cultures. That in turn serves as a nice tie-in to folktales.*—KRISTIN

Some comparisons we use in Senufo, my native language (we call our language Cebaari), are "as clever as a rabbit," and "as dumb as a hyena"–that is the role those animals play in our folktales. We also say, "as terrified as a mouse that fell into the gumbo sauce."–TENENA

The *as–as* sentence frame can also be converted to a comparative sentence, which is also a good practice for ELLs. For example, "She's as fun as a barrel of monkeys" can be changed to "She's more fun than a barrel of monkeys."

The Dictocomp: A Transitional Way to Summarize Main Ideas of a Text

One way to help students learn summary writing while improving listening comprehension is by having them respond in writing to an oral text rather than to a reading. The technique is called a *dictocomp*. In a dictocomp, a teacher preteaches a couple of ideas in the text that he or she is about to read, explains to the students that they will be writing a response to the oral text, and then reads it out loud several times, at a relaxed pace. Then students are asked to write the main idea. A rubric that encapsulates the important points in the text can be designed in advance (Bailey, 1998, pp. 149–150). This is a good transition for ELLs who are not yet swift readers but still need to practice the vital skill of summary writing. Standardized tests in many states require students to demonstrate their comprehension of a text in several content areas, not just in the language arts. Dictocomp helps students to practice this skill.

Getting Out the Scissors

As students learn to organize and move around material, especially in their content-area writing, it helps to have them write on every other line. Doing so gives them enough room to cut up and move around their written work, trying out various potential organization patterns. Often inexperienced writers do include important examples or supporting evidence in their writing, but they put this material in the wrong place in the text, as an afterthought. Cutting up and reassembling sentences rejects the idea that any particular arrangement of words is sacrosanct, and visually demonstrates that reordering sentences and paragraphs is a natural part of the editing process.

Expository Writing Can Begin in the Early Grades

Children can learn the principles of collecting and recording data on topics even before they are reading connected text or doing extensive writing. For example, the life cycle of butterflies can be charted using information gained from different picture books, movies, and measurements taken from the butterfly habitat in the classroom. Then students can write a sentence or paragraph or create a chart to describe their findings. ELL students can learn the foundations of expository writing by the time they are at the Developing level. When students learn new skills using topics with which they are already familiar, they can focus on the writing procedures. Then, by the time the content becomes more challenging, they will have incorporated the procedures into their academic routine.

Filling In Comic Strips: A Way to Transition to Narrative Writing

To make the transition from sentence writing to writing a narrative, teachers can provide paper that has empty cartoon strips with three, six, or nine boxes and ask students to fill them in with drawings about an event in their life. After completing their drawings, they then write captions for the story underneath the cartoon. When the drawings are removed, students have the beginnings of a story, which can then be written again in full sentences with connectors.

Extensive Writing Activities

Extensive writing activities foster a love of writing, confidence about writing and the writing habit, and the motivation to persevere at writing. Even though intensive skills may be practiced alongside extensive writing, extensive writing is mostly used for the purposes of self-expression, and it includes creative writing and other expressive writing activities. Part of the value of extensive writing is the joy of sharing one's writing, whether for publication in a class book, for a performance in the author's chair during writing workshop, or in a digital format.

Dialogue Journals

Dialogue journals are a powerful way for students to use writing to communicate their thoughts and feelings. They can be arranged in different ways according to the teacher's classroom organization. Dialogue journals are kept in a separate notebook, not just on loose-leaf paper, and the entries are usually dated. They can be written in class or as homework. They may be turned in to a teacher, who may write comments and return the journals, or they may be shared with other students. Dialogue journals can even be kept in a digital form, as blogs.

Dialogue journals share these features.

- Topics are freely chosen.
- Journals are read for content, not form.

- Some sort of real dialogue occurs between the reader and the writer.
- Dialogue journals should not be graded, except perhaps for the number of entries or pages.

The Language Experience Approach

The *language experience approach* (LEA; Stauffer, 1970) can be considered one kind of writing for learners at the Entering or Beginning level, usually in early childhood or early elementary settings. In this technique, students narrate sentences or a story to a teacher, who writes it down and then asks the student to read it back. The LEA can be a powerful bridge to writing when learners have something to say but have not mastered enough conventions of the writing system to encode it. Even before they transition to literacy, young ELLs can illustrate their LEA stories. Literate learners can recopy the story the teacher has transcribed for practice in conventions of print. The class can also create an LEA when each student contributes one sentence as the teacher writes the sentences on chart paper, and then all students read the sentences back. Teachers might use this for debriefing from a field trip or a guest speaker.

Encouraging Students to Write in Their Preferred Languages

Giving ELLs the choice of what language (or languages) to write in can be very reassuring to students who are trying to project their identity onto paper. Although L1 writing can help students achieve higher-level writing goals, it is also true that writing about one's life in a new language can be quite liberating (Steinman, 2005). As their education proceeds, there may be a change in ELLs' language writing dominance from their L1 to English. The long-range goal of bilingualism and biliteracy, however, is always to be supported.

Fan Fiction

Fan fiction is a genre of writing made possible by the Internet. When fans of a book or book series can't bear to have it end, they write sequels, or alternate endings, and publish them on the Internet at fan fiction websites. Fan fiction might be based on books, movies, TV shows, or cable or Netflix series. If preteen kids have a passion to write, this is one direction the writing might take. The Harry Potter books, books by Percy Jackson, and books with supernatural themes have hundreds of thousands of fan fiction, or "fanfic," sites, and a lot of reading and writing occurs there. (Caution: There are "dark" fan fiction sites, and teachers should educate themselves about appropriate avenues for fan fiction writing that may be used in the classroom.)

Even when their proficiency is still developing, ELL students can write different endings to books or movies they liked, and if they are strong writers, they can even strive to adopt some of the literary features of the original author, such as Dr. Seuss.

Using a Multimodal Approach

Writing can emanate from many different sources and genres. Adolescents place a high value on music and movies, and they can be used positively in learning situations. At least one study has shown that high school ELLs benefit from writing activities that combine language and content with cooperative group activities that involve incorporating media (Early & Marshall, 2008).

Writing for Learning Activities

Writing for learning activities include metacognitive activities such as showing one's thinking process in finding a solution to a problem or using a graphic organizer to organize study notes. These activities are likely to be found in content-area classrooms, whereas the other two kinds of writing more often reside mainly in the language arts classroom.

Think-Alouds and Modeling Writing

The very best way to model writing conventions and techniques for ELLs is through the use of think-alouds. An effective think-aloud for writing can be set up as follows: A teacher stands at an overhead projector, facing the class, and writes a paragraph on a transparency while thinking aloud. As the paragraph unfolds, ELLs can both see and hear the thinking process that goes into word choices, choosing examples, creating a thesis statement, capitalizing letters, choosing connectors, and other skills. Students get to see the text actually being produced as the teacher handwrites or prints the paragraph. The students can also watch the teacher go back and edit the paragraph, which is equally if not more valuable. When the teacher reconsiders a word choice, corrects spelling or grammar, or reorders sentences, the practices of recasts and uptake are modeled (Doughty & Williams, 1998), making ELLs more aware of error correction. This careful modeling fills in the gaps for ELLs and is a powerful form of real-time learning.

We know a teacher who used this technique every Friday. She wrote paragraphs in response to different writing prompts she provided or she constructed summaries of what the students had learned that week. She modeled different genres, including friendly letters, book reports, and summary paragraphs, thinking aloud as she wrote at the overhead projector. When the composition was completed on the overhead projector, students copied it verbatim into their writing notebooks. This process continued for several months. It provided a foundation on which students could construct their own writing, with the security that they knew what a good paragraph looked like. The students achieved impressive results on the writing portion of their annual test of English proficiency, well above students in the same building that did not use this practice. The teacher pointed out that this seemingly prescriptive method actually helped students grow wings to write more creatively on their own because they had more confidence about the fundamentals of what good writing should look like.

Book Letters

One sixth-grade teacher uses a technique called "book letters" in her literacy class.

> *I use literature in many ways. Students select and read independent-level text, and are required to write book letters to me three times per trimester. In a book letter, they analyze the author's style and point of view, the characters' traits, relationships and motivation, and what emotions they felt while reading. They use evidence from the text to support each part of their analysis, and they have to use a direct quote somehow to explain part of their letter. Because students are reading independent-level text, even a lower-level ELL could write these letters.*—KELLY MIEDWIG

The following academic year we asked Kelly for an update on how the book letters worked out. She answered:

> *I have decided this year to narrow down the focus a bit. Each time we study a new strategy in reading (for example, identifying character traits through textual evidence), students are given resources that help them understand the strategy. Then they are given multiple opportunities to practice the skill through teacher-directed modeling of shared reading, then small-group practice with a shared text. Then, for the book letter, I ask them to respond to a writing prompt that relates to the strategy, but they use their own independent-level text. This way they are only focusing on one strategy at a time. I was not getting enough assessment through the semester in some of the reading skills, so this way I can hit things more often! I plan to do a longer analysis, like the ones I've done in the past, later in the year.*

Practicing literary analysis through informal letters to the teacher is a good entrée into expository writing for ELLs, and pressures them less about the formal features of writing.

Reading Drafts Aloud

Reading drafts aloud, whether alone or to a partner, helps ELL writers become better editors of their work. Sometimes words might not "sound right" even when they look right on the page—a common phenomenon for all students, but especially ELLs from different L1 writing systems. For some learners, their ears are better developed in English than their eyes (and BICS skills generally precede CALP skills), so they can hear and correct mistakes when they listen to themselves read. This can be built into the editing routine.

Graphic Organizers Help Not Only Reading, but Writing

Graphic organizers help readers find main ideas, summarize, extract information from several sources, and compare and contrast ideas. Many of the strategies that help ELLs construct meaning from text while reading also help them construct meaningful text when they write. When students are at the Developing level of proficiency and are beginning to write paragraphs, semantic maps help them brainstorm and organize their ideas. During the writing and revising stages, writers can identify gaps in their organization by representing their main points on outlines, Venn diagrams, T-charts, and the like. Teachers can help ELLs use the graphic organizer for the genre in which they are writing, such as cause–effect charts or timelines. Some graphic organizers have blank templates, such as blank frames for friendly letters, lab reports, and so on. Many of these templates can be found on Pinterest, Teachers Pay Teachers, or in the resources and tools section at Scholastic. Graphic organizers are especially effective when they are displayed around the classroom and referred to frequently, so that students will naturally look at them for guidance.

After students finish writing, rubrics and checklists can help them monitor their own writing by proofreading.

Creating Books with Storybird

Storybird (*https://storybird.com*) allows children to create their own stories and make them into books. It's a nice way to turn a story that students create and illustrate through the Language Experience Approach (LEA) into a book they can take home. This project can also be used as the culmination of writing workshop. Storybird allows the books to be created for free but charges for making copies of the books for parents or teachers.

Arlene Duval, a K–5 ESL pull-out teacher, uses a number of visual aids to support her students' reading and writing activities. Her unique use of "woodland" characters to accompany writing responses to reading can be seen in Figure 9.1.

Arlene Duval holding an Owl of Many Questions
and showing a photo of the bulletin board.

The "Owl of Many Questions."

Word tree, poem, and "Bee-loved" words in Arlene Duval's classroom.

FIGURE 9.1. A tree, a beehive, and an "Owl of Many Questions." The "Owl of Many Questions" activity adapted with permission from CONNECT-IT for *Stranger in the Woods* by Carl R. Sam II and Jean Stoick, EDCO Publishing, Inc.

QUESTIONS FOR FURTHER STUDY

1. If you had to choose three important ideas from this chapter, which would you choose? How can you apply these ideas to your larger knowledge of teaching English as a new language?

2. Think about the writing instruction you received in elementary school, high school, or college. In what ways have those experiences influenced how you think about yourself as a writer and as a teacher of writing?

3. Look at Table 9.2 and think about the areas in which you feel confident or less confident as a teacher of writing. Discuss with a partner.

4. Looking at the right column of Table 9.2, in which areas do you think ELLs require the same amount of scaffolding as L1 writers? In which do they require more?

5. What experiences have you had learning or teaching intensive, extensive, and writing for learning activities? What do you think constitutes a proper balance of the three?

6. If you are currently in the classroom, try to classify the writing activities into expressive, reflective, and expository activities. How does the scaffolding you provide for these three kinds of writing activities differ according to the nature of the activity?

7. Try creating your own activity using "as–as" sentence frames, such as the example earlier in the chapter, and try it out in your classroom. Report on the results.

8. Do you think handwriting is a skill ELLs should be taught? In what ways might handwriting practice enhance understanding of English reading, writing, or spelling, if any? Have you had any experience in teaching, or not teaching, handwriting?

9. Look at Appendix 9.1, showing the TESOL/WIDA writing standards, and compare them with a rubric you might have for writing. To what extent are the three language proficiency standards included in your writing program, rubrics, and assessments?

10. CHALLENGE QUESTION: Alone or with students, find formal language in an advertisement, such as the example of the ad for the watch on p. 232, and convert it to an informal paraphrase that is closer to spoken language. Then, try to change informal language that you find from an informal source, such as a text message or note, into more formal language. Discuss the experience. What did you learn from the process?

11. CHALLENGE QUESTION: If possible, analyze a writing program with which you are familiar and determine what kinds of experiences it provides students to produce expressive, responsive, and expository writing. Look at Table 9.2 and see which activities are included in, or missing from, each of the three levels of writing. In what areas is the writing program strong? In which area(s) does it need strengthening?

Writing Rubric of the WIDA Consortium Grades 1–12

Level	Linguistic Complexity	Vocabulary Usage	Language Control
6 Reaching	A variety of sentence lengths of varying linguistic complexity in a single, tightly organized paragraph or in well-organized extended text; tight cohesion and organization	Consistent use of just the right word in just the right place; precise vocabulary usage in general, specific, or technical language	Has reached comparability to that of English-proficient peers functioning at the "proficient" level in statewide assessments
5 Bridging	A variety of sentence lengths of varying linguistic complexity in a single organized paragraph or in extended text; cohesion and organization	Usage of technical language related to the content area; evident facility with needed vocabulary	Approaching comparability to that of English-proficient peers; errors don't impede comprehensibility
4 Expanding	A variety of sentence lengths of varying linguistic complexity; emerging cohesion used to provide detail and clarity	Usage of specific and some technical language related to the content area; lack of needed vocabulary may be occasionally evident	Generally comprehensible at all times, errors don't impede the overall meaning; such errors may reflect first-language interference
3 Developing	Simple and expanded sentences that show emerging complexity used to provide detail	Usage of general and some specific language related to the content area; lack of needed vocabulary may be evident	Generally comprehensible when writing in sentences; comprehensibility may from time to time be impeded by errors when attempting to produce more complex text
2 Beginning	Phrases and short sentences; varying amount of text may be copied or adapted; some attempt at organization may be evident	Usage of general language related to the content area; lack of vocabulary may be evident	Generally comprehensible when text is adapted from model or source text, or when original text is limited to simple text; comprehensibility may be often impeded by errors
1 Entering	Single words, set phrases, or chunks of simple language; varying amounts of text may be copied or adapted; adapted text contains original language	Usage of highest-frequency vocabulary from school setting and content areas	Generally comprehensible when text is copied or adapted from model or source text; comprehensibility may be significantly impeded in original text

Note. Level 6 is reserved for students whose written English is comparable to that of their English-proficient peers. From Teachers of English to Speakers of Other Languages (2016). Copyright © 2016 Teachers of English to Speakers of Other Languages, Inc. All rights reserved. Reprinted by permission.

CHAPTER TEN

Literacy, Language Learning, and the Digital Revolution

New Vocabulary for This Chapter: *handwritten text, linear text, screen-based linear text, interactive text, emoticon, hashtag, handle, corpus, avatar, metaphor*

It is impossible to overstate the significance of changes resulting from the speed-of-light digital revolution. The landscape is changing so quickly that research on best practices has not been able to keep up with it— technology changes at a fast pace, but research does not. This chapter, therefore, includes a brief literature review combined with a description of some of the new technologies and how they can be applied, based on our understandings of the ways learners come to attain languages and literacy. In addition, we'll share a few suggestions about best practices using digital technology in preparing lessons and classroom activities. We are writing this with a full awareness that any attempts to be "up-to-date" will probably look "dated" in this ever-evolving scenario. The chapter is organized around six topics, each of which is handled only briefly: (1) how the digital revolution is changing literacy; (2) how the digital revolution is changing the teaching and learning of languages; (3) new roles for the teacher and learner; (4) new literacies; (5) digital literacy as a content area; and (6) online teacher resources.

Additional suggestions for classroom practices can be found in the section "How Does This Look in the Classroom?" at the end of the chapter. Other ideas for teaching and learning English with digital resources are woven throughout the book because the digital revolution is part and parcel of teaching today.

Changes to Literacy

The digital revolution has produced new ways of reading, new ways of writing, and new text structures. These changes have major implications for reading comprehension. Even the definition of literacy, as summarized by Leu, Kinzer, Coiro, Castek, and Henry (2013), has changed.

> Thus, to have been literate yesterday, in a world defined primarily by relatively static book technologies, does not ensure that one is fully literate today where we encounter new technologies such as Google docs, Skype, iMovie, Contribute, Basecamp, Dropbox, Facebook, Google, foursquare, Chrome, educational videogames, or thousands of mobile "apps." To be literate tomorrow will be defined by even newer technologies that have yet to appear and even newer discourses and social practices that will be created to meet future needs. Thus, when we speak of new literacies we mean that literacy is not just new today; it becomes new every day of our lives. (p. 1150)

New Ways of Reading

There are four distinct modes for reading written text, and these forms have implications for reading comprehension: handwritten text, linear text, screen-based linear text, and interactive text. *Handwritten text* is text written by a student or teacher using a writing instrument. This text certainly predominates in stages of early literacy in any language and includes labeling, stories, notes, journals, and even handwriting on the board. *Linear text* can be defined as text printed on paper, in the form of books, magazines, posters, newspapers, or even worksheets. Historically, linear text is the text mode students are taught to decode and comprehend, both inside and outside of school. *Screen-based linear text,* now possible on many devices, presents text that looks similar to paper-based text but is read on a screen. These include PDFs and various forms of ebooks. Screen-based linear texts can be read when a screen is offline but may still contain some interactive features from the software loaded into the device, such as dictionaries. The fourth form of text is *interactive text,* which consists of texts specifically created for use in online, screen-based reading with a variety of devices. Each of these forms has advantages and disadvantages, and as technologies evolve, the interplay between them will continue to rapidly evolve. Some characteristics of the four presentation modes of written text can be seen in Table 10.1.

Researchers know quite a bit about how readers interact with linear text in order to achieve reading comprehension, but research is still emerging about screen-based reading, both linear and interactive. *Screen-based reading* is a significant change to the reading field. In a 10-year

TABLE 10.1. Four Presentation Modes for English Written Text

	Print and layout	Progression across text	Studying and annotation methods
Handwritten text	• Fixed placement by writer using writing utensil • Early writers may erase and rewrite	• Normally short, written across page L → R or in writer's own layout	• Might involve handwritten response, such as journaling but not usually "studied"
Linear text	• Fixed font size, color, placement on page • Fixed page layout, including illustrations	• Moves across page L → R • Moves across page top → bottom • Pages turn from R → L as text proceeds	• Handwritten notes on paper • Post-it notes • Dictionary use (paper or online) • Notes on a computer or device
Screen-based linear text	• Changeable font size, color, lighting • Fixed placement on page • Changeable screen brightness • Movable graphics	• Moves across page L → R • Moves across page top → bottom • Page can be advanced by swiping with finger or arrow key	• Highlighting and commenting through embedded software • Handwritten notes • Dictionary use (paper or online) • Notes on a computer or device
Interactive text	• Changeable font size, color, lighting • Flexible page with many moving parts • Often surrounded by other items	• Can be skimmed using keywords • Can be read by moving across text L → R • Can move across text top → bottom • Text can be advanced by scrolling or swiping	• Highlighting and commenting through online extensions and apps • Handwritten notes • Dictionary use (paper or online) • Notes on a computer or device • Downloading and converting to PDF or printing, changing text into linear or screen-based linear text

Note. © 2017 Kristin Lems.

study of digital readers of English, Liu (2005) found that screen-based reading involved a different kind of reading—with more browsing, keyword searching, skimming, backtracking, and skipping. He also found that readers did less in-depth or concentrated reading and had less sustained attention. In addition, the study revealed that those who used screen-based reading (at least in 2005) were less proficient in annotating and highlighting than readers of paper documents. These trends were noted over a 10-year period. In a wide-ranging literature review of screen-based reading, Cull (2011) found that student reading comprehension was lower than in linear paper-based reading, but seemed to be improving over time. He also noted that many cognitive processes are in play when reading on a screen, but that these processes may be hard to maintain due to multiple activities. Cull cautions: "In-depth reading can also take place with printed or digital text, but . . . it is a contemplative cognitive activity somewhat at odds with the Internet's zeitgeist of immediacy" (para. 8).

Text-to-speech apps can also be considered a mode of reading, although they are radically different from reading using the eyes alone. *Text-to-speech* apps were originally designed for the visually impaired, but they are now available on many platforms and devices. In addition, many books can be heard read aloud by expressive human readers. Children's trade book publishers have many interactive titles that can be heard being read aloud by clicking a button. Capstone Interactive titles, for example, give children a choice of activating the read-aloud story one page at a time, or in its entirety, and each word lights up as it is read (Capstone Interactive, 2017). The Starfall educational site (see *www.starfall.com*) also features read-alouds of a number of easy books that can be heard and seen as they are expressively read aloud. An additional valuable feature is that any word can be paused or repeated by the learner controlling the keyboard.

For longer text and older learners, Adobe Acrobat Reader has a "read out loud" plug-in option. In addition, some ebooks have a text-to-speech option, and Amazon's Audible gives subscribers access to thousands of books read aloud by actors.

> *Imagine my surprise when my new book group revealed to me that the books they were reading every month were actually being read aloud for them through downloadable apps from the library while they performed daily activities. When I asked, "Is it reading?" everyone immediately chimed in "Of course it is!"*—KRISTIN

According to the simple view of reading (Gough & Tunmer, 1986), reading comprehension is the product of language/listening comprehension and decoding. Therefore, by this model, when decoding is not involved, it's still possible to "construct meaning." That means that when decoding (or using the eyes) is removed, the construction of meaning moves into the realm of listening comprehension (or using the ears).

Research confirms that ELLs benefit greatly from multiple representations of content (Waxman & Téllez, 2002), which can be provided from digital read-alouds and even text-to-speech software and apps. However, they benefit most when the reading is expressive, whether it is prerecorded or live in the classroom or library. The added advantage of hearing and seeing texts read expressively in a classroom, of course, is the additional information provided by facial features and other paralinguistic cues, as described in Chapter 3. If opportunities for hearing text read orally allow students to access many new texts without needing to decode, it only further advances the case that ELL students need a large and solid listening vocabulary and a strong knowledge of English syntax patterns in order to understand a text.

Getting proficient in constructing meaning from oral text is analogous to the skill of constructing meaning from written text in many ways. For example, we use probabilistic reasoning to predict what is coming next in a story, whether it is written or oral; we notice and remember details about a character in order to form an opinion about the character, whether the details are presented in written or oral form. Although decoding can be supplemented or bypassed in some contexts, listening comprehension cannot. Text-to-speech options reconfirm the need for strong oracy for ELL students.

Each mode has its benefits and deficits, and students should learn to prepare to use each for its optimal purposes. Fourth-grade teacher Janis Michael (2016) notes that it would be inappropriate to take out a library book about a current event unless a student is seeking its historical context, for example. Good paper-based dictionaries may have more scholarly etymology than open-source online dictionaries, but online dictionaries are more likely to keep up with the changing definitions of words that aren't in the latest print edition of the dictionary.

On the other hand, because of all the links and options in interactive texts, it is very easy for readers to lose track of where they are in the text. Along with the strategies related to specific text structures, ELL students are best served when they learn strong metacognitive strategies (Anderson, 2003; Kang, 2014) that will allow them to make wise decisions about the strategies they will need in order to read successfully in each of these modes.

Gordon and Blass (2016) point out that book reading strategies do not automatically transfer over to the reading of interactive texts, and new strategies need to be taught. This is somewhat analogous to the finding that reading comprehension strategies in L2 need to be explicitly taught in order to activate strategies that students already use in their L1.

Michael says that she mixes literacy modes intentionally in the classroom to reduce fatigue and give her students more options. When her students read interactive text on a screen, she asks them to take notes with paper and pencil. When they read linear texts in paper form, she asks them to take notes on their tablets. She believes altering modes keeps the students fresher and relieves eye strain that may come from too much time spent staring at a screen.

New Ways of Writing

There are now many dramatic changes in the ways we can write since the digital revolution. For one thing, it is possible to use "speech-to-text" software to write down words, just as readers can use "text-to-speech" software to hear text read aloud. Dragon and other speech recognition software and apps, including Apple's popular Siri, allow people to "write down" words by speaking into a microphone on their device. Doctors, lawyers, and clinicians use speech recognition software on a daily basis, and it can be programmed to be trained to a speaker's own voice. Most smart devices now have speech recognition capabilities, and this service is becoming standard. It has created interesting interactions between owners of smart devices and the devices themselves. Many of us have seen our spoken words unfold in written form and realized that that wasn't what we meant to say! The words we had spoken were represented quite differently—or "misunderstood"—in print. By watching our speech as it is transformed into print, we become more metalinguistically aware of how we pronounce words. In this way, speech-to-text apps can actually serve as a kind of secondary pronunciation guide for ELLs: if the app "understands" you by displaying the same words you are trying to say, it means you are probably intelligible to a listener, too (although the app does not account for features of stress and intonation). By immediately displaying the written text that the app "thinks" you said, speech-to-text apps also give a learner immediate pronunciation feedback, through a kind of low-stakes formative assessment.

However, as discussed in Chapter 9, writing is "not just frozen speech." When we write, unless we use very simple BICS language such as text messaging, we employ more formal elements of English. Sentences are longer, are more embedded, use more academic vocabulary, have pronoun references, and use a wide variety of tenses, including the passive voice. Also, oral language has a great deal of redundancy—circling back, restating, clarifying—whereas written language is more condensed. For some informational text, such as science writing, the writing is extremely dense, and every word must be understood perfectly to advance through the text. None of these elements are common in the structure of oral speech, and capturing speech in print will not improve a student's ability to compose more academic writing that uses these features.

Look at this excerpt from a paragraph of an assignment submitted through a speech-to-text format.

When an ELL students is reading in a language that is different from their own is difficult . . . I feel more comfortable if I need to talk about a topic or read aloud in class, usually something that ELL do often is ask how you pronounce this word when they are reading . . . the third idea is using audio-assisted oral reading this will help the students to do better in their pronunciation while they read and guided them through the sentences on the story.

If we hear this paragraph read aloud, we can easily get the gist of the sentences because we "forgive" small anomalies, but if we read it silently, a number of errors jump out at us:

1. The introductory clause of the first sentence (beginning with *when*) has a plural subject (*ELL students*) but a singular article (*an*) and verb (*is*).
2. The main clause of the first sentence is missing a subject (needs *it* before *is*).
3. There are no quotation marks, capital letters, or question marks for the question "How you pronounce this word?" and it's missing its auxiliary verb ("How *do* you pronounce this word?").
4. There should be a period between *reading* and *this* because they are two different sentences, resulting in a "run on" sentence.
5. The last sentence puts the word *guide* in the wrong form (*guided*) and uses the wrong preposition (*sentences on the story* instead of *sentences of the story*).

Automatic speech transcription software has many benefits for those who have difficulty with writing or spelling, and the software is getting better all the time. However, students need to be guided to use this kind of software as a way to capture ideas and then convert those initial thoughts into formal language. When teachers receive assignments that have been dictated into an app rather than created through a writing utensil or keyboard, they will see a representation of the way the student speaks. Teachers can help all students, including ELLs, understand the differences and make the transition from capturing spoken ideas into composing expository writing. Oral speech needs to go through several editing processes in order to conform to written conventions. One big advantage, however, of using automatic speech transcription is its ability to capture ideas on the fly, useful for brainstorming a topic or for storing notes to be used later.

ELL students may notice some of their written errors by reading back their compositions out loud to themselves. However, the proofreading must be done in this order: (1) write down the words and (2) read the text aloud to see how it sounds. Sometimes ELL students might not "hear" the grammar errors in their compositions when they read their composition aloud because they made the original errors when speaking.

There are two other dramatic changes to writing in the digital age. One is that it is much easier to publish to a wider audience. In fact, students do this all the time through social media, but they can also publish Google Docs that can be read by the rest of the class, or by their families, in addition to the teacher. Publishing writing is an exhilarating process for a young student, and preparing to publish can be very motivating, as we have learned in writing workshop. Publishing online can heighten that excitement.

The other dramatic change is the ease with which students can engage in collaborative writing. By sharing documents, they can contribute to a group writing project. As discussed in Chapter 9, peer editing and collaboration in ELL writing can be problematic if the learners are not yet at an advanced level, but there is no reason ELLs can't work on collaborative projects, with native English speakers or other ELLs, once they are able to write at the responsive or expository writing level (see Table 9.2; pp. 240–242). Working in collaborative groups is also a strong contributing activity to ELLs' syndrome of success (Waxman & Téllez, 2002).

New Text Structures and Protocols

The third big change in literacy is the profusion of new text structures. These structures need to be introduced systematically and taught explicitly. Guiding ELL learners in learning how to read and write in these new forms of text can be enriching and fun.

Facebook Protocols

Performing operations on social media sites such as Facebook can be practiced in closed classroom community sites such as Edmodo. This enables learners to have a "sheltered" Facebook simulation, giving them practice at uploading photos and graphics, writing posts, and sending messages. We might think that children learn this outside the classroom, but that is not always the case. With a "sheltered" setting, students can practice using new forms of text structures, learn how to set their privacy settings, delete messages, and so forth, in a low-stakes environment. Teachers can and should take part in the sheltered space by actively participating in the exchanges and modeling appropriate linguistic registers. The teacher can assign a discussion question for homework, and students can post their responses through their preferred device.

Email

Email is a text structure that looks like BICS language, due to its relatively short length and rapid back-and-forth exchange. However, email still has some formal protocols and questions of judgment that must be taught. Since email lacks context, it has some CALP elements, and readers must make judgments about the meaning of an email based on the words alone. A 2016 study shows that people are not good at detecting the tone of their friends' emails even though they have confidence that they are (Riordan & Trichtinger, 2017). All students will need to read and write emails to a variety of different recipients, and email, like any other text structure, has plenty of text conventions. Most of us know that the "ALL CAPS" setting in an email is considered to be "shouting," but there are other, more subtle considerations as well. For example, what is the proper salutation for different recipients? How long should a reasonable email be, according to its different purposes? Who should be copied? How do we know when to respond to an email or when the exchange can be considered to be complete? When is it appropriate to put an *emoticon*, a symbol with a face showing an emotion, or another typographic flourish at the end of a message, and when is it not? ELL students need to navigate these questions for future employment, and teachers should not make the mistake of thinking students know how to do this because they are "digital natives."

One of our teachers says:

> When an adult student sends me an email with "smileys" at the end, it's usually about a late assignment or an unexplained absence. Although I recognize that they are sharing an emotion with me, it feels a bit too informal to me. I expect words, not emoticons.

Twitter

Twitter is a form of text structure, and its ability to show quick developments from innumerable sources makes it a staple of today's fast digital world, so ELL students need to learn how to access this information. The genre of Twitter uses the text structure of the tweet. A tweet is very condensed—140 characters to be exact—and those 140 characters contain numerous connections to other places. Tweets may provide up-to-the-minute developments in the news, including important developments in government, scores for sports as they are being played, and much more.

Before or by the time they enter secondary school, students are likely to be looking for information on Twitter or creating their own tweets. Here is some of the background knowledge needed to successfully read or compose a tweet or to follow a series of tweets:

1. Tweets are color coded. The light blue part of a tweet is a link to another location.
2. A *hashtag* labels a topic with a word or short phrase, often humorous or topical in nature. It is preceded by the symbol #. When a person clicks on a hashtag, all other tweets including that hashtag will appear below it. Students need to learn that although the sign is called a "hashtag," it can also be called a "pound sign" on the telephone keypad, or even a "number sign."
3. A Twitter *handle* is the name or identifier of a person with a Twitter account. It begins with the @ sign. When it is in a tweet, all of the people who like and follow the person at that handle will also see the tweet. Students can pronounce the sign as the word "at."
4. Many tweets link to a "tiny URL," which often begins with *goo.gl* or *bit.ly*. Clicking on the tiny URL leads to the place that the tweet is referencing. We can't tell what the tiny URL links to before we click on it because there is no clue in the tiny URL. That can sometimes result in unpleasant surprises. Therefore, the source of the tweet is of some consequence.
5. If a tweet exceeds the 140-character limit, a box appears that shows the writer how many extra characters the tweet contains. When the extra characters are removed, the tweet can be published.

Students can practice reading tweets and orally paraphrase what they understand from them. The teacher can ask questions such as "Who is the intended audience for this tweet?"; "To whom is this tweet addressed?"; "What is its purpose?"; "Do you think this tweet fulfills its purpose?"

Tweets can also be used in writing instruction. Because of their condensed nature, they can be a great vehicle for summary writing, as this middle school teacher observes.

Writing an effective tweet is hard because you're restricted by the amount of characters. Thus, you can have students summarize a main idea of another piece of writing into a tweet.—THOMAS BOCHNIAK

There are other new text structures, such as those involved in blogging and open-source sites, but those just discussed give an illustration of two of the most common and useful. Taken together, the new ways of reading, new ways of writing, and new text structures suggest taking fresh looks at best practices in literacy for ELLs and all students.

Changes in the Teaching and Learning of Languages

Language learning has moved from the language lab into the cloud. Many language-learning programs, both free and subscription-based, are now available for individual use on laptops, tablets, and smartphones, and they are changing the nature of foreign language learning as well as learning English as a new language.

We can apply what we have learned about language acquisition and language learning in previous chapters to judging the quality of an online foreign language program: Is the input comprehensible? Does the learning environment create a low affective filter? Are there ample opportunities for both intensive and extensive practice? Are all five domains of language learning—listening, speaking, reading, writing, and communicative competence—accounted for in the lessons? Is the material challenging? And, are there social interactions to build motivation?

A language-learning program, such as Duolingo, contains stacked modules composed of individual lessons, so learners cannot proceed to the next lesson until they master the previous ones, ensuring comprehensible input. The self-paced and private nature of the lessons means that the affective filter is low. There is a chance to do metacognitive self-checking by revisiting and repeating earlier lessons (Karch, 2016). Krashen (2013) noted that online language learning lacked immediacy and formative feedback, but some now provide immediate feedback, complete with funny noises for errors and trumpet flourishes to celebrate arrival at each new level. Duolingo won a "best foreign language teaching program" in a 2016 Lifehacker poll and introduced "chatbots" in late 2016 to give learners a chance to practice speaking. One student who used Duolingo in order to learn Spanish as a fourth language had these thoughts.

> *What Duolingo does well is easy introduction of new material, plenty of repetition of vocabulary, phrases, and structures, and frequent revisiting of old material. The game is corny but rewarding. It includes all four components of language learning in every lesson (after the first few introductory lessons). After going through about a third of the program, I felt that an additional approach was necessary, so I added a weekly class at my local library. This was taught by a retired high school Spanish teacher, and was at about the second-year level. It added unscripted listening, speaking, and dialogue, as well as reading comprehension with short texts and grammar worksheets. [From Duolingo], I had a*

variety of vocabulary words, basic verb tenses, and negatives already at my disposal . . . however, even with my level of comfort in operating in multiple foreign languages, I am not yet in a position to hold conversations in Spanish.–KATHERINE M. LIN

Katherine recognized that she was missing the interaction with a language community—the comprehensible input—which is indispensable for achieving proficiency in a new language. Other language learning apps such as Memrise have begun to incorporate interactive opportunities, and other foreign-language apps are sure to follow. There are also many places on the Internet to practice English and other languages, including both free sites and those that charge a fee. Fluentu is an app which uses authentic short videos, with a teacher superimposed on them, explaining grammar and vocabulary. Another way to practice is to listen to "slow news" in different languages; the advantage of these sites is that learners can process news they already know in their L1, so it's easier to follow in a new language, especially if words are pronounced somewhat slowly and clearly. There are also many language exchange sites that put people together to chat on Skype. One of the most charming examples of video exchanges is one set up between retirement home residents at a suburb outside Chicago and young people in Brazil (CNA Speaking Exchange, 2016). Now, motivated learners can find many outlets to practice and interact regardless of how many speakers of a language may live in their immediate area.

Online Translators

A few short years ago, it seemed that "machine-assisted translation" would never be able to master the many nuances of rendering speech and text into a new language. Translations were word by word, and they were terrible, owing to incorrect language translations of phrases, idioms, and figurative language. Although even now some translation programs fall short, they have come a long way in the last few years. For example, nearly 100 languages of the world can be used as default languages for Facebook profiles. There are translation options below Facebook posts. Many websites have translation tools available with a dropdown menu, including many school districts and municipalities. Google Translator allows us to point at a word with a smartphone app and identify both its language and its meaning. We can also listen to how a word in another language is pronounced. It's a polyglot's paradise!

It's also a bright new horizon for literacy because social media has brought daily reading into the lives of hundreds of millions of people, regardless of their location or income level. In the digital revolution, reading is just as important as listening, and the sources are very eclectic, from texts and tweets to local restaurant reviews, from instructions at a help desk to articles at thousands of news sites, websites, and blogs. And that's not even taking into account the increased access to millions of books.

In our global village, much translation work can now be done by software, and the state of the art is improving constantly. The grammar translation method that consumed the lives of scholars is confined to a cadre of linguists writing ever-improving software programs. One wonders if there is less motivation for L1 English speakers to learn a new language because translations into English can be easily obtained from so many sources, without needing to learn the languages from which the texts originate. It's tempting, especially in geographically vast English-speaking countries, such as the U.S., Canada, or Australia, to "wait for the world to come to English" rather than exploring the amazing spectrum of languages in existence around the world. However, at the same time that it's easier to get English translations, it is also easier to explore other languages, and globalization has also given us more opportunities for international friendships, travel, and employment, and knowledge of foreign languages still makes a great difference. We hope that all readers of this book consider taking up the exciting challenge!

Those learning English as a new language, however, do not have the luxury of waiting for the world to come to their language. Although these translation aids can be lifesavers, there is still worldwide pressure to learn English, and this is not likely to subside any time soon. Fortunately, people around the world are just as attached to their first languages as English speakers are to theirs, so many people will continue to insist on the preservation and use of their own languages and right to speak and learn in them. Now they have the technology to make that more possible.

New Roles for Teachers and Learners

Only a couple of decades ago, educators declared that teachers had moved from the role of "sage on the stage" to "guide on the side," as students engaged in project-based learning. Now, teachers may be evolving toward a new role: "conductor of the creative" (Lems, personal communication, May, 2017). The digital revolution gives teachers the opportunity—and the obligation—to become expert in designing and managing an engaging, multiuse curriculum that draws eclectically from many sources. This curriculum must be nimble, have high standards, and fan the flame of learners' creativity. Now, a state-of-the-art curriculum encourages young learners to seek out and embrace the learning tools that will help them become college and career ready, and also independent lifelong learners. As teachers help create these conditions, they also need to set up a classroom that affirms and welcomes all learners, as well as their families and caregivers. Setting up a welcoming and nurturing classroom is one area in which technology can never replace a "flesh and blood" teacher.

As the organizer of these many new skills, the teacher becomes a kind of "symphony conductor," orchestrating complex activities through practicing the parts while also bringing out the beauty of the ensemble. Teaching is truly a science and an art.

The role of the learner is changing just as dramatically, if not more so. Learners can access their lessons at a desk or at a roller rink, in front of a giant TV screen, or between serving customers at a part-time job. They can work with their own favorite music in their headphones or work "side by side" with a study buddy on another continent. Young people have many new ways to access their learning, but the best methods to engage with the curriculum and benefit from its lessons still need to be taught. Whereas in the past teachers helped students memorize information and tested them largely on their memories, now we help students to find, choose, use, and apply resources for problem solving. The information does not need to be stored in our heads anymore—but the judgment about how to use the information for specific purposes does.

New Literacies

Emoticons, memes, and in particular, emojis are new developments in "universal" writing systems that can be understood in many countries and languages because they are not based on a fixed pronunciation in any language. Parkin (2016) calls emojis, which originated in 1999 as a set of icons for Japanese cell phones, "the fastest-growing form of communication" (p. 40). An Egyptian-born teacher comments, "We've come full circle with emojis—now it looks like we're back to hieroglyphics."

There are even humorous books about the topic, such as *How to Speak Emoji* (Benenson, 2015).

> *When my daughter texts a string of emojis to me from her cell phone, I have no idea what she is talking about. They are small and she might send a whole string of them. I don't know if it's a story, or a sentence, or just random thoughts. I'm not sure she does either.*—TENENA

The FoxTrot cartoon in Figure 10.1 humorously shows the "disconnect" between those who follow the protocols of handwritten text versus

FIGURE 10.1. Thank-you note. FoxTrot copyright © 2015 Bill Amend. Reprinted with permission of Universal Uclick. All rights reserved.

those who prefer texting with emojis. For additional discussion of emojis, see Chapter 4.

Adding emojis can be considered a way of adding back some of the context that is normally stripped away in writing, which includes "words only." Emoji writing makes "CALP" writing more "BICS-like."

Digital Literacy as a Content Area

Information science, computer science, and their many related fields are important knowledge areas that can lead to many well-paying and powerful jobs. ELL students, like all others, should have an opportunity to learn about them and learn the vocabulary associated with them. Technology vocabulary related to these fields is proliferating as these fields expand, and all of the forms of English word formation described in Chapter 6 are represented. Appendix 10.1, at the end of the chapter, provides a list of technology-based words that can be classified according to one of the 12 forms of word formation, and one additional form.

Online Databases Now Available to Teachers

If there's anything computers are really good at, it's counting (the French name for computers is still "ordinateur," which means "counter")! Because computers are so good at collecting material, then counting it and sorting it, all kinds of new information can be easily stored and accessed—whether it is the performance of your favorite athlete, the sightings of sandhill cranes as they undertake their annual migration, or the detailed scores of individual student performance on tasks and tests, from fitness scores to reading comprehension scores. Collecting and publishing numbers is here to stay—and you can "count on it!" The following three language databases, although not necessarily easy to navigate, will be of interest to language and literacy educators.

1. *wordfrequency.info* is a large database of words in American English that displays the frequency of each word. It contains more than a billion words. It is in a process of constant revision and contains several subcorpora (the plural of *corpus*, which means a large body of words). In addition to showing word frequencies, one can see how each word's occurrence has changed over time, and the distribution of the word across the five main genres of spoken language, fiction, popular magazines, newspapers, and academic language. In addition to being fascinating, the database contains very helpful information to guide teachers in deciding which vocabulary is most important. For example, we can compare the frequency of two different phrasal verbs in order to decide which one to include in a weekly vocabulary list (*think over,* for example, has 1,103 occurrences per million words, but *think upon* has only 66 occurrences) (Word Frequency Data, 2016).

2. *n-grams* result from a large international collaboration of computational linguists who manage and set up parameters for giant lexical databases. They allow us to see the frequency of usage of a word or phrase, changes in word-frequency use over time, and much more. The Google Books n-gram viewer and the Google n-gram viewer can show how often a word is used in each year in both oral and written texts (Google n-gram viewer, 2016). For example, we can visit n-gram sites to see how many babies were given our first names in the year we were born and the trends in baby naming over time. We can look up a compound word, such as *hand plow*, which is connected to a certain time period, and view its tra-

jectory as it hits its peak in the first decade of the 20th century and then declines in usage as newer technologies replace it. Students can use this site for research into their own language studies. (Also, it's fun!)

3. *Readability measures* were originally meant to match readers with books at their reading levels. The most well-known system used before the digital revolution, the Fry readability scale (Fry, 1977), allowed teachers to calculate the difficulty level of a book through a system of counting words in a sentence in a portion of text and locating its grade level on a graph. Fountas and Pinnell (2016) also developed a widely used system of guided reading levels, with an ever-expanding database of books rated by a large group of experts in the reading field. Their book-leveling system, as well as those of Scholastic (Scholastic Teacher, 2016), are very influential. It is also possible to find books coded by their literary genres and by area of interest to help match students with appropriate texts at their current reading levels. Even Microsoft Word software has a readability measure, called Flesch-Kincaid, which classifies text by grade-level year and month. It can be seen by activating its setting.

Renaissance Learning (2016), a publisher of several online reading programs, creates an annual data-based report that offers insights about reading trends. Although the report does not dwell on the ways in which the reading strategies of children reading online might differ from those of children reading paper-based texts, the data collected from its online reading programs confirm that more minutes of independent reading over time results in higher levels of college and career readiness. The 2016 report finds that students who set reading goals have higher achievement levels, which matches well with all the research about metacognitive strategies. The report also categorizes the average difficulty level of informational texts (which are often articles, rather than books) according to grade, and concludes that the informational texts read by first, second, and third graders are actually at a fourth-grade reading level (Renaissance Learning, 2016). This finding suggests that informational text provided to students may present more challenging reading tasks than fiction, and this has implications for ELL children in those grade levels because they may not be ready for the heavy English vocabulary and syntax demands. In addition, informational text may rely on certain background knowledge or cultural assumptions.

Renaissance Learning also has a readability formula, called ATOS Analyzer (2015), that factors in average sentence length, average word length, and average word difficulty level (connected to word frequency).

We briefly mention these large databases to pique your curiosity and increase your own background knowledge about language and literacy in the digital age. Looking at the dynamic new landscape for literacy and language learning, we can clearly see that these revolutionary changes can provide massive benefits to English language learners and indeed, to all learners, because of the greatly improved access, ease, and range of options for learning.

HOW DOES THIS LOOK IN THE CLASSROOM?

We know that teachers teach in many different settings and have varying resources available for use, in addition to their own preferences. Therefore, we'll share only a few effective activities that mention specific apps or software and leave it to you to accommodate the activity to your own situation.

Online Resources

There are many free and affordable learning resources these days, and teachers and students are able to explore, bookmark, and interact with them. The Khan Academy provides thousands of free lessons in math, science, and languages; a nonprofit, CK-12 (2017), offers interactive, free downloadable textbooks in science and math, and there are many others.

Collages, Word Clouds, Avatars

When ELL learners are still at a Beginning or Entering level of English, they can enjoy making artistic representations of themselves through apps and programs such as *piccollage*, an app that allows them to create collages of images on a smart device, and others. Students can drag images into a design that represents their favorite things and use it as a visual identity. Another option is making "word clouds," consisting of words that the students type in, in programs such as *wordle* or *wordcloud.com*. These custom-made images can be printed out and posted on bulletin boards in the room, allowing students to get to know each other a little better. Students can also design their own *avatar*, an artistic personal representation that has its own appearance and voice, through many free programs such as the one at *voki.com*. In all of these ways, ELL students can represent aspects of their identity without needing to use a lot of words and to feel safe and supported as they learn to navigate school and the Internet.

Innumerable other ideas can be found at sites such as *readwritethink.org*, *edutopia.org*, the teacher area at *scholastic.com*, and *educatorstechnology.com*. Just because publishers and organizations don't mention ELLs specifically doesn't mean some of their teaching ideas won't work well with them. However, the reverse is also true—many of the sites that identify themselves as being "ESL sites" are really directed toward college-age students in intensive English programs and not pedagogically appropriate for the PreK–12 students, who are the focus of this book.

Using Photos from Image Banks

There are few things more exhilarating than beholding a great image, and wonderful photos of every aspect of the natural world—from the microscopic to the telescopic—can create inspiring writing and speaking activities in the classroom.

> *I know some teachers who use the image of the day on the Bing search engine and project it up on the screen for 10 minutes each morning. The children use this time to write about the image using as many sensory detail words as possible. Some students are provided with a word bank to help make this task less abstract and more accessible.*—CLARE HOURICAN

There are many online sources for reproductions of great art, including those of major art museums, and students can talk or write about the paintings as they learn about great painters, themes, and periods. Even Beginning-level ELL students can generate some language by describing what they see. More advanced students can compare and contrast two paintings by artists who use different techniques and styles.

Another entertaining source that can spark conversation, for adolescents in particular, is optical illusions. Optical illusions can be a refreshing change of pace after doing concentrated academic work. Optical illusions can be found in Google image searches.

Formative Assessments

Digital technology allows teachers to check student comprehension in real time. *Plickers* is a handy, free classroom app that can be managed by teachers on laptops, iPads, or smartphones to get real-time feedback based on student responses. Besides a smartboard and smart device, no additional technology is needed. The teacher's score sheet is part of the app. The teacher distributes laminated or sturdy barcoded cards to each student. The barcoded cards, which are free downloads, are matched to the class roster by the teacher before the class starts. Citlali Flores, a new teacher in Grayslake, Illinois, used this technology to create an idioms lesson for her ELLs. She shows an idiom on a screen at the front of the room, with four possible definitions. Each student picks their choice and holds up his or her card with either the *a*, *b*, *c*, or *d* side facing up. Citlali then goes around the room and scans the barcoded cards, allowing her to see instantly which answers were chosen and how many students chose each answer.

Nearpod, Kahoot, and *Quizlet Live* are similar to Plickers, but they require the students to have networked devices, which is not always possible. Students respond to quiz questions in the same way—choosing one of four designs that represent the four options—three of which are incorrect answers. The teacher can see instant survey results and get a quick sense of which items need more review. The competition stays friendly because no one but the teacher can see which kids choose which answer. Students love these games, and the games create a lively classroom environment. Once a teacher creates a good quiz, it can be used semester after semester with new students.

Wraparound Digital Services

In addition to all of these individual sites, Google offers a whole suite of services, with some that are available to individual teachers, but many that are licensed to an entire school. Teachers we work with find great value in the Google Classroom features, ranging from apps to calendars that students and families can view to ways to submit and edit compositions. Teachers can use Google Classroom as a platform for Writer's Notebook, a journaling activity. Third-grade teacher Kevin Wardzala sets up individual student files, and students add to their own notebooks using a template Kevin provides on Google Slides (Wardzala, 2016). The big advantage of using an online format for Writer's Notebook is that students can add to it from any location, through many kinds of devices and at any time, even when they are absent from school.

Connecting with Families through Texting

Although some families of ELLs do not have Wi-fi in their homes, most have smartphones. Sending parents and caregivers voice messages or text messages is a very effective way to increase family involvement. Maria Marquez wrote songs about science with her bilingual kindergarten students and recorded the class singing the songs on her cell phone, then forwarded the recording as an attachment to each of the families. Using voice messages is more appropriate, Maria explains, for those families who are not literate in any language and cannot read text messages. However, when they can hear messages about classroom activities, they are eager to visit their child's class and take part in them. "The cell phone messages have made a huge difference," she says. "Now families feel like they are part of the class."

WebQuests

WebQuests are curricular projects related to a unit of study for students usually in grades 5 and above. The sources and activities are designed in advance by the teacher so that students have guidance and scaffolding as they embark on their online research. WebQuests can be considered superior examples of "sheltered" instruction because they provide more scaffolding and direction than students usually get when doing independent research. For this reason, they are especially helpful for ELLs. Sox and Rubinstein-Avila (2009) stress that creating a good WebQuest for ELL students requires paying attention to the language difficulty level in the featured sites as well as providing practice in using strategies needed for reading interactive texts. WebQuests can be accomplished individually, in pairs or in small groups. The topics are endless, as long as the teacher commits to preparing the necessary set of resources, and keeps it updated from year to year. One good free site teachers often use for WebQuests is *zunal.com*, which curates thousands of teacher-created WebQuests.

Students as Tech Resources

You don't need to be the one explaining how digital media works—sometimes your students will be as tech-savvy as you are, or more so. When students explain technology applications to others, as well as to you, whether in a whole class or small-group format, they practice their spoken English and develop leadership skills. Because there are so many jobs in information technology, from help desks to coding, from maintaining websites to cybersecurity, practicing these skills can be the first step toward a career path. Students may need assistance in the academic tasks within technology, but they are less likely to need assistance with the actual operations because these students are digital natives.

Clearing Away the Clutter for Online Reading

To cut down on the distractions from reading online, teachers can use a good tool, Mercury Reader, a free Google extension. Once it is installed using the Chrome browser, when you find an article on the Internet that you'd like to have your students read, just click on the Mercury icon in the corner of the screen, and it will miraculously remove the clutter so that students will see only a clean copy of the text. A clean copy makes reading blogs and other online content much easier for distractible students— and teachers. The same service is also available under different names in Safari and Firefox.

Finding the Apps You Need

There is an endless supply of new apps popping up, some of which are free, and reviews of them abound. Those apps that a preschool teacher using a tablet finds useful are quite different from those that work well for a learner at the junior high or high school level. Our only rule of thumb is to keep in mind best practices in teaching ELLs: comprehensible input, keeping the affective filter low, working in all five domains, providing many opportunities for instructional conversation, and keeping the difficulty level within the zone of proximal development. At this time, and in the foreseeable future, it's truly an "embarrassment of riches." Find a few good apps and make them your own, and add new ones deliberately and mindfully. Once you have a stable core collection, you can share what you know with your colleagues and continue to learn from each other.

QUESTIONS FOR FURTHER STUDY

1. What are three ideas from the chapter that you found interesting or provocative, and why?

2. Think about something connected to your academic life (as a learner or a teacher) that has dramatically changed because of technology, and reflect on the consequences of the change. What do you miss about the "old way"? What do you consider to be better about the "new way"? What else?

3. Have you ever misunderstood an email, or been misunderstood from an email you sent? What do you think accounted for the misunderstanding? What did you learn from it, if anything? Have you also been misinterpreted on Facebook? How would you help your young ELLs learn to navigate Facebook?

4. Look at the descriptions of screen-based reading described in Liu's research. Does it correspond to your own perception about your reading? In what ways do you believe you read differently if you are doing screen-based reading?

5. Thinking about the computer as a "counter," what kinds of things do you count in your daily life? In your job? What are the instruments you use to count these things? In what ways has the ability—and the necessity—to count more things had an effect on the quality of life you lead?

6. Look at your own teaching (present, future, or past) and assign approximate percentages to the attention you have paid to designing curricula and access to resources, delivering the lessons, and creating a low affective filter to create classroom community. In what ways you do think this approach will change as technology in education changes? What do you predict will stay the same?

7. Using the descriptions of the 12 forms of English word formation in Chapter 6, do the activity in Appendix 10.1 and compare your answers with a classmate, if possible.

8. "Unpack" the background knowledge for a different text structure than email or Twitter and share it with others. Was it difficult to think of all the steps to perform a routine function?

9. CHALLENGE QUESTION: Look at Table 10.1, which sketches characteristics of the four presentation modes for English written text. Create additional columns that analyze these four forms according to additional criteria. Which mode is appropriate for different classroom activities? Homework? Student writing? What are the implications of using one or another of these modes? Share your analysis with others.

10. CHALLENGE QUESTION: If you are monolingual, ask a bilingual friend to help you with the question. Choose an online translator tool and set English as the source and the other language as the destination. First, choose 10 individual English vocabulary words and look at their translations. Next, choose five English idioms and look at their translations. Then, enter a short paragraph from an English literary work, such as a novel at the grade level in which you teach or plan to teach, and look at the translation. Finally, enter a paragraph from a STEM area, such as biology or physics. Discuss the results. What were the strengths and weaknesses of the translator for these different kinds of words and phrases? What encouragement and/or cautions would you give ELL students about using an online translator?

Technology Terms Demonstrating
English Word Formation

Classify the technology vocabulary below using the chart on p. 282 according to the 12 kinds of English word formation you have studied in Chapter 6, and add a 13th—"metaphors" (using an image or action already known to the reader in a completely new context). Since "backformation" is one kind of multiple process, we include it with multiple processes. In many cases, more than one answer can be correct, but there is usually a best answer. (See p. 283 for suggested answers, but only after you've filled in the chart.)

gigabyte	*to message*	*troll*	*cached*	*blog*	*doc*	*phishing*
online	*iTunes*	*keyboarding*	*GIF*	*to boot*	*majordomo*	*PDF*
pinterest	*to upload*	*meltdown*	*web*	*surfing*	*menu*	*geek*
ebook	*to "friend"*	*firewall*	*to text*	*techie*	*pixel*	*DVD/DVR*
keyword	*avatar*	*cyberspace*	*logon*	*ROM*	*mouse*	*newbie*
spam	*help desk*	*fax*	*nerdette*	*Skype*	*stream*	*cloud*
snail mail	*clickbait*	*dropdown*	*reboot*	*app*	*podcast*	*Google*

(*continued*)

Coinage (neologisms)	Borrowing (loan words)	Clipping	Blending (portmanteau words)
Compounds	Acronyms	Paired-word sound play	Metaphors
Abbreviations	Conversion (category shift)	Scale change	Multiple processes (backformation)

Which forms predominate? Which are less common?

(continued)

Suggested Answers for APPENDIX 10.1

Coinage (neologisms)	Borrowing (loan words)	Clipping	Blending (portmanteau words)
Google phishing geek pixel Skype	avatar cached menu majordomo	app doc fax web	spam blog podcast cyberspace pinterest ebook iTunes

Compounds	Acronyms	Paired-word sound play	Metaphors
dropdown help desk keyword logon online firewall clickbait	ROM GIF	snail mail	mouse cloud stream meltdown surfing troll

Abbreviations	Conversion (category shift)	Scale change	Multiple processes (backformation)
DVD/DVR PDF	to message to friend to boot to text to upload	gigabyte techie nerdette newbie	keyboarding reboot

Note. In many cases, more than one answer can be correct, but there is usually a best answer.

Glossary

abbreviation: creating a new word by pronouncing each of the first letters of a group of words separately; one of the processes for forming new words in English (e.g., *CEO* for chief executive officer).

accuracy: proportion of words read aloud correctly; core measure of Oral Reading Fluency.

acronym: creating a word from the first letters of a series of words, pronounced as a new word; one of the processes for forming new words in English (e.g., NASA [National Aeronautics and Space Administration], *radar* [radio detecting and signaling device]).

affect: social–emotional variables that influence language learning and acquisition.

affective filter: one of six hypotheses that form Krashen's (1982) theory of second-language acquisition. The emotional response to a language learning or other situation, characterized as either high or low.

affix: morpheme attached to a root (base) to form words or change grammatical categories; in English, they are prefixes and suffixes.

alphabet: writing system in which letters (*graphemes*) represent sounds (*phonemes*).

alphabetic/letter name spelling: stage of English spelling for students in which the sound of the letter name is written, such as "c" for the word "sea."

alphabetic orthography: writing system having a symbol or symbols to represent vowel and consonant sounds.

assimilative motivation: the incentive to learn a new language or anything else in order to join a group or community and construct a new personal identity, as in a "melting pot."

auding: active construction of meaning while listening to an oral text, similar to the way a reader actively constructs meaning from a written text. Also called active listening.

audio imaging: using sounds or music to prompt visualization in order to remember a word, event, or idea.

audiolingualism (or audiolingual method)/ALM: language teaching method widely used in the 1960s and 1970s in which oral skills (oracy) take precedence over reading and writing skills.

auditory comprehension: See *listening comprehension.*

automaticity theory of reading: theory claiming that learning to read proficiently requires moving from effortful decoding of words to unconscious and automatic decoding of words (LaBerge & Samuels, 1974).

avatar: in the digital context, an icon or image a user adopts as a visible identity for video games and other Internet contexts.

backformation: removing the end of a word (usually a noun) and creating a new word from it, usually a verb; one of the processes for forming new words in English (e.g., *televise* from *television; teach* from *teacher; opt* from *option*).

balanced literacy: a pedagogical approach combining the teaching of discrete reading and writing skills within a framework of large meaning-based activities (e.g., shared reading, interactive read-aloud, writer's workshop).

basic interpersonal communicative skills (BICS): conversational language, primarily oral, that young ELLs pick up in informal and social situations (Cummins, 1981).

blending (portmanteau words): combining two or more morphemes to form a new hybrid word; one of the word formation processes of English (e.g., *spam, brunch*).

borrowing: taking a word from another language and adopting it into a new one; one of the word formation processes of English (e.g., *tortilla, pajamas*).

bottom-up skills: word-level skills required for decoding.

bound morpheme: morpheme that must attach to a root (base) to make a word. Bound morphemes are composed of prefixes, suffixes, and bound roots.

bound root: root that must attach to another root or affix in order to create a single morpheme (unit of meaning).

caretaker speech: See *motherese*.

chunking (parsing): separating written text into meaningful phrase or clause units.

clipping: shortening a word, one of the processes for forming new words in English (e.g., *gym* from *gymnasium*; *pedi* from *pedicure*).

closed class: linguistic term indicating that new morphemes cannot be added to a lexicon; a function word is an example of a closed class.

cloze: activity in which students supply missing words from a text, either oral or written. Also called fill-in-the-blank or gap-fill activities.

cognate: a word having a similar form and meaning in different languages and coming from the same root. Languages belonging to the same language family share more cognates.

cognitive academic language learning approach (CALLA): content-based instructional model focusing on English features and strategies (Chamot & O'Malley, 1986).

cognitive academic language proficiency (CALP): academic language proficiency, oral and written, of school, professions, and literate venues (Cummins, 1979, 1991, 2008).

cognitive load: amount of mental work required to perform a task.

cognitive processing strategies: inferencing, predicting, problem solving, constructing meaning, part of the processing strategies of the hypothetical model of the reading process (Birch, 2015).

coinage (neologisms): one of the processes for forming new words in English; "making up" new words (e.g., *Google*, *Tylenol*, *Kleenex*).

collocation: words occurring together in a fixed order (e.g., listemes, phrasal verbs, and idioms); usually acquired or learned as a memorized unit.

communicative approach: a language teaching approach in which learners take part in interactive, meaningful activities.

communicative competence: the synergistic knowledge language users develop to make appropriate language choices in different contexts.

compensatory model of second-language reading: Bernhardt model in which L2 proficiency (30%), L1 literacy (20%), and unexplained variables (50%) contribute to L2 reading and can affect each other in bidirectional ways (Bernhardt, 2011).

compounding: creating a new word from two or more free morphemes (existing words); one of the processes for forming new words in English (e.g., *toothbrush, butterfly, snapdragon*).

comprehensible input: See *input hypothesis*.

comprehensible output: See *output hypothesis*.

concept of word: the ability to tell where words begin and end within the flowing stream of speech.

consonantal alphabet: a writing system that relies primarily on consonants; some of the vowels are left for the readers to fill in (e.g., Arabic).

content area: academic subject area such as math, science, social studies, or computers.

content-based instruction (CBI): a language teaching methodology in which students learn English while learning academic content.

content frame (semantic feature analysis grid): graphic organizer with several items classified according to a number of separate characteristics using a matrix format.

content word: nouns, verbs, adjectives, adverbs, and some prepositions. In English, the last content word of a phrase or clause receives the strong stress. Most vocabulary study focuses on content words. See also *lexical morpheme*.

context-reduced oral language: conversation lacking cues that can compensate for breakdowns in auditory comprehension, such as telephone calls (Cummins, 1981). This language is difficult for ELLs.

contrastive analysis (CA): predicting or understanding errors produced by learners of a new language based on the structure of their first language. CA has a strong form and a weak form.

contrastive stress: changing normal stress patterns to emphasize a particular part of a phrase or clause.

conversion (category shift): creating a new word by changing its function; one of the processes for forming new words in English (e.g., "Are we out of *butter*?" "Yes, I used it to *butter* the toast.").

corpus (plural corpora): very large collection of words, comprising the foundation for corpus linguistics.

cross-linguistic homograph: a word that shares the same letters in L1 and L2 but not the same meaning (e.g., *pie* in English and Spanish).

cross-linguistic homophone: a word that shares the same sounds and the same pronunciation in L1 and L2 but not the same meaning (e.g., *drei*, the number 3 in German, but *dry*, the opposite of wet, in English).

cross-linguistic influence: the action, conscious or unconscious, of applying the features of a first language to the learning of a new language. This can be positive, negative, or neutral.

cultural capital: the social assets, including literacy, that promote social mobility, including but not limited to economic means (Bourdieu, 1991).

decodable word: word with easy-to-match phonemes and graphemes.

decoding: identifying words, part of "bottom-up" reading skills.

deep orthography (opaque orthography): a writing system in which graphemes do not closely represent the phonemes of the language (e.g., Chinese, English).

deficit theory: the idea that students have deficiencies to be "fixed" or "corrected," rather than capabilities and resources to be developed. The deficit hypothesis underlies attitudes and teaching practices that consider learners to be "an empty vessel to be filled."

derivational morpheme: prefix(es) or suffix(es) combined with a root (base) to create words, change word meanings, or change grammatical categories.

diacritics: markings attached to or around a written symbol to clarify pronunciation features such as tone, syllable stress, vowel quality, or nasalization. Diacritic marks can also alter meaning.

dialect: systematic, rule-governed variations in pronunciation, grammar, vocabulary, phrases, or language usage spoken by members of a language community. Dialects can be based on factors such as geographic region, race, religion, age, economic class, politics, sex, gender, social class, or other factors.

dictation: intensive listening activity in which students write down words or phrases spoken or read by a teacher or a recording; used for practicing listening comprehension, phonological awareness, and concept of word.

dictocomp: writing exercise asking students to summarize an oral text in writing.

digraph: sound represented by two letters, such as *ph*.

discourse marker: in oral texts, conversational fillers, sounds, and paralinguistic cues that help listeners keep track of the speaker's direction at a given moment. Also applies to written text; discourse markers might include numbering, punctuation, signal words, text features, etc.

drop everything and read (DEAR): one sustained silent reading/extended reading technique.

ellipsis: missing words that proficient listeners or readers are able to fill in from context.

emoji: image that can be inserted into texts to express emotions, attitudes, or situations.

emoticon: short image added to texts to represent the writer's emotions with a set of round yellow faces. An earlier form of the emoji.

English as a foreign language (EFL): the study of English in countries where English is not the primary language of communication or schooling.

English as a second language (ESL): designates the study of English in countries where English is the primary language of communication or schooling.

English language learner (ELL): a learner of any age whose first language is not English.

etymology: the study of the origin of words and how they evolve.

expository writing: purposeful composing for presenting information about a given nonfiction topic.

expressive writing: the early stages of writing, usually narrative and descriptive, based on the writer's observations, feelings, and experiences.

extensive listening activity: getting the gist of oral texts through practice and strategies. See also *gist*.

extensive reading: reading large amounts of text for general comprehension.

false cognate: words in two language that are derived from the same root and appear to look or sound similar but have taken on different meanings over time.

fluency: the ability to recognize written words while simultaneously constructing meaning from connected text; also called *reading fluency*.

focus on form (FoF): methods in which learners and teachers pay in-depth attention to grammatical forms and their meanings in context.

free morpheme: morpheme that can stand by itself as a word; composed of lexical morphemes and functional morphemes.

free voluntary reading (FVR): an extensive reading technique in which readers choose their own texts.

frontloading: preteaching vocabulary or other knowledge prior to reading a text or beginning a unit of study.

functional morpheme: class of free morphemes made up of articles, conjunctions, auxiliary verbs, pronouns, and some prepositions; also referred to as *function word*.

function word: articles, conjunctions, auxiliary verbs, pronouns, and some prepositions; also called *functional morpheme*.

generative: producing many elements with a given set of rules, such as a generative grammar.

gist: synthesizing a text, either oral or written, down to its main idea. A skill acquired over time through extensive listening or extensive reading.

grammar: the overarching structure of a language, which includes its phonology, morphology, syntax, and semantics.

grammar translation approach: a language teaching approach using texts to teach grammar with little or no attempt to build oral skills or communicative competence.

grammatical category: classes of words having certain features in common, such as verbs or nouns, sometimes called "parts of speech."

grapheme: a written symbol that represents speech.

graphic organizer: a visual system for organizing information.

handwritten text: text created with a writing utensil of some kind, such as labeling, writing on the board by the teacher, student writing in early literacy, creative writing, or journaling. Contrasts with linear text, screen-based linear text, and interactive text.

handle: a name or identifier used by a person with a Twitter account. It is preceded by the @ sign.

hashtag: a word or short phrase used on Twitter, often humorous, to characterize a topic. It is preceded by the # sign.

H-chart: graphic organizer with two long overlapping rectangles for representing common features; similar to a Venn diagram.

homograph: two words with the same spelling but different sounds and meanings (e.g., *bass* for *bass fishing* or *bass guitar*).

homonym: term used to describe two words that look or sound alike; the three kinds of homonyms are homophones, homographs, and polysemous words.

homophone: words sharing the same pronunciation but different meanings and spellings (e.g., *bear/bare*; *to/too/two*).

hypothetical model of the reading process: reading model focusing on activating an interaction between processing strategies and knowledge bases in order to process a text (Birch, 2015).

idiom: expression that cannot be understood from the meaning of the individual words; memorized as a unit (e.g., *straight from the horse's mouth, raining cats and dogs*); idioms are one kind of collocation.

independent writing: stage in process writing for developing ideas more fully.

inferencing: ability to read "between the lines" or make connections within a text, whether oral or written.

inflectional morpheme: grammar markers that show the categories of tense, number (singular/plural), possession, or comparison of a word. They are bound morphemes and are the last suffix of a word.

input hypothesis: one of six hypotheses that form Krashen's (1982) theory of second-language acquisition. Enormous amounts of spoken or written language just above the learner's current level facilitate the acquisition of a new language.

instructional conversation: questioning and sharing ideas and knowledge through structured academic dialogue.

instrumental motivation: the incentive to learn a new language or anything else for a specific purpose (e.g., school, work, relationships).

integrative motivation: the incentive to learn a new language or anything else in order to integrate into a community while keeping one's identity, as in a "salad bowl."

intensive listening activity: listening practice focusing on small elements of an oral text.

interactive process: a description of reading as a process combining bottom-up and top-down skills and strategies and the active construction of meaning of a text by a reader.

interactive read-aloud (IR): a core early literacy technique using picture books, done over several days. Many skills can be practiced through skillful prereading, mid-reading, and postreading activities.

interactive text: text designed to be read online, including features such as links to graphics, definitions, keywords, videos, or blogposts. Also called branched text. Contrasts with handwritten text, linear text, and screen-based linear text.

interdependence hypothesis: knowledge of one language assists the learning of another language (Cummins, 1979, 1981).

interference: impeding effects of the first language on second-language acquisition.

intonation pattern: the vocal changes of pitch occurring in the normal course of speaking. These may vary among different dialects of a language and among different speakers.

intrinsic motivation: the incentive to learn a new language or anything else "for its own sake" or for curiosity.

invented spelling: the spelling used by learners who are just learning to put letters together to make words. Also known as inventive spelling.

keyword method: a word-learning technique based on forming mental images and connecting them to new words, often through the word's sound.

language acquisition: innate, universal, and automatic human endowment; all normally endowed children acquire a native language.

language-based theory of learning: Halliday's theory (1993) that all learning is a linguistic process with three interconnected areas: learning language, learning through language, and learning about language.

language control: WIDA writing standard regarding amount of grammatical accuracy available to produce comprehensible written text.

language distance: the amount of similarity between two languages with regard to their phonology, morphology, syntax, semantics, and cognates. Also called *linguistic proximity*.

language experience approach (LEA): early literacy approach using a student's dictated stories as the basis for reading a text.

language knowledge: sounds, letters, words, phrases, and sentences, the language-specific part of the knowledge base of the hypothetical model of the reading process (Birch, 2015).

language learning: effortful and conscious attainment of a language, usually through school, including literacy.

language loss: decline or disappearance of language knowledge due to lack of use of the language.

language processing strategies: letter recognition, word identification, accessing word meaning, and chunking into phrases, part of the processing strategies of the hypothetical model of the reading process (Birch, 2015).

language-specific: a linguistic feature that is particular to a given language.

learning logs: journals kept by students to keep track of their metacognitive awareness.

lemma: is a single form of a word, a "dictionary entry" of a word.

lexeme: the set of variations of a lemma that come from adding different derivational and inflectional morphemes to a root or stem. Sometimes called "word families."

lexical morpheme: class of free morphemes making up the majority of words in a language. See also *content word*.

lexicon: all of the words in a language.

linear text: a text printed on paper, with fixed font size, page layout, and pages that progress from beginning to end. Includes picture books, textbooks, posters, worksheets, and all texts printed on paper. Contrasts with handwritten text, screen-based linear text, and interactive text.

lingua franca: a language used by speakers of diverse languages to communicate.

linguistic capital: the amount of nonmonetary social capital based on one's linguistic ability and use (Kanno & Kangas, 2014).

linguistic complexity: complex, organized, coherent, and varied sentences and paragraphs; a highly proficient composing skill.

linguistic proximity: See *language distance*.

listeme: a memorized string of words occurring in a fixed order (e.g., *up* and *down*) that do not follow a general rule; a listeme is one kind of collocation.

listening comprehension: the ability to understand spoken language (oral text). Key concept in the simple view of reading (SVR). See also *oral text*.

listening vocabulary: the storehouse of known words in a language; a larger listening vocabulary facilitates learning to read.

literacy: historically, the designated skills of reading and writing and all of their associated activities, but more recently, includes oral skills and metalinguistic skills as well.

literacy advantage: the knowledge and benefits that accrue to those literate in a language; L1 literacy is a critical foundation for creating success for reading in a new language.

logograms: symbols, or signs that stand for or represent a whole word, a concept, or an idea.

logographic writing system: a writing system having characters, or logograms, that represent morphemes but may or may not contain phonological information (e.g., Chinese).

metacognition: conscious awareness of one's own thinking and learning processes. Also called metacognitive awareness.

metalinguistic awareness: ability to think about, reflect on, and manipulate the forms and functions of language.

metaphor: words extended from a literal, material meaning to a more abstract association. Metaphors are important in understanding poetry and literature as well as informational text.

miscues: term used in the reading field to describe errors in oral reading that may, or may not, be based on misunderstandings.

modal auxiliary verbs: verbs that precede main verbs and are used to indicate likelihood, ability, permission, and obligation (e.g., *can, may, should*). They are functional morphemes and are also called modal auxiliaries.

morpheme: the smallest linguistic unit of meaning.

morphology: one of the four language universals. The study of units of meaning and the ways they combine to make new words.

morphophonemic: containing both phonemic and morphological information; a morpheme may have different pronunciations due to surrounding sounds in a word (e.g., *please, pleasure*).

motherese: simplified speech, exaggerated intonation, and slow, deliberate pacing used with young children or beginning language learners to aid comprehension.

multiple processes: combination of word formation processes (e.g., *dashcam; epipen*).

non-effect: the lack of influence, or irrelevance, of features of the first language on second-language acquisition, and in particular, literacy.

numeracy: the ability to understand and to use simple numerical concepts like addition, subtraction, multiplication, and division. Numeracy and literacy are both necessary to function fully in our global world.

numeric spelling: the combination of a written alphabetic letter along with a number (e.g., d8 for "date.").

onset: the vowel or consonant(s) beginning a syllable in English.

opacity: the degree to which the symbols or graphemes of a written language match closely with the phonemes of the language; a language can be classified as more transparent (close correspondence) or opaque (not a close correspondence).

open class: descriptive term indicating that new morphemes can be added to a lexicon; a content word is an example of an open class category.

oracy: the combined skills of listening and speaking; used as a parallel to literacy.

oral proficiency: the speaking skill.

oral reading fluency (ORF): skill of reading text aloud, often measured by appropriate rate, accuracy, and expression; shown to correlate closely with silent reading comprehension in native speakers of English.

oral text: words that are being spoken (as opposed to written text, words that are written).

orthographic depth hypothesis: idea that shallow orthographies (like Italian or Spanish, among others) are easier for beginning readers to learn to decode while deep orthographies (like English) take longer and are harder to learn to decode.

orthographic distance: similarities and differences between two or more writing systems, a subcategory of language distance.

orthographic transparency or depth: See *opacity*.

orthography: the written system of a language.

output hypothesis: opportunities for producing spoken and written language are essential for second-language acquisition (Swain, 2005).

paired-word sound play: one of the processes for forming new words in English; the second word sounds like the first except for a vowel or consonant (e.g., *hip-hop, wishy-washy, humdrum*).

paralinguistic features or cues: non-word-based behaviors, such as facial expressions, gestures, or body language, which convey meanings. These are language specific and culture specific.

performance definitions for ELLs: descriptors of language behaviors moving toward an agreed-upon language proficiency level. ELL performance definitions form part of the TESOL standards and WIDA standards.

phoneme: smallest unit of sound having meaning; each language has a different set.

phoneme segmentation: the process of being able to break down individual phonemes of a word and put them back together. This is a key skill for reading and writing in English.

phonics: the letter–sound and sound–letter relationships and spelling patterns in a language; opaque alphabetic orthographies require more phonics practice.

phonological awareness: the ability to recognize sounds, an important skill for reading success in any language.

phonological decoding: recognizing the sounds of a word and being able to pronounce it.

phonological loop: taking visual or auditory data and transferring it into short-term and then long-term memory storage through repetition, or retrieving it from memory through phonological recognition.

phonology: one of the four language universals. Phonology consists of the sounds and sound patterns of a language and the rules governing how they combine; the distinct auditory identity of a language.

phrasal verb: the combination of a verb and one or more prepositions or occasionally a verb and an adverb (e.g., *get up*, *sit down*); these can be considered collocations.

pinyin: use of the Roman alphabet to represent Chinese characters based on their pronunciation; a temporary scaffold. "Pin Yin" literally means "spell sound."

polysemous word: word with the same spelling and pronunciation but multiple meanings (e.g., *bank* [for money], *bank* [land at the side of a stream], *bank* [to tilt an airplane wing in order to turn], *bank* [safe place for storage]).

positive cross-linguistic influence (PCI): the facilitating effects of the first language on second-language acquisition and, in particular, literacy.

prefix: affix(es) placed at the beginning of a word or root.

preteaching: for vocabulary study, introducing vocabulary before students read a text.

prewriting: one of four phases of writing workshop, including brainstorming, scribbling, and gathering ideas.

probabilistic reasoning: a cognitive skill developed by learners as their knowledge of a new language increases, allowing them to make increasingly accurate predictions in listening, reading, spelling, and other language functions.

process writing: model focusing on the process of writing rather than the end product; stages include prewriting, drafting, revising, editing, and publishing.

processing efficiency: term used by Koda (2005) to describe the ease experienced when one is proficient at something, such as fluent reading.

prompt: an oral or written cue to which students are asked to respond in speaking or writing.

proposition: the way the brain processes input and stores it in memory in reduced form. A mental proposition consists of the predicate, or verb, of the message and the information attached to it.

prosody: vocal patterns and inflections used in speaking or reading aloud; they are language specific.

publishing: sharing writing with an audience; a stage in process writing.

punctuation: written conventions representing oral speech in written form (e.g., commas, periods, exclamation marks).

rate: speed at which words are read aloud or silently; core measure of Oral Reading Fluency.

reading comprehension: the ability to construct meaning from a given written text.

reading comprehension strategy: term used to represent numerous conscious and unconscious processes for understanding a written text.

reading logs: journals kept by students during or after reading to apply reading comprehension strategies.

realia: using real-world objects or artifacts, such as tools, food items, seeds, flowers, menus, etc., to build background knowledge.

reasoning by analogy: the ability to predict the meaning of unknown words through familiarity with the frames that surround the unknown element.

recasts: creating a grammatically correct form by restating or rewriting an incorrect form.

recoding: representing spoken words in written form.

redundancies: the built-in overlap in oral and written texts that allows a person to discern a meaning even if some of his or her cueing is incomplete; more redundancies are available to aid comprehension in oral text than in written text.

resilience: the ability to persevere to overcome obstacles or recover from setbacks.

responsive writing: writing, such as descriptions, directions, book or movie reviews, interviews, newsletter articles, reports, and summaries made in response to something seen, heard, or read.

revising and editing: refining ideas and preparing text for publishing; a critical stage in the process writing model.

rime: in an English syllable, its vowel and any consonants coming after it (e.g., *-ang* is the rime for *sang, bang*). See also *onset*.

root: morpheme containing the primary meaning of a word; constitutes the base for attaching affixes.

scale change: one of the processes for forming new words in English; adding a prefix or suffix can show quantity, size, or familiarity (e.g., *macroeconomics, minimart, hoodie, Bobbie*).

screen-based linear text: text resembling the appearance of a paper-based text, but read on a screen, such as PDFs or ebooks. They can be read when a screen is offline but may include some interactivity within a device's software. Contrasts with handwritten text, linear text, and interactive text.

second-language acquisition (SLA): the content area related to acquiring, learning, or teaching a new language (e.g., SLA theory, SLA research, SLA methodology) and its educational discipline.

semantic feature analysis grid: See *content frame*.

semantic field: a group of words related to the same subject or concept.

semantic map: a graphic organizer used to connect a word with many associations; often used as a prewriting activity or for activation of prior knowledge; has a spider web format.

semantics: one of the four language universals. It is the study of the combination of the meanings contributed by phonology, morphology, and syntax in understanding oral and written text.

shallow orthography (transparent orthography): a writing system having symbols or graphemes that closely match the phonemes of the language (e.g., Spanish, Turkish).

sheltered instruction: subject matter content adapted to ELLs' language proficiency levels; used in content-based instructional models.

sheltered instruction observation protocol (SIOP): widely used and research-supported eight-part model of sheltered instruction (Echevarria, Vogt, & Short, 2000).

short-circuit hypothesis: high levels of second language proficiency are necessary for first-language reading skills to facilitate second-language reading (Clarke, 1980).

sight word: a word that is not easily decodable. These are often conflated with high-frequency words.

signal words, transitions, and connectors: discourse signals conveying information at numerous levels in texts—for example, *because, additionally* (signal words), *thus, therefore* (transitions), *so, although, but* (connectors). Often used synonymously.

silent period: an early stage of language acquisition focusing on listening to and understanding language. Although no language production may occur, it is an active period of language learning and acquisition.

simple view of reading (SVR): theory that reading comprehension is the product of decoding times language/listening comprehension. Language/listening comprehension is what remains when decoding has been accounted for (Gough & Tunmer, 1986).

socially constructed: description of understandings based on social interactions that provide frameworks for learning.

sociocultural theory: focus on social nature of language and its uses in order to "do things in the world."

specially designed academic instruction in English (SDAIE): instructional program used in California for content-based instruction of English (California Department of Education, 1993).

story grammar: predictable pattern of events that occur over the course of a story. Knowing story grammar can help children predict events in a story. Story grammars may vary among cultures.

strategies: deliberate actions that readers take to establish and enhance their comprehension.

stress patterns: audible differences in how long, and how loudly, any speaker of a language pronounces a word or a group of words. Stress patterns are part of the phonology of a language.

suffix: affix(es) placed at the end of a word or root. There are two kinds of suffixes, derivational and inflectional; inflectional morphemes come only at the end of a word.

sustained silent reading (SSR): students and teacher reading silently on a regular basis; an extensive reading technique.

syllabary: the set of syllables making up a syllabic writing system, equivalent to an alphabet for an alphabetic writing system (e.g., Korean, Gujarati).

syllabic writing system: a writing system in which each symbol represents a consonant–vowel combination (e.g., Korean and Japanese Hiragana and Katakana).

syllable: a consonant–vowel pattern. All syllables have a vowel. English words contain one or more syllables.

syndrome of success: factors that, alone and in combination, enable success in developing language and literacy in a new language.

syntax: one of the four language universals. It consists of the word order of phrases and clauses in a language based on word order; sometimes used erroneously as a synonym for *grammar* in language arts and ESL/ EFL classrooms.

systemic functional linguistics (SFL): branch of linguistics based partly on Halliday's (1993) language-based theory of learning. The sociocultural focus explains language use as a set of choices that improve as learners' linguistic repertoires increase; also called *functional linguistics.*

T-chart: graphic organizer for organizing information with two sets of information alongside each other.

Teachers of English to Speakers of Other Languages (TESOL): worldwide professional organization of ESL experts and educators; authors/ publishers of the TESOL Standards and other publications; holds annual international convention, and has state and national affiliates.

telling versus composing: using one's own experiences as a basis for writing (telling) versus engaging in academic tasks (composing) as a basis for writing.

text structure: organization of texts by genre (e.g., fiction, nonfiction, drama, research paper, editorial) or by presentation (handwritten, linear, screen-based linear, or interactive); also a prereading strategy focusing on analyzing text structures of a document.

think-aloud: metacognitive technique in which readers orally model their own reading process. When teachers do this, it can serve as a model for students; think-alouds can also be used as a formative assessment (also called *verbal report*).

threshold theory: theory that L2 proficiency, more than L1 literacy, determines reading and writing proficiency in the second language (Alderson, 1984, 2000).

top-down skills: analytical and cognitive skills needed for reading comprehension.

total physical response (TPR): widely used listening comprehension strategy in which students demonstrate their comprehension of language and lessons through movement. This is a key technique for beginning and early learners and can also be used in high-level content areas.

transfer: influence resulting from similarities and differences between a target language and a language previously acquired.

transparency: a close match in a writing system between phonemes and graphemes.

transparent orthography (shallow orthography): writing systems having a close match between phonemes and symbols (e.g., Spanish, Dutch).

uptake: accepting and using recasts in which students correct their own grammatical errors.

Venn diagram: graphic organizer with overlapping ovals for representing similarities and differences; can be used to guide reading or writing. See also *H-chart*.

visualization: forming a visual image in the mind in order to remember or evoke a word, event, or idea.

vocabulary usage: the use of a repertoire of words for reading and composing.

wait time: amount of time a teacher waits after asking students a question or after listening to student responses. Longer wait time helps ELLs.

washback: effects on teaching and learning from a practice or an assessment that can be positive or negative.

word calling: decoding words of a text aloud with little or no comprehension of their meaning.

word recognition: various ways of recognizing and accessing individual words.

World Class Instructional Design and Assessment (WIDA) Consortium: a multistate working group that created PreK–12 language proficiency standards that describe performance definitions for ELLs.

world knowledge: people, places, events, and activities, part of the knowledge base of the hypothetical model of the reading process (Birch, 2015).

writing workshop: name used for well-known process writing method; emphasizes collaboration and support during all stages of composing.

zone of proximal development (ZPD): the level at which learners can perform tasks with the assistance of a peer or "expert other," resulting in the ability to move to a higher level of learning (Vygotsky, 1986).

References

Abdelhadi, S., Ibrahim, R., & Eviatar, Z. (2011). Perceptual load in the reading of Arabic: Effects of orthographic visual complexity on detection. *Writing Systems Research, 3*(2), 117–127.

Achugar, M., Schleppegrell, M., & Oteiza, T. (2007). Engaging teachers in language analysis: A functional linguistics approach to reflective literacy. *English Teaching: Practice and Critique, 6*(2), 8–24.

Alderson, J. C. (1984). Reading in a foreign language: A reading problem or a language problem? In J. C. Alderson & A. H. Urquhart (Eds.), *Reading in a foreign language* (pp. 1–24). London: Longman.

Alderson, J. C. (2000). *Assessing reading.* Cambridge, UK: Cambridge University Press.

The American heritage dictionary of the English language (4th ed.). (2000). Boston: Houghton Mifflin.

Anderson, N. J. (1999). *Exploring second language reading.* Boston: Heinle & Heinle.

Anderson, N. J. (2003, November). Scrolling, clicking, and reading English: Online strategies in a second/foreign language. *The Reading Matrix, 3*(3), 1–33.

Applegate, M. D., Applegate, A. J., & Modla, V. B. (2009). "She's my best reader; She just can't comprehend": Studying the relationship between fluency and comprehension. *The Reading Teacher, 62*(6), 512–521.

Asher, J. (1988). *Learning another language through actions: The complete teacher's guidebook.* Los Gatos, CA: Sky Oaks.

ATOS Analyzer. (2015). Wisconsin Rapids, WI: Renaissance Learning. Retrieved from www.renaissance.com/products/accelerated-reader/atos-analyzer.

Atwell, N. (1987). *In the middle: Writing, reading, and learning with adolescents.* Portsmouth, NH: Heinemann.

Atwell, N. (2002). *Lessons that change writers.* Portsmouth, NH: Heinemann.

August, D., Calderon, M., & Carlo, M. (2002). *Transfer of skills from Spanish to English: A study of young learners. Report for practitioners, parents, and policy makers.* Washington, DC: Center for Applied Linguistics.

August, D., & Shanahan, T. (Eds.). (2006). *Developing literacy in second-language learners: Report of the National Literacy Panel on language-minority children and youth.* Mahwah, NJ: Erlbaum.

Azar, B. S. (2003). *Fundamentals of English grammar* (3rd ed.). London: Longman.

Baddeley, A., Gathercole, S., & Papagno, C. (1998). The phonological loop as a language learning device. *Psychological Review, 105,* 1158–1173.

Bailey, K. (1998). *Learning about language assessment.* Pacific Grove, CA: Newbury House.

Baker, C. (1993). *Foundations of bilingual education and bilingualism.* Clevedon, UK: Multilingual Matters.

Baker, C. (2011). *Foundations of bilingual education and bilingualism* (5th ed.). Clevedon, UK: Multilingual Matters.

Baker, S. K., & Good, R. (1995). Curriculum-based measurement of English reading with bilingual Hispanic students: A validation study with second-grade students. *School Psychology Review, 24*(4), 561–578.

Bamford, J., & Day, R. R. (1997). Extensive reading: What is it? Why bother? *The Language Teacher, 21*(5), 6–8, 12.

Baumann, J. F., & Kame'enui, E. J. (1991). Research on vocabulary instruction: Ode to Voltaire. In J. Flood, J. J. D. Lapp, & J. R. Squires (Eds.), *Handbook of research on teaching the English language arts* (pp. 604–632). New York: Macmillan.

Bear, D. R., Templeton, S., Helman, L., & Baren, T. (2003). Orthographic development and learning to read in different languages. In G. Garcia (Ed.), *English learners: Reaching the highest level of English literacy* (pp. 71–95). Newark, DE: International Reading Association.

Beeman, K., & Urow, C. (2012). *Teaching for bi-literacy: Strengthening bridges between languages.* Philadelphia, PA: Caslon.

Benenson, F. (2015). *How to speak emoji.* Kansas City, MO: Andrews McMeel.

Bernhardt, E. B. (2011). *Understanding advanced second language reading.* New York: Routledge.

Bernhardt, E. B., & Kamil, M. (1995). Interpreting relationships between L1 and L2 reading: Consolidating the linguistic threshold and the linguistic interdependence hypotheses. *Applied Linguistics, 16,* 15–34.

Berninger, V. W., Abbott, R. D., Jones, J., Wolf, B. J., Gould, L., Anderson-Youngstrom, M., et al. (2006). Early development of language by hand: Composing, reading, listening, and speaking connections; three letter-writing modes; and fast mapping in spelling. *Developmental Neuropsychology, 29*(1), 61–92.

Biemiller, A. (1970). The development of the use of graphic and contextual information as children learn to read. *Reading Research Quarterly, 6,* 75–96.

Biemiller, A. (1999). *Language and reading success.* Cambridge, MA: Brookline Books.

Birch, B. M. (2007). *English L2 reading: Getting to the bottom* (2nd ed.). Mahwah, NJ: Erlbaum.

Birch, B. M. (2015). *English L2 reading: Getting to the bottom* (3rd ed.). New York: Routledge.

Bounds, G. (2010, October 5). How handwriting trains the brain. Retrieved from *www.wsj.com/articles/SB10001424052748704631504575531932754922518#.*

Bourdieu, P. (1991). *Language and symbolic power* (J. B. Thompson, Ed.; G. Raymond & M. Adamson, Trans.). Cambridge, MA: Harvard University Press.

Boushey, G., & Moser, J. (2014). *The daily 5* (2nd ed.). Portland, ME: Stenhouse.

Bowers, P., Golden, J., Kennedy, A., & Young, A. (1994). Limits upon orthographic knowledge due to processes indexed by naming speed. In V. W. Berninger (Ed.), *The varieties of orthographic knowledge, I: Theoretical and development issues* (pp. 173–218). Dordrecht, The Netherlands: Kluwer.

Brazil, D. (1995). *A grammar of speech.* Oxford, UK: Oxford University Press.

Bremner, P., & Leonards, U. (2016). Iconic gestures for robot avatars, recognition and integration with speech. *Frontiers in Psychology, 10,* 3389.

Brown, D. (1950). "And having ears, they hear not." *Journal of the National Education Association, 39,* 586–587.

Brinton, D. M., Snow, M. A., & Wesche, M. B. (2003). *Content-based second language instruction.* Ann Arbor, MI: University of Michigan Press.

Brown, G., & Yule, G. (1983). *Teaching the spoken language: An approach based on the analysis of conversational English.* Cambridge, UK: Cambridge University Press.

Brown, H. D. (2001). *Teaching by principles: An interactive approach to language pedagogy* (2nd ed.). White Plains, NY: Longman.

Bryson, B. (1990). *Mother tongue: English and how it got that way.* New York: HarperCollins.

Bryson, B. (1994). *Made in America: An informal history of the English language in the United States.* New York: Morrow.

Buehl, D. (1995). *Classroom strategies for interactive learning: A monograph of the Wisconsin State Reading Association.* Schofield, WI: Wisconsin State Reading Association.

Calderon, M. (2006). Quality instruction in reading for English language learners. In K. Téllez & H. Waxman (Eds.), *Preparing quality educators for English language learners* (pp. 121–144). Mahwah, NJ: Erlbaum.

Calkins, L. (1984). Learning to think through writing. In A. Jagger & M. T. Smith-Burke (Eds.), *Observing the language learner* (pp. 190–198). Newark, DE: International Reading Association.

Calkins, L. (2006). *A guide to the writing workshop.* Portsmouth, NH: Heinemann.

California Department of Education. (1993, November). A report on specially designed academic instruction in English (SDAIE). Sacramento, CA: Prepared by the work group of the Commission on Teacher Credentialing and the California Department of Education.

Canale, M. (1983). From communicative competence to communicative language pedagogy. In J. Richards & R. Schmidt (Eds.), *Language and communication* (pp. 2–27). New York: Longman.

Canale, M., & Swain, M. (1980). Theoretical bases of communicative approaches to second language teaching and testing. *Applied Linguistics, 1,* 1–47.

Capstone Interactive. (2017). Retrieved from *Capstone.com.*

Caravolas, M., & Bruck, M. (1993). The effect of oral and written language input on children's phonological awareness: A cross-linguistic study. *Journal of Experimental Child Psychology, 55*(1), 1–30.

Caravolas, M., Lervåg, A., Mousikou, P., Efrim, C., Litavský, M., Onochie-Quintanilla, E., et al. (2012). Common patterns of prediction of literacy development in different alphabetic orthographies. *Psychological Science 23*(6), 678–686.

Carle, E. (2017). Welcome to the official Eric Carle website. Retrieved from *www. eric-carle.com/home.html*.

Carlisle, J. F., Beeman, M. B., & Shah, P. P. (1996). The metalinguistic capabilities and English literacy of Hispanic high school students: An exploratory study. In D. J. Leu, K. Kinzer, & K. A. Hinchman (Eds.). *45th Yearbook of the National Reading Conference* (pp. 306–316).

Carver, R. P. (1981). *Reading comprehension and auding theory.* Springfield, IL: Charles C Thomas.

Chall, J. S. (1983). *Stages of reading development.* New York: McGraw-Hill Book Company.

Chall, J. S. (1996). *Stages of reading development* (2nd ed.). Fort Worth, TX: Harcourt.

Chamot, A. U., & O'Malley, J. M. (1986). *A cognitive academic language learning approach: An ESL content-based curriculum.* Wheaton, MD: National Clearinghouse on Bilingual Education.

Chamot, A. U., & O'Malley, J. M. (1994). *The CALLA handbook.* Reading, MA: Addison-Wesley.

Chaney, C. (1992). Language development, metalinguistic skills, and print awareness in 3-year-old children. *Applied Psycholinguistics, 13*(4), 485–514.

Cherry, M. (2008, March–April). *The Humanist* interview: Emel Gokcen. *The Humanist, 68*(2), 24–26.

Chomsky, N. (1965). *Aspects of the theory of syntax.* Cambridge: The MIT Press.

Chomsky, N. (1972). *Language and mind.* New York: Harcourt.

CK-12. (2016). Retrieved from *www.ck12.org/features#dashboard*.

Clarke, M. A. (1980). The short-circuit hypothesis of ESL reading—or when language competence interferes with reading performance. *Modern Language Journal, 64*(2), 203–209.

Clay, M. (1968). A syntactic analysis of reading errors. *Journal of Verbal Learning and Verbal Behavior, 7,* 434–438.

Cloud, N. (2016). *Learning about students' prior experiences.* Colorincolorado.com. Retrieved from *www.youtube.com/watch?v=De7JkhvWfvs*.

Clyne, M., Hunt, C. R., & Isaakidis, T. (2004). Learning a community language as a third language. *International Journal of Multilingualism, 1*(1), 33–52.

CNA Speaking Exchange. (2016). FCB Brazil. Retrieved from *www.youtube.com/watch?v=3ka8SEny7ws&feature=youtu.be*.

Cobb, C., & Blachowicz, C. (2007). *Teaching vocabulary across the content areas.* Alexandria, VA: Association for Supervision and Curriculum Development.

Collins, M. (2005). ESL preschoolers' English vocabulary acquisition from storybook reading. *Reading Research Quarterly, 40*(4), 406–408.

Comrie, B., Matthews, S., & Polinsky, M. (Eds.). (1996). *The atlas of languages.* New York: Facts on File.

Conboy, B. T., & Kuhl, P. K. (2011). Impact of second language experience in infancy: Brain measures of first and second language speech perception. *Developmental Science, 14,* 242–248.

Crosson, A., & Lesaux, N. (2010). Revisiting assumptions about the relationship of fluent reading to comprehension: Spanish-speakers' text-reading fluency in English. *Reading and Writing, 23*(5), 475–494.

Cull, B. W. (2011, June). Reading revolutions: Online digital text and implications for reading in academe. Retrieved from *firstmonday.org/ojs/index.php/fm/article/view/3340/2985.*

Cummins, J. (1979). Linguistic interdependence and the educational development of bilingual children. *Review of Educational Research, 49*(2), 222–251.

Cummins, J. (1981). The role of primary language development in promoting educational success for language minority students. In Office of Bilingual Bicultural Education, *Schooling and language minority education: A theoretical framework* (pp. 3–49). Sacramento, CA: State Department of Education.

Cummins, J. (1991). The development of bilingual proficiency from home to school: A longitudinal study of Portuguese-speaking children. *Journal of Education, 173*(2), 85–98.

Cummins, J. (1996). *Negotiating identities: Education for empowerment in a diverse society.* Los Angeles: California Association for Bilingual Education.

Cummins, J. (2007, April). *Accelerating second language and literacy development.* Presentation made for SDR Associates, Rosemont, IL.

Cummins, J. (2008). Putting language proficiency in its place: Responding to critiques of the conversational/academic language distinction. Retrieved May 23, 2008, from *www.iteachilern.com/cummins/converacademlangdisti.html.*

Delpit, L. (1995). *Other people's children.* New York: New Press.

deJong, E. J. (2011). *Foundations for multilingualism in education: From principles to practice.* Philadelphia: Caslon.

De Jong, P. F., & van der Leij, A. (2002). Effects of phonological abilities and linguistic comprehension on the development of reading. *Scientific Studies of Reading, 6*(1), 51–77.

Deno, S. L. (1985). Curriculum-based measurement: The emerging alternative. *Exceptional Children, 52,* 219–232.

De Zutter, H. (1993). *Who says a dog goes bow wow?* New York: Doubleday.

Dorner, L., Orellana, M., & Li-Grining, C. (2007). "I helped my Mom," and it helped me: Translating the skills of language brokers into improved standardized test scores. *American Journal of Education, 113*(3), 451–478.

Doughty, C. J., & Long, M. H. (Eds.). (2003). *The handbook of second language acquisition.* Malden, MA: Blackwell.

Doughty, C. J., & Williams, J. (Eds.). (1998). *Focus on form in classroom second language acquisition.* Cambridge, UK: Cambridge University Press.

Dowhower, S. (1991). Speaking of prosody: Fluency's unattended bedfellow. *Theory into Practice, 30*(3), 165–175.

Dressler, C., & Kamil, M. (2006). First- and second-language literacy. In D. August & T. Shanahan (Eds.), *Developing literacy in second language learners* (pp. 197–238). Mahwah, NJ: Erlbaum.

Dulay, H. C., & Burt, M. K. (1974). Natural sequences in child second language acquisition. *Language Learning, 24,* 37–53.

Dulay, H. C., & Burt, M. K. (1977). Remarks on creativity in language acquisition. In M. Burt, H. Dulay, & M. Finocchiaro (Eds.), *Viewpoints on English as a second language* (pp. 95–126). New York: Regents.

Dymock, S. (1993). Reading but not understanding. *Journal of Reading, 37*(2), 86–91.

Early, M., & Marshall, S. (2008). Adolescent ESL students' interpretation and appreciation of literary texts: A case study of multimodality. *Canadian Modern Language Review, 64*(3), 377–397.

Echevarria, J., Vogt, M. E., & Short, D. (2000). *Making content comprehensible for English language learners: The SIOP model.* White Plains, NY: Pearson.

Eller, R. G. (1989). Johnny can't talk, either: The perpetuation of the deficit theory in classrooms. *Reading Teacher, 42*(9), 670–674.

Ellis, N. (1997). *Second language acquisition.* Oxford, UK: Oxford University Press.

Ellis, N., & Beaton, A. (1993). Psycholinguistic determinants of foreign language vocabulary learning. *Language Learning, 43*, 559–617.

Ellis, N. C., Natsume, M., Stavropoulou, K., Hoxhallari, L., Van Dall, V. H. P., Polyzoe, N., et al. (2004). The effects of orthographic depth on learning to read alphabetic, syllabic and logographic scripts. *Reading Research Quarterly, 39*, 438–468.

Epstein, A. (2007). *The intentional teacher: Choosing the best strategies for young children's learning.* Washington, DC: National Association for the Education of Young Children.

Essley, R. (2008). *Visual tools for differentiating reading and writing instruction.* New York: Scholastic.

Fang, Z. (2008). Going beyond the "Fab Five": Helping students cope with the unique linguistic challenges of expository reading in the middle grades. *Journal of Adolescent and Adult Literacy, 51*(6), 476–487.

Field, J. (2008). Bricks or mortar: Which parts of the input does a second language listener rely on? *TESOL Quarterly, 42*(3), 411–432.

Fender, M. (2001). A review of L1 and L2/ESL word integration skills and the nature of L2/ESL word integration development involved in lower-level text processing. *Language Learning, 51*(2), 319–396.

Fitzgerald, J. (1995). English-as-a-second-language reading instruction in the United States: A research review. *Journal of Reading Behavior, 27*(2), 115–152.

Fletcher, R., & Portalupi, J. (1998). *Craft lessons: Teaching writing K–8.* Portland, ME: Stenhouse.

Fletcher, R., & Portalupi, J. (2001). *Writing workshop: The essential guide.* Portsmouth, NH: Heinemann.

Fountas, I., & Pinnell, G. S. (2016). Fountas and Pinnell leveled books website. Retrieved from *www.fountasandpinnellleveledbooks.com/.*

Fox, M. (2016). Possum magic read-aloud. Retrieved from *http://memfox.com/for-everyone-current-read-alouds/.*

Fraser, C. A. (1999). Lexical processing strategy use and vocabulary learning through reading. *Studies in Second Language Acquisition, 21*, 225–241.

Freeman, D. E., & Freeman, Y. S. (2004). *Essential linguistics: What you need to know to teach reading, ESL, spelling, phonics, and grammar.* Portsmouth, NH: Heinemann.

Freeman, D. E., & Freeman, Y. S. (2014). *Essential linguistics: What teachers need to know to teach ESL, reading, spelling, grammar* (2nd ed.). Portsmouth, NH: Heinemann.

Freire, P. (1970). *Pedagogy of the oppressed*. New York: Continuum.

Fries, C. C. (1945). *Teaching and learning English as a foreign language*. Ann Arbor, MI: University of Michigan.

Fry, E. (1977). Fry's readability graph: Clarifications, validity, and extension to level 17. *Journal of Reading, 21*(3), 242–252.

Fuchs, L. S., Fuchs, D., Hosp, M., & Jenkins, J. R. (2001). Oral reading fluency as an indicator of reading competence: A theoretical, empirical, and historical analysis. *Scientific Studies of Reading, 5*(3), 239–256.

Fuchs, L. S., Fuchs, D., & Maxwell, L. (1988). The validity of informal reading comprehension measures. *Remedial and Special Education, 9*(2), 20–29.

Garcia, G. E. (2000). Bilingual children's reading. In M. Kamil, P. B. Mosenthal, P. D. Pearson, & R. Barr (Eds.), *Handbook of reading research* (Vol. 3, pp. 813–834). Mahwah, NJ: Erlbaum.

Garcia, J. R., & Cain, K. (2014). Decoding and reading comprehension: A meta-analysis to identify which reader and assessment characteristics influence the strength of the relationship in English. *Review of Educational Research, 84*, 74–111.

Gardner, R. C., & Lambert, W. E. (1972). *Attitude and motivation in second language learning*. Rowley, MA: Newbury House.

Genesee, F., Geva, E., Dressler, C., & Kamil, M. (2006). Synthesis: Cross-linguistic relationships. In D. August & T. Shanahan (Eds.), *Developing literacy in second-language learners* (pp. 153–183). Mahwah, NJ: Erlbaum.

Gersten, R., & Baker, S. K. (2000). *Practices for English-language learners. An overview of instructional practices for English-language learners*. Newton, MA: National Institute for Urban School Development.

Gersten, R., Baker, S. K., Shanahan, T., Linan-Thompson, S., Collins, P., & Scarcella, R. (2007). *Effective literacy and English language instruction for English learners in the elementary grades*. Washington, DC: National Center for Education Evaluation and Regional Assistance.

Geva, E. (2006). Second-language oral proficiency and second-language literacy. In D. August & T. Shanahan (Eds.), *Developing literacy in second-language learners* (pp. 123–139). Mahwah, NJ: Erlbaum.

Goodman, K. (1970). Reading: A psycholinguistic guessing game. In D. Gunderson (Ed.), *Language and reading: An interdisciplinary approach* (pp. 107–122). Washington, DC: Center for Applied Linguistics.

Google n-gram viewer. (2016). Retrieved from *https://books.google.com/ngrams/info*.

Gordon, D., & Blass, L. (2016, April). *Digital vs. print reading: Teaching appropriate skills for both modalities*. Presentation at the annual meeting of Teachers of English to Speakers of Other Languages, Baltimore, MD.

Goswami, U. (2013). The development of reasoning by analogy. In P. Barrouillet & C. Gauffroy (Eds.), *The development of thinking and reasoning* (pp. 49–70). East Sussex, UK: Psychology Press.

Gottlieb, M. (2006). *Assessing English language learners*. Thousand Oaks, CA: Corwin.

Gottlieb, M., Cranley, E., & Oliver, A. R. (2007). *Writing rubric of the WIDA Consortium, grades 1–12. ELP standards and resource guide, 2007 Edition*. The WIDA

Consortium. Retrieved August 22, 2008, from *www.wida.us/standards/RG_ Speaking%20Writing%20Rubrics.pdf*.

Gottlieb, M., Katz, A., & Ernst-Slavit, G. (2009). *Paper to practice: Using the TESOL English language proficiency standards in pre-K–12 classrooms.* Alexandria, VA: Teachers of English to Speakers of Other Languages.

Gough, P. B., & Tunmer, W. E. (1986). Decoding, reading, and reading disability. *Remedial and Special Education, 7*(1), 6–10.

Grabe, W. (2001). Reading-writing relations: Theoretical perspectives and instructional practices. In D. Belcher & A. Hirvela (Eds.), *Linking literacies: Perspectives on L2 reading-writing connections* (pp. 15–47). Ann Arbor, MI: University of Michigan Press.

Grabe, W. (2003). Reading and writing relations: Second language perspectives on research and practice. In B. Kroll (Ed.), *Exploring the dynamics of second language writing* (pp. 242–262). Cambridge, UK: Cambridge University Press.

Grabe, W., & Stoller, F. (2002). *Teaching and researching reading.* Harlow, UK: Longman & Pearson.

Graves, D. (1973). Children's writing: Research directions and hypothesis based upon an examination of the writing process of seven-year-old children (Doctoral dissertation, University of New Hampshire). *Dissertation Abstracts International, 34,* 6255A.

Graves, D., & Hansen, J. (1983). The author's chair. *Language Arts, 60,* 176–183.

Guilloteaux, M. J., & Dornei, Z. (2008). Motivating language learners: A classroom-oriented investigation of the effects of motivational strategies on student motivation. *TESOL Quarterly, 42*(1), 55–78.

Gwynne, F. (1970). *The king who rained.* New York: Aladdin Books, Simon & Schuster.

Gwynne, F. (1976). *A chocolate moose for dinner.* New York: Aladdin Books, Simon & Schuster.

Halliday, M. A. K. (1993). Towards a language-based theory of learning. *Linguistics and Education, 5*(2), 93–116.

Hamilton, C., & Shinn, M. R. (2003). Characteristics of word callers: An investigation of the accuracy of teachers' judgments of reading comprehension and oral reading skills. *School Psychology Review,* (32), 228–240.

Hanley, R., Masterson, J., Spencer, L. & Evans, D. (2004). How long do the advantages of learning to read a transparent orthography last? An investigation of the reading skills and reading impairment of Welsh children at 10 years of age. *Quarterly Journal of Experimental Psychology Section A–Human Experimental Psychology, 57*(8), 1393–1410.

Hart, B., & Risley, T. R. (1995). *Meaningful differences in the everyday experience of young American children.* Baltimore: P.H. Brookes.

Heath, S. B. (2012). *Words at work and play: Three decades in family and community life.* Cambridge, UK: Cambridge University Press.

Helman, L. (2005). Spanish speakers learning to read in English: What a large-scale assessment suggests about their progress. In E. Maloch, J. V. Hoffman, D. L. Schallert, C. M. Fairbanks, & J. Worthy (Eds.), *54th yearbook of the National Reading Conference* (pp. 211–226). Oak Creek, WI: National Reading Conference.

Hess, K. (2013). A guide for using Webb's Depth of Knowledge with Common Core State Standards. Retrieved from *https://education.ohio.gov/getattachment/Topics/Teaching/Educator-Evaluation-System/How-to-Design-and-Select-Quality-Assessments/Webbs-DOK-Flip-Chart.pdf.aspx.*

Hiebert, E. H., Brown, Z. A., Taitague, C., Fisher, C. W., & Adler, M. A. (2004). Texts and English language learners: Scaffolding entrée to reading. In F. Boyd, C. Brock, & M. S. Rozendal (Eds.), *Multicultural and multilingual literacy and language* (pp. 32–53). New York: Guilford Press.

Hiebert, E. H., & Fisher, C. W. (2006). Fluency from the first: What works with first graders? In T. Rasinski, C. Blachowicz, & K. Lems (Eds.), *Fluency instruction: Research-based best practices* (pp. 279–294). New York: Guilford Press.

Hoffman, J. V. (1987). *The oral recitation lesson: A teacher's guide.* Austin, TX: Academic Resource Consultants.

How many words are there in English? (2017). Retrieved from *www.merriam-webster.com/help/faq-how-many-english-words.*

How many words are there in the English language? (2017). Retrieved from *www.oxforddictionaries.com/us/words/how-many-words-are-there-in-the-english-language.*

Hoyt, L. (2002). *Make it real: Strategies for success with informational text.* Portsmouth, NH: Heinemann.

Hymes, D. (1981). On communicative competence. In C. J. Brumfit & K. Johnson (Eds.), *The communicative approach to language teaching* (pp. 5–26). Oxford, UK: Oxford University Press. (Original work published 1971)

Igoa, C. (1995). *The inner world of the immigrant child.* Mahwah, NJ: Erlbaum.

International Children's Digital Library. (2016). Retrieved from *http://en.childrenslibrary.org/.*

Jimenez, F. (1997). *The circuit: Stories from the life of a migrant child.* Albuquerque, NM: University of New Mexico Press.

Jimenez, R. T., Garcia, G. E., & Pearson, D. P. (1996). The reading strategies of bilingual Latino/a students who are successful English readers: Opportunities and obstacles. *Reading Research Quarterly, 31*(1), 90–112.

Johnson, R., & Moore, R. (1997). A link between reading proficiency and native-like use of pausing in speaking. *Applied Language Learning, 8*(1), 25–42.

Jones, J. N., Abbott, R. D., & Berninger, V. W. (2014). Predicting levels of reading and writing achievement in typically developing, English-speaking 2nd and 5th graders. *Learning and Individual Differences, 1*(32), 54–68.

Kang, H. (2014). Understanding online reading through the eyes of first and second language readers: An exploratory study. Retrieved from *http://krex.ksu.edu.*

Kanno, Y., & Kangas, S. E. N. (2014). "I'm not going to be like, for the AP": English language learners' limited access to advanced college-preparatory courses in high school. *American Educational Research Journal, 51*(5), 848–878.

Karch, A. (2016). Duolingo review: The quick, easy and free way to learn a language. Retrieved from *www.fluentin3months.com/duolingo/.*

Katz, L., & Frost, R. (1992). The reading process is different for different orthographies: The orthographic depth hypothesis. In R. Frost & L. Katz (Eds.),

Orthography, phonology, morphology, and meaning (pp. 67–84). Amsterdam: Elsevier North Holland Press.

Kempen, G., & Huijbers, P. (1983). The lexicalization process in sentence production and naming: Indirect election of words. *Cognition, 14*(2), 185–209.

Kieffer, M. J., & Lesaux, N. K. (2008). The role of derivational morphology in the reading comprehension of Spanish-speaking English language learners. *Reading and Writing, 21*(8), 783–804.

Kieffer, M. J., & Lesaux, N. K. (2009). Breaking down to build meaning: Morphology, vocabulary and reading comprehension in the urban classroom. *The Reading Teacher, 61*(2), 134–144.

Kim, Y. S. (2012). The relations among L1 (Spanish) literacy skills, L2 (English) language, L2 text reading fluency, and L2 reading comprehension for Spanish-speaking ELL first grade students. *Learning and Individual Differences, 22,* 690–700.

Kimmel, E. C. (1999). *Balto and the great race.* New York: Random House.

Koda, K. (2005). *Insights into second language reading.* Cambridge, UK: Cambridge University Press.

Konnikova, M. (2014, June 3). What's lost as handwriting fades. Retrieved from *www.nytimes.com/2014/06/03/science/whats-lost-as-handwriting-fades.html?_r=0.*

Koskinen, P. S., Blum, I. H., Tennant, N., Parker, E. M., Straub, M. W., & Curry, C. (1995). Have you heard any good books lately? Encouraging shared reading at home with books and audiotapes. In L. M. Morrow (Ed.), *Family literacy: Connections in schools and communities* (pp. 87–103). Newark, DE: International Reading Association.

Kozub, R. (2000). Reader's theatre and its effect on oral language fluency. Retrieved from *www.readingonline.org/editorial/august2000/rkrt.htm.*

Krashen, S. (1977). Some issues relating to the Monitor Model. In H. D. Brown, C. A. Yorio, & R. H. Crymes (Eds.), *On TESOL '77* (pp. 144–158). Washington, DC: TESOL.

Krashen, S. (1982). *Principles and practice in second language acquisition.* New York: Pergamon Press.

Krashen, S. (1985). *The input hypothesis.* Beverly Hills, CA: Laredo.

Krashen, S. (1987). Applications of psycholinguistic research to the classroom. In M. H. Long & J. C. Richards (Eds.), *Methodology in TESOL: A book of readings* (pp. 33–44). New York: Newbury House.

Krashen, S. (2004). *The power of reading: Insights from the research* (2nd ed.). Portsmouth, NH: Heinemann.

Krashen, S. (2013). Rosetta Stone: Does not provide compelling input, research reports at best suggestive, conflicting reports on users' attitudes. Retrieved from *www.sdkrashen.com/content/articles/rosetta_stone_review_krashen.pdf.*

Kucer, S. B. (2001). *Dimensions of literacy: A conceptual base for teaching reading and writing in school settings.* Mahwah, NJ: Erlbaum.

Kucer, S. L. (1985). The making of meaning: Reading and writing as parallel processes. *Written Communication, 2*(3), 317–336.

LaBerge, D., & Samuels, S. J. (1974). Toward a theory of automatic information processing in reading. *Cognitive Psychology, 6,* 293–323.

Labov, W. (1972). *Language in the inner city: Studies in the Black English vernacular* (Vol. 3). Philadelphia: University of Pennsylvania Press.

Lado, R. (1977). *Lado English series.* New York: Regents.

Lakoff, R. (1973). Language and woman's place. *Language in Society, 2*(1), pp. 45–80.

Lantolf, J. P., & Thorne, S. L. (2006). *Sociocultural theory and the genesis of second language development.* Oxford, UK: Oxford University Press.

Learner's Dictionary. (2017). Retrieved from *http://learnersdictionary.com.*

Lems, K. (2001a). An American poetry project for low intermediate ESL adults. *English Teaching Forum, 39*(4), 24–29.

Lems, K. (2001b). *Using music in the adult ESL classroom.* ERIC Digest EDO-LE-01-03.

Lems, K. (2002). Music hath charms for literacy . . . in the ESL classroom. *Indiana Reading Journal, 34*(3), 6–12.

Lems, K. (2005). A study of adult ESL oral reading fluency and silent reading comprehension. In E. Maloch, J. V. Hoffman, D. L. Schallert, C. M. Fairbanks, & J. Worthy (Eds.), *54th yearbook of the National Reading Conference* (pp. 240–256). Oak Creek, WI: National Reading Conference.

Lems, K. (2008). *Inverted morphemes pyramid.* Unpublished diagram.

Lems, K. (2012). Reading fluency and comprehension in English language learners. In T. Rasinski, C. Blachowicz, & K. Lems, Eds., *Fluency instruction: Research-based best practices* (2nd ed., pp. 243–254). New York: Guilford Press.

Lems, K. (2016). Learning English through music in the digital age. *TESOL Video News.* Alexandria, VA: Teachers of English to Speakers of Other Languages. Retrieved from *http://newsmanager.commpartners.com/tesolvdmis/issues/2016-07-26/4.html.*

Lems, K., & Abousalem, S. (2014). Interactive read-aloud: A powerful technique for young ELLs. In P. Spycher (Ed.), *The Common Core Standards in English language arts* (pp. 5–16). Arlington, VA: TESOL Publications.

Lesaux, N. K., Kieffer, M. J., Faller, S. E., & Kelley, J. G. (2010). The effectiveness and ease of implementation of an academic vocabulary intervention for linguistically diverse students in urban middle schools. *Reading Research Quarterly, 45*(2), 196–228.

Leu, D. J., Kinzer, C. K., Coiro, J., Castek, J., & Henry, L. A. (2013). New literacies: A dual-level theory of the changing nature of literacy, instruction, and assessment. In D. E. Alvermann, N. J. Unrau, & R. B. Ruddell (Eds.), *Theoretical models and processes of reading* (6th ed., pp. 1150–1181). Newark, DE: International Reading Association.

Lewis, J., Aydin, A., & Powell, N. (2013–2016). *March trilogy.* New York: Top Shelf Productions.

Li, D., & Nes, S. (2001). Using paired reading to help ESL students become fluent and accurate readers. *Reading Improvement, 38*(2), 50–62.

Li, L. (2002). The role of phonology in reading Chinese single characters and two-character words with high, medium and low phonological regularities by Chinese grade 2 and grade 5 students. *Reading Research Quarterly, 37,* 372–374.

Lightbown, P., & Spada, N. (2011). *How languages are learned* (3rd ed.). Oxford, UK: Oxford University Press.

Literacy. (2013). United Nations Educational, Scientific, and Cultural Organization. Retrieved from *www.unesco.org/new/en/education/themes/education-building-blocks/literacy/.*

Liu, Z. (2005). Reading behavior in the digital environment. *Journal of Documentation. 61*(6), 700–712.

Long, M. H., & Robinson, P. (1998). Focus on form: Theory, research, and practice. In C. Doughty & J. Williams (Eds.), *Focus on form in classroom second language acquisition* (pp. 15–41). Cambridge: Cambridge University Press.

Markell, M. A., & Deno, S. L. (1997). Effects of increasing oral reading: Generalization across reading tasks. *Journal of Special Education, 31*, 233–250.

McCarthey, S. J., Garcia, G. E., Lopez-Velasquez, A. M., & Shumin, G. Y. (2004). Understanding writing contexts for English language learners. *Research in the Teaching of English, 38*(4), 351–394.

McCauley, J. K., & McCauley, D. S. (1992). Using choral reading to promote language learning for ESL students. *The Reading Teacher, 45*(67), 526–533.

McCrum, R., MacNeil, R. & Cran, W. (2002). *The story of English* (3rd rev. ed.). New York: Penguin.

McGuinness, D. (2004). *Early reading instruction: What science really tells us about how to teach reading.* Cambridge, MA: MIT Press.

McTague, B., Lems, K., Butler, D., & Carmona, E. (2012). ELL fluency scores— What can they tell us? In T. V. Rasinski, C. Blachowicz, & K. Lems (Eds.), *Fluency instruction: Research-based best practices* (2nd ed., pp. 278–288). New York: Guilford Press.

Mercer, N. (2014). Oracy skills framework. Retrieved from: *www.educ.cam.ac.uk/research/projects/oracytoolkit/oracyskillsframework/OracySkillsFramework.pdf.*

Meisinger, E. B., Bradley, B. A., Schwanenflugel, P. J., Kuhn, M. R., & Morris, R. D. (2009). Myth and reality of the word caller: The relation between teacher nominations and prevalence among elementary school children. *School Psychology Quarterly, 24*(3), 147–150.

Meyer, B. J. F., Brandt, K. M., & Bluth, G. J. (1980). Use of top-level structure in text: Key for reading comprehension on ninth grade readers. *Reading Research Quarterly, 16*, 72–103.

Michael, J. (2016, October 1). *Is the medium the message? Effects of reading digital text on comprehension.* Paper presented at the annual meeting of the Illinois Reading Council, Peoria, IL. Handout retrieved from *https://docs.google.com/document/d/1uTV2fsKGkeg-oiv7Vl90ZoYBVP9ZuJHKKJ2N_X2oYQg/edit.*

Miller, J., & Schwanenflugel, P. J. (2006). Prosody of syntactically complex sentences in the oral reading of young children. *Journal of Educational Psychology, 98*(4), 839–843.

Mohammad, A. (2015). Tanzania dumps English as its official language and opts for Kiswahili. Retrieved from *http://qz.com/355444/tanzania-dumps-english-as-its-official-language-in-schools-opts-for-kiswahili/).*

Mohr, K., & Mohr, E. (2007). Extending English-language learners' classroom interactions using the response protocol. *The Reading Teacher, 60*(5), 440–450.

Moll, L. C., Amanti, C., Neff, D., & Gonzalez, N. (1992). Funds of knowledge for teaching: Using a qualitative approach to connect home and classrooms. *Theory into Practice, 31*(2), 132–141.

Moll, L., Estrada, E., Díaz, E., & Lopez, L. (1997). The organization of bilingual lessons: Implications for schooling. In M. Cole, Y. Engeström, & O. Vásquez (Eds.), *Mind, culture, and activity: Seminal papers from the Laboratory of Comparative Human Cognition* (pp. 254–268). Cambridge, UK: Cambridge University Press.

Morris, D. (1993). The relationship between children's concept of word in text and phoneme awareness in learning to read: A longitudinal study. *Research in the Teaching of English, 27*(2), 133–154.

Most confusing two-letter word. (2016). Proofreadnow.com. Retrieved from *www.proofreadnow.com/blog/bid/48170/Most-Confusing-Two-Letter-Word*.

Myles, J. (2002). Second language writing and research: The writing process and error analysis in student texts. Retrieved from *tesl-ej.org/ej22/a1.html*.

Nakamoto, J., Lindsey, K. A., & Manis, F. R. (2007). A longitudinal analysis of English language learners' word decoding and reading comprehension. *Reading and Writing, 20*(7), 691–719.

Nation, I. S. P. (2001). *Learning vocabulary in another language.* Cambridge, UK: Cambridge University Press.

National Institute of Child Health and Human Development of the National Institutes of Health. (2004, September 15). Children follow same steps to learn vocabulary, regardless of language spoken. Retrieved July 11, 2008, from *www. sciencedaily.com/releases/2004/09/040915113243.htm*.

National Reading Panel. (2000). *Teaching children to read: An evidence-based assessment of the scientific research literature on reading and its implications for reading instruction.* Washington, DC: National Institute of Child Health and Human Development.

Oded, B., & Walters, J. (2002). Deeper processing for better EFL reading comprehension. *System, 29*(3), 357–370.

Odlin, T. (1989). *Language transfer: Cross-linguistic influences in language learning.* Cambridge, UK: Cambridge University Press.

Odlin, T. (2003). Cross-linguistic influences. In C. J. Doughty & M. H. Long (Eds.), *The handbook of second language acquisition* (pp. 436–486). Malden, MA: Blackwell.

Ogle, D., Blachowicz, C. L. Z., Fisher, P. J., & Lang, L. (2015). *Academic vocabulary in middle and high school: Effective practices across the disciplines.* New York: Guilford Press.

Olson, C. B., & Land, R. (2007). A cognitive strategies approach to reading and writing instruction for English language learners in secondary school. *Research in the Teaching of English, 41*(3), 269–303.

O'Malley, J. M., & Valdez-Pierce, L. (1996). *Authentic assessment for English language learners.* Boston: Addison-Wesley.

Omniglot. (2017). Omniglot. Retrieved from *www.omniglot.com*.

Online etymology dictionary. (2016). Retrieved from *www.etymonline.com/index.php*.

O'Shea, L. J., & Sindelar, P. T. (1983). The effects of segmenting written discourse on the reading comprehension of low- and high-performance readers. *Reading Research Quarterly, 18*, 458–465.

Oxford Dictionaries. (2016). Oxford dictionaries word of the year is . . . (2015). Oxford Dictionaries. Retrieved from *http://blog.oxforddictionaries. com/2015/11/word-of-the-year-2015-emoji/*.

Padrón, Y. N., Waxman, H. C., Powers, R. A., & Brown, A. (2002). Evaluating the effects of the pedagogy to improve resiliency program on English language learners. In L. Minaya-Rowe (Ed.), *Teacher training and effective pedagogy in the context of student diversity* (pp. 211–238). Greenwich, CT: Information Age.

Pang, E., & Kamil, M. (2003, March). *Cross-linguistic transfer of reading skills in bilingual children*. Paper presented at the meeting of the American Association of Applied Linguistics (AAAL), Arlington, VA.

Parish, H. (1963–2013). *Amelia Bedelia* (series). New York: HarperCollins.

Park, B. (1992–2013). *Junie B. Jones* (series). New York: Random House.

Parkin, S. (2016, September 3). How emojis outgrew the aubergine allotment. *The Guardian Weekly, 195*(17), 40.

Paulesu, E., McCrory, E., Fazio, F., Menoncello, L., Brunswick, N., Cappa, S. F., et al. (2000). A cultural effect on brain function. *Nature Neuroscience, 3*(1), 91–96.

Pearl, J. (2014). *Probabilistic reasoning in intelligent systems: Networks of plausible inference*. San Mateo, CA: Morgan Kaufmann Publishers.

Peebles, J. L. (2007). Incorporating movement with fluency instruction: A motivation for struggling readers. *The Reading Teacher, 60*(6), 578–581.

Peregoy, S. F., & Boyle, O. F. (2005). *Reading, writing and learning in ESL* (4th ed.). Boston: Pearson.

Perfetti, C. A., & Dunlap, S. (2008). Learning to read: General systems and writing system variations. In K. Koda & A. M. Zehler (Eds.), *Learning to read across languages: Cross-linguistic relationships in first- and second-language literacy development* (pp. 13–38). New York: Routledge.

Pinker, S. (1999). *Words and rules: The ingredients of language*. New York: Basic Books.

Pinker, S. (2000). *The language instinct: How the mind creates language*. New York: Harper.

Pinker, S. (2007). *The language instinct: How the mind creates language*. New York: Harper.

Pinker, S. (2008). *The stuff of thought*. New York: Viking Penguin.

Pluck, M. (2006). "Jonathon is 11 but reads like a struggling 7 year old": Providing assistance for struggling readers with a tape-assisted reading program. In T. Rasinski, C. Blachowicz, & K. Lems (Eds.), *Fluency instruction: Research-based best practices* (pp. 192–208). New York: Guilford Press.

Pratt, C., & Grieve, R. (1984). The development of metalinguistic awareness: An introduction. In W. Tunmer, C. Pratt, & M. Herriman (Eds.), *Metalinguistic awareness in children: Theory, research, and implications* (pp. 2–35). New York: Springer-Verlag.

Pre-K–12 English Language Proficiency Standards. (2016). Retrieved from *www. tesol.org/advance-the-field/standards/prek-12-english-language-proficiency-standards*.

Prince, R. E. C. (2009). *Morphological analysis: New light on a vital reading skill*.

Usable knowledge. Retrieved January 8, 2009, from *www.uknow.gse.harvard. edu/teaching/TC102-407.html.*

Pritchard, R., & O'Hara, S. (2008). Reading in Spanish and English: A comparative study of processing strategies. *Journal of Adolescent and Adult Literacy, 51*(8), 630–638.

Puente de Hózhó Trilingual Magnet School. (2016). Retrieved from *www.fusd1. org/Page/1942.*

Quirk, M., & Beem, S. (2012). Examining the relations between reading fluency and reading comprehension for English language learners. *Psychology in the Schools, 49*(6), 539–553.

Quirk, R., & Greenbaum, S. (1973). *A concise grammar of contemporary English.* New York: Harcourt Brace Jovanovich.

Rafael, T. E., & Au, K. H. (2005). QAR: Enhancing comprehension and test taking across grades and content areas. *The Reading Teacher, 59*(3), 206–221.

Raimes, A. (1998). *How English works: A grammar handbook with readings.* Cambridge, UK: Cambridge University Press.

Ramirez, C. M. (2001). An investigation of English language and reading skills on reading comprehension for Spanish-speaking English language learners. Unpublished doctoral dissertation. Portland, OR: University of Oregon.

Rasinski, T. (2000). Speed does matter in reading. *Reading Teacher, 54*(2), 146–151.

Rasinski, T. (2003). *The fluent reader: Oral reading strategies for building word recognition, fluency, and comprehension.* New York: Scholastic.

Rasinski, T., Blachowicz, C., & Lems, K. (Eds.). (2012). *Fluency instruction: Research-based best practices* (2nd ed.). New York: Guilford Press.

Rasinski, T. V. (1990). Investigating measures of reading fluency. *Educational Research Quarterly, 14*(3), 37–44.

Read, C. (1975). *Children's categorization of speech sounds in English.* Urbana, IL: ERIC Clearinghouse on Reading and Communication Skills and National Council of Teachers of English. ED 112–426.

Renaissance Learning. (2016). What kids are reading, and the path to college and careers, 2016 Edition. Retrieved from *http://doc.renlearn.com/KMNet/ R004101202GH426A.pdf.*

Richards, J. C. (1983). Listening and comprehension: Approach, design, procedure. *TESOL Quarterly, 17*(2): 219–240.

Richard-Amato, P. A. (2010). *Making it happen: From interactive to participatory language teaching: Theory and practice* (4th ed.). White Plains, NY: Longman.

Riedel, B. W. (2007). The relation between DIBELS, reading comprehension, and vocabulary in urban first-grade students. *Reading Research Quarterly, 42*(4), 546–567.

Riordan, M. A., & Trichtinger, L. A. (2017). Overconfidence at the keyboard: Confidence and accuracy in interpreting affect in e-mail exchanges. *Human Communication Research, 43*(1), 1–24.

Rivers, W. M. (1981). *Developing foreign-language skills* (2nd ed.). Chicago, IL: University of Chicago Press.

Rodriguez, R. (1982). *Hunger of memory: The education of Richard Rodriguez.* Boston: BantamDell.

Rothenberg, C., & Fisher, D. (2007). *Teaching English language learners: A differentiated approach.* Upper Saddle River, NJ: Pearson Merrill Prentice Hall.

Rowe, M. B. (1986). Wait time: Slowing down may be a way of speeding up. *Journal of Teacher Education, 37*(1), 43–50.

Rowling, J. K. (1997–2016). *Harry Potter* (series). New York: Scholastic.

Royer, J. M., & Carlo, M. S. (1991). Transfer of comprehension skills from native to second language. *Journal of Reading, 34*(6), 450–455.

Rumelhart, D. E. (1994). Toward an interactive model of reading. In R. B. Ruddell, M. R. Ruddell, & H. Singer (Eds.), *Theoretical models and processes of reading* (4th ed., pp. 864–894). Newark, DE: International Reading Association. (Original work published 1977)

Samuels, S. J. (1979). The method of repeated readings. *The Reading Teacher, 32,* 403–408.

Samuels, S. J. (2007). Afterword for B. W. Riedel, The relation between DIBELS, reading comprehension and vocabulary in urban first-grade students. *Reading Research Quarterly, 42*(4), 546–567.

Satrapi, M. (2003–2004). *Persepolis* (series). New York: Pantheon Books.

Saunders, W., & Goldenberg, C. (1999). *The effects of instructional conversations and literature logs on the story comprehension and thematic understanding of English proficient and limited English-proficient students.* Santa Cruz, CA: Center for Research on Education, Diversity & Excellence, University of California.

Savignon, S. (1983). *Communicative competence: Theory and classroom practice: Texts and contexts in second language learning.* Reading, MA: Addison-Wesley.

Scarborough, H. (2001). Connecting early language to later reading (dis)abilities. In S. Neuman & D. Dickensen (Eds.), *Handbook of early literacy research* (pp. 97–110). New York: Guilford Press.

Scholastic Teacher. (2016). Guided reading leveling resource chart. Retrieved from *http://teacher.scholastic.com/products/guidedreading/leveling_chart.htm.*

Schoonen, R., Hulstijn, J., & Bossers, B. (1998). Metacognitive and language-specific knowledge in native and foreign language reading comprehension: An empirical study among Dutch students in grades 6, 8, and 10. *Language Learning, 48,* 71–106.

Shanahan, T., & Beck, I. (2006). Effective literacy teaching for English language learners. In D. August & T. Shanahan (Eds.), *Developing literacy in second-language learners: Report of the National Literacy Panel on language-minority children and youth* (pp. 415–488). Mahwah, NJ: Erlbaum.

Share, D. L., & Stanovich, K. E. (1995). Cognitive processes in early reading development: Accommodating individual differences into a model of acquisition. In J. S. Carlson (Ed.), *Issues in education: Contributions from psychology* (Vol. I, pp. 1–57). Greenwich, CT: J.A.I. Press.

Shinn, M. R., Knutson, N., Good, R. H., Tilly, W. D., & Collins, V. (1992). Curriculum-based measurement of oral reading fluency: A confirmatory analysis of its relation to reading. *School Psychology Review, 21,* 459–479.

Silva, T. (1993). Toward an understanding of the distinct nature of L2 writing: The ESL research and its implications. *TESOL Quarterly, 27,* 657–677.

Silverman, R. D. (2007). Vocabulary development of English-language and

English-only learners in kindergarten. *The Elementary School Journal, 107*(4), 365–383.

Silverstein, S. (1964). *The giving tree.* New York: Harper & Row.

Silverstein, S. (1974). *Where the sidewalk ends.* New York: Harper & Row.

Silverstein, S. (1981). *A light in the attic.* New York: Harper & Row.

Skutnabb-Kangas, T., & Toukomaa, P. (1976). *Teaching migrant children's mother tongue and learning the language of the host country in the context of the sociocultural situation of the migrant family.* Helsinki: Finnish National Commission for UNESCO.

Sobol, D. (1967). *Two-minute mysteries.* New York: Apple Paperbacks.

Sokolowski, P. (2016, February 16). Keynote address given at the annual meeting of Illinois Teachers of English as a Second Language/Bilingual Education, Lisle, IL.

Sox, A. & Rubinstein-Avila, E. (2009). WebQuests for English-language learners: Essential elements for design. *Journal of Adolescent and Adult Literacy, 53*(1), 38–48.

Stamper, K. (2017). *Word by word: The secret life of dictionaries.* New York: Pantheon.

Stanovich, K. E. (1986). Matthew effects in reading: Some consequences of individual differences in the acquisition of literacy. *Reading Research Quarterly, 21*, 360–407.

Stanovich, K. (1996). Word recognition: Changing perspectives. In R. Barr, M. Kamil, P. B. Mosenthal, & P. D. Pearson (Eds.), *Handbook of reading research* (Vol. 2, pp. 418–452). Mahwah, NJ: Erlbaum.

Stauffer, R. (1970). *The language-experience approach to the teaching of reading.* New York: Harper and Row.

Steig, W. (1987). *CDB!* New York: Simon & Schuster.

Steig, W. (2003). *CDC?* New York: Farrar, Straus & Giroux.

Steinman, L. (2005). Writing life 1 in language 2. *McGill Journal of Education, 40*(1), 65–79.

Sticht, T. G., & James, J. H. (1984). Listening and reading. In P. D. Pearson, R. Barr, M. L. Kamil, & P. Mosenthal (Eds.), *Handbook of reading research* (pp. 293–317). Mahwah, NJ: Erlbaum.

Stoller, F. L., & Grabe, W. (1997). A six T's approach to content-based instruction. In M. A. Snow & D. M. Brinton (Eds.), *The content-based classroom: Perspectives on integrating language and content* (pp. 78–94). White Plains, NY: Longman.

Sulzby, E. (1991). Assessment of emergent literacy: Storybook reading. *The Reading Teacher, 44*(7), 498–500.

Swain, M. (2000). The output hypothesis and beyond: Mediating acquisition through collaborative dialogue. In J. P. Lantolf (Ed.), *Sociocultural theory and second language learning* (pp. 97–114). Oxford, UK: Oxford University Press.

Swain, M. (2005). The output hypothesis: Theory and research. In E. Hinkel (Ed.), *Handbook of research in second language teaching and learning* (pp. 471–483). Mahwah, NJ: Erlbaum.

Tafa, E., & Manolitsis, G. (2008). A longitudinal literacy profile of Greek precocious readers. *Reading Research Quarterly, 43*(2), 165–185.

Taguchi, E., Gorsuch, G., Lems, K., & Rozzwell, R. (2016). How repetition and an auditory model helps readers. *Reading in a Foreign Language, 28*(1), 101–117.

Taguchi, E., Takayasu-Maass, M., & Gorsuch, G. J. (2004). Developing reading fluency in EFL: How assisted repeated reading and extensive reading affect fluency development. *Reading in a Foreign Language, 16*(2), 70–96.

Tan, L. H., Xu, M., Chang, C. Q., & Siok, W. T. (2013). China's language input system in the digital age affects children's reading development. *PNAS 110*(3), 1119–1123.

Teachers of English to Speakers of Other Languages (TESOL). (2016). PreK–12 English Language Proficiency Standards. Retrieved from *www.tesol.org/ advance-the-field/standards/prek-12-english-language-proficiency-standards.*

Téllez, K., & Waxman, H. C. (2006). A meta-synthesis of qualitative research on effective teaching practices for English language learners. In J. M. Norris & L. Ortega (Eds.), *Synthesizing research on language learning and teaching* (pp. 245–277). Philadelphia: John Benjamins.

Tharp, R. G., Doherty, R. W., Echevarria, J., Estrada, P., Goldenberg, C., Hilberg, R. S., et al. (2003, March). Research evidence: Five standards for effective pedagogy and student outcomes. Technical Report No. G1. Center for Research, Education, Diversity and Excellence. Retrieved from *www.joanwink.com/scheditems/CREDE08.pdf.*

Thomas, W. P., & Collier, V. P. (2002). *A national study of school effectiveness for language minority students' long-term academic achievement.* Santa Cruz, CA: Center for Research on Education, Diversity and Excellence, University of California-Santa Cruz.

Thorndike, R. L. (1973). *Reading comprehension in fifteen countries.* New York: Wiley.

Tierney, R. J., & Pearson, P. D. (1983). Toward a composing model of reading. *Language Arts, 60,* 568–579.

Tierney, R. J., & Pearson, P. D. (1985). New priorities for teaching reading. *Learning, 13*(8), 14–18.

Tierney, R. J., & Shanahan, T. (1990). Research on the reading–writing relationship: Interactions, transactions, and outcomes. In R. Barr, M. L. Kamil, P. Mosenthal, & P. D. Pearson (Eds.), *Handbook of reading research* (Vol. 2, pp. 246–280). White Plains, NY: Longman.

Torgeson, J. K., & Burgess, S. R. (1998). Consistency of reading-related phonological processes throughout early childhood: Evidence from longitudinal-correlational and instructional studies. In J. L. Metsala & L. C. Ehri (Eds.), *Word recognition in beginning literacy* (pp. 161–188). Mahwah, NJ: Erlbaum.

Tracey, D. H., & Morrow, L. M. (2002). Preparing young learners for successful reading comprehension: Laying the foundation. In C. C. Birch & M. Pressley (Eds.), *Comprehension instruction: Research-based best practices* (pp. 219–233). New York: Guilford Press.

Trelease, J. (2016). Free parent brochures on reading. Retrieved from *www. trelease-on-reading.com/brochures.html.*

Truss, L. (2003). *Eats, shoots and leaves: The zero tolerance approach to punctuation.* New York: Penguin Books.

Truss, L. (2006). *Eats, shoots and leaves: Why commas really do make a difference!* New York: Penguin Young Readers.

Vanderwood, M. L., Linklater, D., & Healy, K. (2008). Nonsense word fluency and future literacy performance for English language learners. *School Psychology Review, 37*(1), 5–17.

Van Dijk, T. A., & Kintsch, W. (1983). *Strategies of discourse comprehension.* New York: Academic Press.

Van Gelderen, A., Schoonen, R., De Glopper, K., Hulstijn, J., Simis, A., Snellings, P., et al. (2007). Linguistic knowledge, processing speed, and metacognitive knowledge in first- and second-language reading comprehension: A componential analysis. *Journal of Educational Psychology, 96*(1), 19–30.

Venezky, R. L. (1970). *The structure of English orthography.* The Hague: Mouton.

Vygotsky, L. (1978). *Mind in society.* Cambridge, MA: Harvard University.

Vygotsky, L. (1986). *Thought and language.* Cambridge, MA: MIT Press.

Wagner, R. G., Torgeson, J. K., & Rashotte, C. A. (1994). The development of reading-related phonological processing abilities: New evidence of bidirectional causality from a latent variable longitudinal study. *Developmental Psychology, 30*, 73–87.

Wang, M., & Koda, K. (2007). Commonalities and differences in word identification skills among learners of English as a second language. *Language Learning, 57*(1), 201–222.

Wardzala, K. (2016, September 29). *Integrating writer's notebooks with Google classroom.* Presentation at the annual meeting of Illinois Reading Conference, Peoria, IL.

Waxman, H. C., & Téllez, K. (2002). Research synthesis on effective teaching practices for English language learners. (ERIC Document Retrieval No. ED474821). Philadelphia: Temple University, Mid-Atlantic Regional Educational Laboratory, Laboratory for Student Success.

Webb, N. L. (2002). *Depth-of-knowledge levels for four content areas.* Madison, WI: University of Wisconsin Center for Educational Research.

White, E. B. (1952). *Charlotte's web.* New York: Harper and Brothers.

The WIDA Consortium. (2016). *ACCESS for ELLs.* Oshkosh, WI: Wisconsin Department of Public Instruction.

Wilford, J. N. (2009, June 22). Carvings from Cherokee script's dawn.. Retrieved from *www.nytimes.com/2009/06/23/science/23cherokee.html?ref=science&_r=1&mtrref=undefined.*

Williams, T., Hakuta, K., Haertel, E., et al. (2007). *Similar English learner students, different results: Why do some schools do better? A follow-up analysis, based on a large-scale survey of California elementary schools serving low-income and EL students.* Mountain View, CA: EdSource.

Wong-Fillmore, L. (2000). Loss of family languages: Should educators be concerned? *Theory into Practice, 34*(4), 203–210.

Woodall, B. (2010). Simultaneous listening and reading in ESL: Helping second language learners read (and enjoy reading) more efficiently. *TESOL Journal, 1*(2), 186–205.

Word Frequency Data. (2016). Word frequency data: Corpus of contemporary American English. Retrieved from *www.wordfrequency.info/free.asp?s=y.*

Yigsaw, A. (2013). Students first language writing skills and their English language proficiency as predictors of their English language writing performance. *Journal of Language and Culture, 4*(6), 109–114.

Yuan, G. (2008). *American born Chinese.* New York: Squarefish Macmillan.

Yuan, G. (2017). American born Chinese. Retrieved from *https://www.youtube. com/watch?v=FYCZqt5WSOM.*

Yule, G. (2006). *The study of language* (3rd ed.). Cambridge, UK: Cambridge University Press.

Zimmer, B. (2011, February 4). If worst comes to worst. Retrieved from *www. nytimes.com/2011/02/06/magazine/06FOB-onlanguage-t.html?_r=0.*

Zipke, M. (2008). Teaching metalinguistic awareness and reading comprehension with riddles. *The Reading Teacher, 62*(2), 128–137.

Zutell, J., & Allen, J. (1988). The English spelling strategies of Spanish-speaking bilingual children. *TESOL Quarterly, 22,* 333–340.

Zutell, J., Donelson, R., Bevans, J., & Todt, P. (2006). Building a focus on oral reading fluency into individual instruction for struggling readers. In T. Rasinski, C. Blachowicz, & K. Lems (Eds.), *Fluency instruction: Research-based best practices* (pp. 265–278). New York: Guilford Press.

Zwiers, J. (2006). Integrating academic language, thinking, and content: Learning scaffolds for non-native speakers in the middle grades. *Journal of English for Academic Purposes, 5*(4), 317–332.

Zwiers, J. (2007). Teacher practices and perspectives for developing academic language. *International Journal of Applied Linguistics, 17*(1), 93–116.

Zwiers, J. (2008). *Building academic language: Essential practices for content classrooms.* Newark, DE: International Reading Association.

Index